Woman's Work

Ann Oakley

WOMAN'S WORK

The Housewife, Past and Present

Vintage Books
A Division of Random House
New York

VINTAGE BOOKS EDITION, February 1976

Library of Congress Cataloging in Publication Data

Oakley, Ann.
  Woman's work.

  British ed. published in 1974 under title: Housewife.
  Bibliography: p.
  Includes index.
  1. Housewives—Case studies.   I. Title.
[HQ759.03 1976]   301.41'2   75–28281
ISBN 0–394–71960–3

Manufactured in the United States of America

For my mother
and my daughter

Contents

Preface

First of all, this is a book about *women*. It is not a book about marriage or the family, and it does not aim to look at the situations of men and women equally. In current social imagery 'housewife' is a term often used casually to mean 'woman', 'wife', or even 'mother'. In this book, the term 'housewife' refers only to women's unpaid work role in the home.

A vast number of books have been written about men and their work; by contrast, the work of women has received very little serious sociological or historical attention. Their unpaid work in the home has scarcely been studied at all. This book is an attempt partially to redress this balance. Its perspective is feminist: it challenges the set of conventional values which label work a masculine activity and assign women to the home.

The book – or, rather, the project of which it is a part – has had a confused history. In 1969, when I first decided to do a study of housework, I was interested not only in women's attitudes to housework in industrial society now, but in the historical background to the housewife role, in the cross-cultural patterning of the division of labour, and in ideologies of women's domesticity. Three books have resulted. *Sex, Gender and Society* (London: Maurice Temple Smith, 1972) looks at sex differences/similarities generally, with particular emphasis on cross-cultural variations in the roles of men and women. The historical and ideological material (and some cross-cultural material, as well) is included in the present book, together with case-studies of four housewives and their situation today. A more detailed analysis of the survey from which these case-studies are taken is to be published in a third volume, *The Sociology of Housework* (Martin Robertson, in press).

Because the housewife role is the shared experience of most women in modern industrialized societies, this book is relevant not only to British women, but to all women. In particular, there appear essential parallels between the British situation, and the situation in the United States. The role of housewife is feminine in both countries, and the context of the housewife's work – the patterning of marriage and family relationships – is broadly the same. The privatization of the family, and the home with the housewife in it, is a shared ideal: so is the feminine ideal of fulfilment in marriage, motherhood and housewifery. Though the historical chapters focus on Britain, they do so because what happened in Britain illustrates the way the role of housewife emerged with the development of industrial capitalism: it is one example of a general process.

During the writing of the book I have benefited, as many other women have done, from the collective confidence of the women's movement: I am immensely grateful for this. I would also like to thank those who have helped in more specific ways: the housewives who generously agreed to be interviewed; Valerie Allport and other library staff of Bedford College, London University, for their patient provision of literature; and all those individuals who have read, and commented on, various drafts of the manuscript. I owe particular debts to Elyse Dodgson, Juliet Mitchell and Robin Oakley, for their constant advice and support. My parents, Kay and Richard Titmuss, read much of the manuscript at a very distressing time in their lives, and I am grateful for the help they gave. None of these people are, of course, directly responsible for the book's final form.

Lastly, it is obligatory for me to thank my own family for the experience of my own oppression as a housewife. Without this, I would never have wanted to write the book in the first place.

Woman's Work

One

What is a Housewife?

A housewife is a woman: a housewife does housework. In the social structure of industrialized societies, these two statements offer an interesting and important contradiction. The synthesis of 'house' and 'wife' in a single term establishes the connections between womanhood, marriage, and the dwelling place of family groups. The role of housewife is a family role: it is a feminine role. Yet it is also a work role. A housewife is 'the person, other than a domestic servant, who is responsible for most of the household duties (or for supervising a domestic servant who carries out these duties)'.[1] A housewife is 'a woman who manages or directs the affairs of her household; the mistress of a family; the wife of a householder'.[2]

The characteristic features of the housewife role in modern industrialized society are (1) its *exclusive allocation to women*, rather than to adults of both sexes; (2) its association with *economic dependence*, i.e. with the dependent role of the woman in modern marriage; (3) its *status as non-work* – or its opposition to 'real', i.e. economically productive work, and (4) its *primacy* to women, that is, its priority over other roles.

A man cannot be a housewife. A man who says he is a house-wife is an anomaly. On the level of fact his statement may be true: he may indeed do housework and assume the responsibility for it. But on another level his claim rings of absurdity, or deviation. It runs counter to the social customs of our culture.

In 1970, Albert Mills of Coventry claimed to be a housewife. His wife, Vera, who was employed, wished to claim the dependent wife's benefit for her husband under the National

Insurance Act of 1965. Albert had kept house for five years, while Vera brought home the money: Albert was the housewife. But the Mills lost their battle. As the lawyer representing the Department of Health and Social Security interpreted the relevant section of the Act: 'When the Act refers to a person as a wife, the word is used with the meaning given to it in English law – a matrimonial partnership of a monogamous character. In law it is a man and a woman who make a natural pair.'[3] Within this 'natural' partnership, it is the woman 'naturally' who takes the role of housewife.

A woman's performance of the housewife role is thus not a random event. It is possible, of course, to be a housewife and to be unmarried, but the majority of housewives are married women, and the allocation of the housewife role to the woman in marriage is socially structured. Marriage is not simply a personal relationship: rather it is 'an institution composed of a socially accepted union of individuals in husband and wife roles'.[4] A biological male cannot legally take the social role of wife–housewife, and a biological female cannot legally take the role of husband:

Detectives today prepared a report for the Director of Public Prosecutions on the couple who went through a form of marriage at Southend register office knowing they were both women . . . The couple are Terry Floyd, 24, and blonde 23-year-old Carole Mary Lloyd . . . Floyd said, 'I am technically female. But I feel and I always have felt like a man.' Carole said, 'I have known all along that my husband is a woman . . . but it does not make the slightest difference to us.'[5]

To society, however, biological sex is the all-important criterion.

Through the location of the housewife role in marriage, housewifery is an economically dependent occupation. As the Registrar General neatly and condescendingly puts it, married women 'engaged in unpaid home duties are not regarded as retired, but treated as "others economically inactive" '.[6]

Within this definition lie three aspects of the economics of housework. Firstly, the housewife does not herself produce commodities of direct value to the economy. Her primary economic function is vicarious: by servicing others, she enables them to engage in productive economic activity. Secondly, instead of a productive role, the housewife acts as the main consumer in the family. The tools of her trade are mostly bought by her outside the home – the food with which meals are made, the furniture with which the home is filled, the clothes with which the family are dressed, the appliances with which housework is done. 'Shopping' is one of the housewife's main work activities. The reality of the equation 'woman = housewife = consumer' is clearly illustrated by the role the housewife is allocated in the anti-inflationary campaigns of governments. The government 'appeals' to the housewife to report rising prices, to buy 'wisely' and so on and so forth. In the 1972 British Government price-freeze, the onus was put entirely on 'the housewife' to report illicit price rises: 'The suggestion is that they [housewives] should first challenge the shopkeeper if they think a price is being unfairly raised,' explained Prime Minister Heath: 'The housewife is quite capable of doing this . . .'[7]

The third aspect of the Registrar General's definition is that the housewife's work is not regarded as work because she receives no wage or salary for it. Not only is the housewife not paid for her work, but in almost all industrialized countries the housewife as a houseworker has no right to the financial benefits – sickness benefit, unemployment benefit, and so on – which accrue to other workers through state insurance systems.* Any benefits for which she qualifies come to her indirectly, through marriage, and because, in marriage, she acknowledges her condition of economic dependence. As a worker, she does not exist. The situation once established is self-perpetuating. The housewife is not paid, is not insured, cannot

---

* An exception is Sweden where taxation and national insurance systems aim to treat people as individuals, not on the basis of sex or marital status. See Wynn, *Family Policy*, pp. 217–18.

claim sickness benefit, etc.: therefore the housewife does not work. The alternative logic is: the housewife does not work and *therefore* she has no right to any financial benefit or reward. In either case, the modern concept of work, as the expenditure of energy for financial gain, defines housework as the most inferior and marginal work of all.

This central contradiction – housework is work, housework is not work – appears as a constant theme in the analysis of the housewife's situation. On the one hand, she is a privileged person: she is exempt from the need, binding on other adult members of society, to prove her worth in economic terms. 'Both my husband and I,' said one reader of a newspaper article on housewives and their work, 'think the housewife is one of the privileged classes.' Or as another reader expressed it:

To my mind she [the housewife] is a queen and her husband and children are her adoring subjects. Tradespeople are her courtiers whom she can dispense with at will if they displease her. Her home gives her scope to try out her artistic ability, the culinary arts, her sociability. She is free to work eighteen hours a day . . . or just take things easy . . . At least she is not a slave to an employer . . . [8]

But while the assertion, 'I am a housewife,' acts as a validation of the right to withdraw from economic activity, the admission, 'I am just a housewife,' disclaims any right to feel pride in this status. From privilege stems deprivation.

Housework is low-status work. 'Menial', a term used to describe low-status work generally, should properly be used to describe only housework. As the dictionary says: 'Menial (1) adjective of service, servile (of servant, usually derogatory), domestic (2) noun, servant. From old French *mesnie*, household.'

Some of housework's low status is due to the low status of the people who do it – women. A phonetic reduction of the term 'housewife' produces the appellation 'hussy'. 'Hussy' means 'worthless woman'. This equation of linguistic meaning reflects the equation of social meaning. A housewife and a woman are one and the same: one and the same, they are subject to deprivation and oppression in relation to the position of the dominant group in society. Neither housewives in their work roles nor women in their social and economic roles generally, are incorporated into the image and ideology of this group: if they were they would not have 'a situation'. They would not be set apart, different, unequal.

The status of housework is interwoven specifically with the status of married women. As a member of the British Government explained in 1970: 'The role of housewife is an extremely honourable profession, but the normal responsibility for looking after her welfare falls to her husband.'[9] In other words, however honourable the housewife's role, hers is, and must be, a situation of economic dependence, which marriage, by definition, involves. Feminists might well ask what kind of honour this is, and what other profession places its (unpaid) workers in the precarious situation of depending for economic survival on the beneficence of those with whom they share their beds.

The primacy of the housewife role in women's lives today is perhaps less obvious than its associations with femininity, economic dependence, and low-status work. Yet a growing mass of evidence points to the conclusion that progress towards sex equality is hampered by women's domestic responsibilities, even when legal or other institutional barriers have been removed. (Some of this evidence is discussed in Chapter 4.) A major problem is the failure to appreciate that housework *is* work in terms of the time and energy it involves, a fact which is nicely epitomized in the following anonymous rhyme, entitled 'On a Tired Housewife':

> Here lies a poor woman who was always tired,
> She lived in a house where help wasn't hired.
> Her last words on earth were: 'Dear friends, I am going
> To where there's no cooking, or washing, or sewing.
> For everything there is exact to my wishes,
> For where they don't eat there's no washing of dishes.

I'll be where loud anthems will always be ringing
But having no voice, I'll be quit of the singing.
Don't mourn me for now, don't mourn me for never,
I am going to do nothing for ever and ever.'[10]

No precise figures are available for the number of women who are housewives, but a British survey found that 85 per cent of all women aged between sixteen and sixty-four in a random sample of over 7,000 women were housewives – they carried the responsibility for running the household in which they lived. While nine out of ten women who were not employed were housewives, so were seven out of ten of those with a job outside the home. Housework is clearly the major occupational role of women today. Employment does not itself alter the status (or reduce the work) of being a housewife.

With the virtual disappearance of the 'underclass' of private domestic servants, housewife and houseworker roles have merged. The average housewife spends between 3,000 and 4,000 hours a year on housework.* Housewives in the urban British sample studied by the author in 1971 reported an average of 77 hours weekly housework.[11] The amount of time housework takes shows no tendency to decrease with the increasing availability of domestic appliances, or with the expansion of women's opportunities outside the home. A comparison of data available from different countries over the last four decades (shown in the table below) demonstrates a remarkable consistency in housework hours.

The social trivialization of housework (and of women) is in part responsible for the tendency to underestimate or ignore the amount of time women spend doing it. But other features of the housewife role also conspire to conceal it. Housework differs from most other work in three significant ways: it is private, it is self-defined and its outlines are blurred by its integration in a whole complex of domestic, family-based roles

---

*This average – 3,796 hours a year of housework time – is calculated from five studies: Girard 1958, Girard 1959, Mass Observation 1951, Moser 1950 and Stoetzel 1948.

which define the situation of women as well as the situation of the housewife. Housework is an activity performed by housewives within their own homes. The home is the workplace, and its boundaries are also the boundaries of family life.

A Comparison of Data on Housework Hours[12]

Study	Date	Average Weekly Hours of Housework
1 Rural Studies		
United States	1929	62
United States	1929	64
United States	1956	61
France	1959	67
2 Urban Studies		
United States	1929	51
United States	1945	
Small city		78
Large city		81
France	1948	82
Britain	1950	70
Britain	1951	72
France	1958	67
Britain	1971	77

In modern society, the family and the home are private places, refuges from an increasingly impersonal public world. There are no laws which oblige the housewife to make the home a safe place for her family, although, by contrast, industrial employers are subject to a mass of controls. There are regulations governing the safety of domestic appliances, but the housewife as the manager of the domestic environment is not bound to see that their safety is maintained (or, indeed, to buy them in the first place). Accidents are now the prime cause of death for people under forty-five in most Western countries, and domestic accidents make up the bulk of all accidents. What people do in their own homes is their affair. Physical violence or dangerous neglect subject the lives of six children in every thousand to the risk of mortality.[13]

The physical isolation of housework – each housewife in her own home – ensures that it is totally self-defined. There are no public rules dictating what the housewife should do, or how and when she should do it. Beyond basic specifications – the provision of meals, the laundering of clothes, the care of the interior of the home – the housewife, in theory at least, defines the job as she likes. Meals can be cooked or cold; clothes can be washed when they have been worn for a few hours or a few weeks; the home can be cleaned once a month or twice a day. Who is to establish the rules, who is to set the limits of normality, if it is not the housewife herself?

Housewives belong to no trade unions; they have no professional associations to define criteria of performance, establish standards of excellence, and develop sanctions for those whose performance is inadequate or inefficient in some way. No single organization exists to defend their interests and represent them on issues and in areas which affect the performance of their role.* These facts confirm the diagnosis of self-definition in housework behaviour.

The housewife's isolation emphasizes her differences from other workers. She lacks the sociability of a work-group: informal associations of workers engaged on the same job are an important source of standards of performance in employment work. The housewife lacks the opportunity to associate with her co-workers and to reach agreement with them on the shape and substance of work activity. Although other people – friends, neighbours, relatives – may be an important source of housework standards and routines, the work itself has to be

---

*Organizations like the Housewives' Register meet certain needs, especially the need for social contact, but they are neither professional organizations nor trade unions.

done in the individual home. (Shopping as a work activity is an exception to this rule.)

So infinitely variable and personal a role as the housewife's might well seem to contravene accepted definitions of what a 'role' is. (A role is 'a set of rights and obligations, that is, an abstraction to which the behaviour of people will conform in varying degree'.)[14] In the social image of a woman, the roles of wife and mother are not distinct from the role of housewife. Reflections of this image in advertising, and in the media generally, portray women as some kind of statistical mean of all three roles combined. A particularly clear presentation of this image appears in women's magazines, which show women 'how to dress, eat, housekeep, have their babies and even make love' all at the same time. 'In psychological terms they [women's magazines] enable the harassed mother, the overburdened housewife, to make contact with her ideal self: that self which aspires to be a good wife, a good mother, and an efficient home-maker.'[15] 'Housewife' can be an umbrella term for 'wife' and 'mother'. Women's expected role in society is to strive after perfection in all three roles.

A study of housework is consequently a study of women's situation. How did the present position of women as house-wives come about? Has housewifery always been a feminine role? Housewives are neither endemic to the structure of the family, nor endemic to the organization of human society. Societies and family systems differ: human beings have no species-specific environment and no species-specific form of behaviour: 'It is an ethnological commonplace that the ways of becoming and being human are as numerous as man's [woman's] cultures.'[16] Other people in different cultures may live in families, but they do not necessarily have housewives.

The question, 'What is a housewife?' is specifically a question about *industrialized* society. The two chapters which follow en-large this statement. Chapter 2 looks at the roles of women in non-industrialized societies and Chapter 3 examines the way in which the role of housewife emerged with industrialization.

Two

Women's Roles in Pre-Industrial Society

The role of housewife reconciles two opposed structures in modern society: home and work. Industrialization, which calls for the concentration of economically productive effort in large-scale organizations outside the family, is the primary agent in this opposition between the private, economically non-productive life of the home, and the public world of wage- or salary-earning work.

'In traditional [non-industrialized] societies, work and family structures tend to be linked as parts of an integrated cultural whole . . . '[1] The unit of production is the unit of kin relationships, and life is not divided into what one does to earn a living – called work – and what one does the rest of the time. The location of work does not entail separation from family life, and the values relating to performance in the work role and the family role do not prescribe different and conflicting goals in each. All adults work, and status in the community, for adults of both sexes, derives as much from identification with a family as from identification with a particular kind of work.

Roles in traditional non-industrialized societies are often defined to some extent by sex status. Social rules for the division of labour by sex are common, though these rules vary a great deal between societies, and some have almost no division of labour by sex. Even where division of labour by sex exists, it is not an invariable rule that women's tasks are domestic and men's are not: the economic and social structure of traditional societies permits no clear distinction between labour which is publicly productive and labour which is domestic, performed in the home.

Two African societies with very different versions of the division of labour between men and women provide illustrations of the lack of distinction between non-productive household labour and publicly productive labour in traditional societies.

The Mbuti pygmies live in the north-east Congo, and are the largest single group of pygmy hunters and gatherers in Africa.[2] They inhabit a dense equatorial rain forest, where they hunt game and gather vegetable foods. They have no rules for the division of labour by sex. In practice, however, women's work consists of gathering vegetable foods, building the huts, preparing food and making baskets and nets (for hunting). Men make other hunting equipment, bark cloth and gather honey. Women and men go hunting together. Men gather vegetable foods when they have the opportunity: no social ridicule or disapproval attaches to the performance of one sex's customary activity by the other sex.

With a minimal division of labour by sex, the Mbuti also stress the differences between the sexes very little in other areas of life. The roles of mother and father are not sharply differentiated; women are not alone, or even chiefly, responsible for childcare. Infants may accompany their parents on the hunt for game or for vegetable foods or may be left in the camp to be looked after by youths or elders of either sex. On days when the entire band stays in the camp, infants are allowed to crawl where they like, and are not restricted to the area around each family's hut. They may be picked up, fondled or fed by anyone. (Mbuti language distinguishes the sex of individuals only at the parental level, in the terms for 'mother' and 'father': the language has no terms for 'male' and 'female', 'boy' and 'girl' and so on.)

For these people the economic unit of social life is the band, a group of related families who hunt and gather within a territorial area recognized as their own. Work relationships coincide with kin relationships, and although work activities often require travel away from the collection of huts which forms the camp, the criterion dividing those who go (to hunt and gather) and those who stay (to care for children) is not sex, but age. The responsibilities carried by young and middle-aged adults of both sexes are the provision of food and the rearing, though not the continuous care, of children. For the women there is no conflict or question of choice between a domestic role and an economically productive role – just as there are no such alternative possibilities for the man.

In contrast to the Mbuti, their geographical neighbours, the Lele of Kasai,[3] provide an example of a society with a relatively rigid system of rules for the division of labour by sex. However, like the Mbuti, the differentiation of sex roles among the Lele is not based on an opposition between home, domestic work and family life on the one hand, and the area of non-family work activity outside the home, on the other.

Living in the south-west Congo, on the extreme edge of the equatorial forest belt, the Lele's main economic activity is the cultivation of the raffia palm. This is an exclusively masculine task, and all other work-tasks are also assigned exclusively to one sex or the other. Women draw water, gather and chop firewood, cultivate fish ponds and salt-yielding plants, prepare salt and palm oil, clear undergrowth, and help to plant, weed and harvest the crops. Men perform all the tasks connected with the use of the raffia palm, including preparing the raffia, setting up the looms, and weaving and sewing it. They cut oil palm fruits, and are responsible for the provision of meat by hunting.

The most basic division in social life is between the forest, which is a masculine sphere, and the grassland on the edges of the forest, which belongs to the women. Women are prevented from even entering the forest on every third day and on all important religious occasions. Similarly, the only crop which thrives on the grassland, the groundnut, is exclusively cultivated by the women. No man must ever set eyes on a woman involved in groundnut cultivation.

In the work they do, there is a clear separation between the roles of men and women: the division of labour is protected and enforced by a system of sexual taboos. The physical layout of their villages shows the same separation. Round the edge of the village are palm groves, divided into men's groves (used to give shade for the weaving looms) and women's groves (used for pounding grain). The four corners of the village are reserved for the four men's age-sets. At meals and during leisure time, the sexes are separated, as they are in their work.

The situation among the Lele (and among the Mbuti) is the same as that in the majority of traditional African societies: the work done by the women is essential to the economic survival of the society. Despite the ritual allocation of some tasks to men and some to women, men's work and women's work are equal in status and importance. The women's work takes them away from the village as much as the men's work requires that they stay within it. It is not possible to draw a line of demarcation between domestic work and economically productive work: 'work' and 'home' are integrated in the total life of the culture.

These two examples of traditional societies present a picture of women's role which is very different from that given by industrialized societies today. In traditional societies generally the integration of domestic life with productive work life is a constant feature. Many other societies could have been cited to show that the separation between home and work is not a feature of human society as such, but of industrialized society specifically. In the great majority of these traditional societies, the division of labour by sex is neither so inflexibly specified nor so minimally articulated as it is in Lele and Mbuti cultures respectively.

The differentiation of home and productive work worlds which occurs with economic development has consequences not only for women's work, but for the work and family roles of both sexes, and for the relationship between the family and the economy. In societies where women's productive work has traditionally been vital these areas are radically altered by the introduction of new technology and the development of complex patterns of labour specialization.[4] Western society during the period of industrialization provides a case-study in these processes of change, culminating in the modern differentiation of gender roles and the modern division between domestic life and productive work. This is the subject of the next chapter.

The remainder of this chapter is devoted to a description of women's roles in pre-industrial society in the West. The account is restricted to Britain for the sake of simplicity, although the outlines are shared by other societies, including the United States. The period of intensive industrialization in Britain covers roughly 1750–1850; in the following account references are, therefore, to the seventeenth and early eighteenth century unless otherwise specified.

1 Women's Work in Pre-Industrial Britain

Before industrialization, agriculture and textiles were the chief occupations of the British people. Both occupations were engaged in by women and in both the work of women was indispensable.

In their role as agriculturalists, women produced the bulk of the country's food supply. The entire management of the dairy, including the milking of cows and the making of butter and cheese, was in women's hands, and women were also responsible for the growing of flax and hemp, for the milling of corn, for the care of the poultry, pigs, orchards and gardens. On the larger farms, the woman would not undertake all the work herself, but would employ, train and organize both male and female servants. The practice of allotting twice as much land to married men as to single in the early American colonies is an incidental demonstration of women's accepted importance as agriculturalists during this period.

Where women worked the land for wages, the custom of paying women labourers less than men appears to date only from about the mid sixteenth century. Medieval records contain references to women 'villeins' and 'cotters' living on their own holdings and rendering the same services to the lord of the manor as men: some are widows, but some are unmarried women. Until the eighteenth century, women performed virtually every kind of agricultural labour, including thatching and sheepshearing. Folklore ceremonies dating from medieval times associate women as witches with the symbols of agriculture, the pitchfork and the plough, suggesting that women's role in agriculture may once have dominated the role of men. If this were so, it would suggest a parallel with the division of labour in many traditional small-scale societies today, where women are the agriculturalists and men occupy their time with drinking and talk.[5]

The role women played as agriculturalists in pre-industrial British society may, to some extent, be counted as part of their domestic role. As Alice Clark points out in her invaluable account of *The Working Life of Women in the Seventeenth Century*:

Under modern conditions, the ordinary domestic occupations of English women consist in tending babies and young children . . . in preparing household meals, and in keeping the house clean . . . In the seventeenth century it [the domestic role] embraced a much wider range of production; for brewing, dairy-work, the care of poultry and pigs, the production of vegetables and fruit, spinning flax and wool, nursing and doctoring, all formed part of domestic industry.[6]

By 'domestic industry' Clark means 'the form of production in which the goods produced are for the exclusive use of the family'. This includes the work which the modern housewife does unpaid as a service to her family. But side by side with such work, in the seventeenth century, was a system of 'family industry' in which the family was the unit of production and the goal of production was goods or services intended for sale or exchange.

Contemporary accounts of the duties of women make it clear that production for sale or exchange was usually integrated with production for the family's own use. The 'family' consisted of father, mother, children, household servants and apprentices – servants and apprentices being children and young people of both sexes. The two basic characteristics of family industry were the unity of capital and labour: the family both owned the stock and tools and contributed the labour (receiving the monetary return for labour as a 'family' wage); and the location of the workplace within the precincts of the home. 'From the point of view of the economic position of women,' observes Alice Clark, 'a system can be classed as family industry while the father works at home, but when he leaves home to work . . . family industry disappears and industrialism takes its place.'[7]

Women's work in textiles (second in national importance to agriculture) was also performed under a system of family industry. In the production of cotton, for instance:

most processes of production were fused with the nuclear family. Under this domestic system, the father wove and apprenticed his sons into weaving. The mother was responsible for preparatory processes; in general she spun, taught the daughters how to spin, and allocated the picking, cleaning, drying, carding, etc. among the children.[8]

The home of the family engaged in cotton production was like a miniature factory: the entire process of production, from raw material to finished cloth, was contained within it. The primary role of women in textile production was compared by contemporaries to the service rendered by men who ploughed: 'Like men that would lay no hand to the plough, and *women that would set no hand to the wheele*, deserving the censure of wise Solomon, He that would not labour should not eat' [italics added].[9]

While all spinning was done by women and children, women

also took part in weaving and in other processes. Later on, in the eighteenth century, when the textile trades were in the process of industrialization, this tradition of male and female working side by side appears to have continued, for a time at least.

Women's work in the woollen trade was equally important, though in the seventeenth century female spinners of wool were paid much less than their counterparts in the cotton trade. The married woman, of course, spun both wool and flax for domestic use. When spinning for monetary return, the woman herself would sometimes buy the wool, spin it and sell the yarn. Sometimes she was supplied with wool by a clothier, receiving piece wages for her labour. The wives of farmers and husbandmen would work in the wool trade in this way, supplementing the income the family received from other work. But there were also women – 'spinsters' – who relied on spinning for their living.

Aside from their contribution to agriculture and textiles, women's other traditional occupations included work in the skilled trades and in the retail and provision trades. In the seventeenth century, they produced most of the bread and beer in England. On larger farms the chief woman servant was expected both to bake and to brew, and in the towns brewing and baking existed as trades from the earliest times. Women were members of the ancient bakers' companies on the same terms as men. As a baker (and also in other trades) a woman generally helped her husband in his business and carried it on after his death, but brewing appears to have been originally an entirely feminine occupation. (It became a masculine trade by the end of the seventeenth century, though women still continued to brew for domestic purposes.) Most of the beerhouses in London were owned by women, and the 'ale wife' was a noted character in rural England. Brewing was important, since before cheap sugar became available, beer was an essential nutrient; it was drunk at every meal by everyone, including small children.

Other roles performed by women in the provision trades included those of miller, innkeeper, butcher and fishwife. In the retail trades, women played a prominent part: 'In fact the woman who was left without other resources turned naturally to keeping a shop, or to the sale of goods in the street, as the most likely means for maintaining her children . . . '10 The woman shopkeeper appears frequently in writings of the time: a pamphlet of the Civil War era, for instance, describes a 'Mistresse Phillips' with ten children 'most of them being small, one whereof she at the same time suckled', whose shop ('which enabled her to keep all those') was ransacked. Significantly, earlier in the account it is said that when Mistresse Phillips was sent for she 'was found playing the good house-wife at home (a thing much out of fashion)'.11

Opening and running a shop in the seventeenth century was not a particularly easy thing to do. People who had not served an apprenticeship in this trade were often tried and fined or imprisoned for doing so. The same kind of restrictions were imposed on those who wished to work in the skilled trades – another sphere in which women's work was important.

Most skilled trades in the seventeenth century were specialized crafts subject to the organization of the guilds. These associations – the forerunners of today's trade unions – covered such occupations as stationer, bookseller, printer, leatherseller, carpenter, grocer, merchant taylor, goldsmith, draper, apothecary, pewterer and blacksmith. In their earliest charters, and certainly in those of the sixteenth and seventeenth centuries, there is evidence of the real equality of the sexes. The charters expressly mention 'sisters' as well as 'brothers': women were admitted on an equal basis with men. Toulmin Smith, in her history of English guilds, observes that only about 5 of the 500 whose records survive were *not* formed equally of men and women.12 Entrance to the guilds was obtained by apprenticeship, patrimony, redemption or marriage. The first three methods were open to women, but probably little used by them, the latter method predominating. Here is an instance of entry by patrimony:

Katherine Wetwood, daughter of Humphrey Wetwood of London, Pewterer, was sworn and made free by the Testimony of the Masters and Wardens of the Merchant Taylors' Company, and of two silk weavers, that she was a virgin and 21 years of age. She paid the usual patrimony fine of 9s 2d.[13]

In London and the other cities, there were also separate women's trades, for which there were guilds to protect their interests. Girls apprenticed often continued to exercise their trade after marriage. References in contemporary documents to women who were following skilled or semi-skilled trades in London are very frequent.

Although it is clear from the records of the guilds that women workers were common, few figures exist to indicate their rate of participation. Poll-tax returns for Oxford in 1380 mention six trades followed by women; 37 were spinsters, 11 were tailors, 9 innkeepers, 3 shoemakers, 3 hucksters, and 5 washerwomen. (Six other trades were shared by both sexes: butchers, brewers, chandlers, ironmongers, netmakers, and woolcombers.) Similarly, a return for the West Riding of Yorkshire in 1379 shows 6 women as chapmen, 11 as innkeepers, 1 farrier, 1 shoemaker, 2 nurses, 39 brewsters, 2 farmers, 66 websters, 2 listers or dyers, 2 fullers or walkers, and 22 seamstresses. These would all be women carrying on their trades separately from their husbands, or as widows.

Returns made for different regions in the next two centuries show that women were working in some occupations that would contravene our twentieth-century ideas about the proper differentiation of tasks by sex. A list of the smiths at Chester in 1574, for example, includes 5 women's names, together with those of 35 men. Work pursued by women in the seventeenth century appears perhaps even less congruent with modern ideas of the feminine role. Women worked as pawnbrokers, money-lenders, shipping agents, contractors to the Army and Navy, as glassmakers and managers of insurance offices. They also owned ships and collieries. (The employment of women in coalmines continued until the mid nineteenth century.) 'Able business women might be found in every class of English society throughout the seventeenth century . . . '[14]

A telling comment on the quality of independence associated with women's work in the seventeenth century is a petition of women to Parliament dated 1641. The Queen's proposal to leave London in that year was greeted with active dismay, not by the men of the capital, but by the women, who claimed that their material welfare was dependent on the court's presence. They therefore petitioned Parliament to reverse the Queen's decision:

> That your petitioners, their husbands, their children and their families, amounting to many thousands of soules, have lived in plentiful and good fashion by the service of several trades and venting of diverse works . . . All depending wholly for the sale of their commodities (which is the maintenance and very existence and beeing of themselves, their husbands and families) upon the splendour and glory of the English court, and principally upon that of the Queen's majesty.[15]

2 Women's Role in the Family

In seventeenth-century England, marriage was essential for full membership of adult society, and it was expected that all men and women would marry, and that all who could would have children. Many couples did in fact not marry until they had established their fertility, and the number of prenuptial conceptions was probably higher than it is today.[16]

Marriage and parenthood were important because it was not the individual who mattered, nor even the nuclear family of two parents and children, but the larger unit:

> . . . the extended family, to whose interests those of the interrelated nuclear families of parents and children were subordinated. The promotion of family ambition, the advancement of family interest,

not the realisation of private ambition and the achievement of personal success, were seen as the common all-important social task.[17]

Marriage was founded, not on the basis of a personal and romantic love between man and woman, but on a concern to advance the extended family's interests. The marriage relationship was not, as it is in the twentieth century, something to be valued for itself: 'Marriage was an act of profound importance to the social structure. It meant the creation of a new economic unit, as well as a lifelong association of persons previously separate . . . '[18]

Under these circumstances, the state of marriage discriminated less between the roles of man and woman than it does today. When married, women as well as men were expected to carry on with productive work – whether in agriculture, in textiles, or in some particular trade. Consequently, there was no idea of the woman's economic dependence on the man in marriage; it was not the duty of the husband to support the wife, nor was it the duty of the husband to support the children. 'Men did not at this time regard marriage as necessarily involving the assumption of a serious economic burden, but, on the contrary, often considered it to be a step which was likely to strengthen them in life's battles . . . '[19] In practice the woman usually supported herself and her children through her own work. 'If the father earned enough money to pay the rent and a few other necessary expenses, the mother could and did feed and clothe herself and her children by her own labours.'[20] In the employment of agricultural labourers during this period there was no discrimination between the married and the single man, since it was assumed that a wife and children would provide for themselves. When no land was available for the wife to work it was taken for granted that the wage-earner's family must then be dependent on the poor rate.

This expectation that the married woman would support herself became less true of the upper classes towards the end of the seventeenth century, but it continued to underlie the marriage contracts of the working classes well into the eighteenth and nineteenth centuries. 'Consider my dear girl,' advises *A Present for a Servant Maid* (1743), 'that . . . you cannot expect to marry in such a manner as neither of you will have occasion to work, and none but a fool will take a wife whose bread must be earned solely by his labour, and will contribute nothing towards it herself.'[21]

A list of the occupations of married couples taken from the Sessions Papers of the Old Bailey (couples who were either witnesses, prosecutors or prisoners of the court) shows that only one out of eighty-six married women did not have an occupation of her own. In the list covering the period 1737 to 1800 the range of married women's occupations is very wide. It includes 'keeps a house for lodgers' (a woman married to a coalheaver); 'sells old clothes' (married to a recruiting sergeant); 'keeps the Feathers public house, Broadway, Westminster' (married to a soldier); 'plumber' (married to a tallow chandler); and 'poultry dealer' (married to a butter salesman). The one woman who said her husband maintained her also said she occasionally sold old clothes for a living.[22]

The economic independence of married women was reflected in the system of state provision for the poor and unemployed. Until 1795, this consisted mainly of workhouse accommodation, and did not differentiate between men and women. After this date, a system of 'outdoor' relief was adopted which recognized the burden of responsibility for family support carried by the husband–father. The procedure was to make up the difference between a man's earnings and the minimum he and his family could be expected to live on, taking into account the number of his 'dependants'. The rules were phrased so that it was the husband–father who was entitled to assistance for the support of 'his' family, rather than entitlement resting with the wife–mother, or with the family as a collectivity.

The work women did, and were expected to do, in the seventeenth century, had to be reconciled with responsibilities towards the maintenance of the home and towards children.

But the provision of food itself was regarded as the shared responsibility of husband and wife. Housework as a separate activity did not exist.

The pre-industrial home was a simple establishment: the space which housed the family was not divided into rooms with particular functions. Separate areas within the home, where these existed, were merely called 'chambers'. The history of domestic architecture is the history of the evolution of family life: the bedroom, the kitchen, the drawing room, and the corridor are all relatively recent innovations. Until the late seventeenth century, beds were to be found all over the house, and the upstairs chamber was likely to contain the tools of a family's trade in addition to, or instead of, a bed. Only in the eighteenth century did the bedroom as such feature in upper-class homes, but until a corridor between rooms was regularly incorporated into the design of houses, bedrooms were entered one from another and so afforded their inhabitants little privacy.

In the pre-industrial home, there was no differentiation between cooking, eating and sitting rooms. The hall, that is the entrance to the home, was the centre of domestic activity: here the family cooked, ate their meals, and relaxed together. The furnishing and decoration of the home was a relatively simple affair in all social classes. A yeoman farmer living in Kent in the late sixteenth century possessed goods amounting to £128 in all, but his household goods were worth less than £7, though 'his home was comfortable enough'. In the central hall, the only ornament was a painted cloth on the wall. The farmer and his family had a table in the hall, with one chair and a bench, for their meals. Most of the cooking was done on the hall fire, and cooking implements comprised two kettles, two iron pans and three brass pots. For lighting, they had three pewter candlesticks. The marital bedroom was one of the two rooms off the hall, and its furniture consisted of two feather beds and two linen chests. The other room off the hall had a flock bed in it, but was used to store two spinning wheels – one for linen, one for wool – a flour bin, two tubs and two more old chests. Above these rooms, a loft held a truckle bedstead and a feather bed. At the opposite end of the hall was a room the family called the 'kitchen' which contained mainly brewing gear and dairy vessels, although it also boasted a hearth against a wall with two spits and a dripping pan for roasts. 'Here in fact we catch a family in process of changing their habits; the hearth in the hall is ceasing to be a focus of family life, and cooking (and the housewife) are being relegated to the kitchen.'[23] The evolution of a kitchen – in its modern sense – was protracted and uneven. Like the bedroom, the idea of the kitchen as a separate space began to emerge among the gentry in the late sixteenth century but was not general to the structure of the working-class home until the late nineteenth and early twentieth centuries.

The one- or two-room house was the most usual dwelling for the working-class family before, throughout and for some time after the period of industrialization. Under these circumstances, housework was not the isolated activity it now is. The absence of modern labour-saving devices may have added to household work, but the absence of the kitchen, for the mass of the population, ensured that housework remained integrated with the main work of the family. The making of clothes, and the preparation of food – items in the ordinary housewife's role – were part of a communal work-activity.

A further striking difference between the seventeenth-century housewife's domestic responsibilities and those of her twentieth-century counterpart involved her attitudes towards children, and her concept of childcare.

Accustomed as we now are to the centrality of the child in the family and to exhaustive studies of the motives, thoughts and activities of children, the lack of importance attached to childhood in Tudor England seems on first acquaintance astonishing. It becomes less astonishing, however, when one remembers how brief the total span of life – particularly of infant life – could be in the sixteenth century.[24]

The average expectation of life was between thirty and forty years. Women bore something between twelve and twenty children, but the average family was much smaller. Usually only two or three children survived. The high rate of mortality

militated against the individual child being the focus and principal object of parental interest and affection. Indeed, [it] sustained the centuries old belief that if many children were begotten, a few might be preserved and bred – a curiously detached attitude to the death of children. 'I have lost two or three children at nurse', wrote Montaigne, 'not without regret, but without grief.'[25]

Childhood in this society was short: children were treated as diminutive adults. (When special dress for children appeared at the end of the eighteenth century it was considered very eccentric.) The age of marriage was twelve for a girl and four-teen for a boy. At the age of seven or eight most children left home to become servants or apprentices to other families: the custom was general among the upper and middle classes, but was also followed by some working-class families.

Infancy was but a biologically necessary prelude to the sociologic-ally all-important business of the adult world . . . Since childhood was of so little importance in contemporary affairs, children them-selves pushed forward with eager anticipation in the affairs of the outside world.[26]

Children had few toys, and childhood games and pastimes ceased beyond the age of three or four, when children were considered ready to engage in the same leisure pursuits as adults. There was no literature written especially for children's entertainment until about 1780.

Whereas for the modern mother, motherhood is a fulltime vocation, the seventeenth-century mother expected to rear only some of her many children past infancy, and did so with simple ideas of childcare. She regarded her children as an asset, not as an economic burden. Her household work was lightened by the help of children from an early age; children would mind their younger siblings and help with daily domestic routines, as well as working in the family industry. The children of a London baker, for instance,

were not free to go to school . . . or even to play as they wished . . . they would find themselves doing what they could in . . . sieving flour, or in helping the maidservant with her panniers of loaves on the way to the market stall, or in playing their small parts in preparing the never-ending succession of meals . . . [27]

Sometimes the housewife's helper would be a child servant or apprentice from another family. Girls and boys were apprenticed to learn trades and also to do household work. This meant that almost every married woman, except for the very poor, would have someone to help with the housework and care of children. The situation was changing around the beginning of the seventeenth century. Daniel Defoe, writing in 1725, noted that women servants were then so scarce that 'their wages are increased of late to six, seven and eight pounds per annum and upwards . . . an ordinary tradesman cannot well keep one, but his wife, who might be useful in his shop or business, must do the drudgery of Household Affairs.' [28]

With the coming of industrialization, the roles of married and unmarried women have been reversed. In the seventeenth century, domestic work proper – cooking, cleaning, mending and childcare – would have been performed by the unmarried girl (and boy) under the supervision of the married woman who herself worked in the family industry. Under modern conditions, it is the married woman who does the domestic work, while the unmarried female is employed in productive work outside the home.

In pre-industrial Britain, male child servants and apprentices were as likely to be involved in housework and the care of children as females, and the role of the father in the family brought men and children into much more intimate contact with each other than is the case in most families today. When the place of work was the home or the area round the home,* it was possible both for mothers to be engaged in productive work and for fathers to spend time with their children. If there was no sharp division between the domestic and economic roles of the woman, neither was there for the man. The father was not separated from his children, and they played around him while he worked: 'Men in all classes gave time and care to the education of their children . . . although now it is taken for granted that domestic work will be done by women, a considerable proportion of it in former days fell to the share of men.'[29]

The diary of Ralph Josselin, a seventeenth-century clergyman, stands out as painting a vivid picture of the close and long relationship between father and child. Josselin had ten children, and charted their progress carefully in his diary from before birth throughout their, sometimes brief, lives. He describes the ages at which they teethed, walked, and talked, and is concerned with the timing and success of their weaning, which in one case at least was a joint decision taken by both husband and wife.[30]

In the seventeenth-century family, women were not subject to the arbitrary authority of their husbands; they were equal partners. In the home and outside it, and particularly in the market place, female opinion was voiced and respected. As late as 1816 the heritage of this tradition expressed itself in the form of 'housewives' riots' – countrywomen, angry at the high price of food, held up wagons full of provisions on their way to the town markets, and compelled the owners to sell their goods at lower rates. Such a phenomenon is unknown today, although twentieth-century housewives face precisely the same problem of price-inflation.

The actual equality of the sexes within marriage in the seventeenth century contrasted with the doctrine of women's

* As Laslett points out (*The World We Have Lost*) the identity of home and workplace was not universal in the seventeenth century, but it was by far the most usual arrangement.

subjection preached by the church and increasingly enshrined
in the laws of the country. Indeed, the church's conception of
woman's role, as described by St Paul ('Let women be subject
to their husbands, as to the Lord: for the husband is the head
of the woman as Christ is the head of the Church') appears
to have influenced the formation of English law as early as the
seventh century. From the Reformation on, it had a mounting
effect on the status of women, particularly when expressed in
its more extreme Calvinist and Puritan forms.

But the theory that women ought to be subject to men,
although embodied in the common law, did not affect the
ordinary domestic relations of English people until considerably later. 'Common law' was the law of the nobles. Farming
people and artisans depended in their dealings with one another
on customs which decreed the independence of women and
their equality with men. These customs dated back to the
beginnings of English society, to the Anglo-Saxon era, when
not only was there equality between the sexes in practice, but
also, effectively, in law.

3 Women's Status as Individuals

In their work, and in their position in the family, the situation of
seventeenth-century women as individuals is apparent. To a
large extent, their activities in society were independent of
their position as wives and mothers: a situation which is in
marked contrast to their situation today.

Though declining as the century came to an end, women's
independence in this pre-industrial society took many forms.
The legal position of the woman engaged in trade gave her the
same rights and responsibilities as men in equivalent positions,
establishing her identity as a responsible individual irrespective
of marital status. The married woman trader could go to law
as a 'femme sole' – a term meaning an adult unmarried or
widowed woman – and her husband was not responsible for
her debts. This right was laid down in the early customs of

many boroughs; a fifteenth-century custom of the City of London, for example, states that:

> Where a woman coverte de baron follows any craft within the said city by herself apart, with which the husband in no way intermeddles, such woman shall be bound as a single woman in all that concerns her said craft. And if the wife shall plead as a single woman in a Court of Record, she shall have her law and other advantages by way of plea just as a single woman. And if she is condemned she shall be committed to prison until she shall have made satisfaction; and neither the husband nor his goods shall in such cases be interfered with. If a wife, as though a single woman, rents any house or shop within the said city, she shall be bound to pay the rent of the said house or shop, and shall be impleaded and sued as a single woman, by way of debt if necessary, notwithstanding that she was coverte de baron at the time of such letting, supposing that the lessor did not know thereof . . . [31]

This practice paralleled both the independence of women in the early craft guilds and the right which married women possessed to have young people apprenticed to them for the purpose of learning a trade. Though the law subjected the married woman to the authority of her husband in some respects, it also allowed women some choice in the matter of whether their legal status was to be that of 'femme sole' or 'femme couverte'. A contemporary exposition of the laws affecting women, *The Lawes Resolution of Women's Rights or The Lawes Provision for Women* (published in 1632), points this out, as it also points out several legal areas in which women possessed definite rights – more rights than they had in the nineteenth century. A married woman could, for instance, sue out of Chancery if she was 'threatened by her husband to bee beaten, mischieved or slaine . . . to compell him to finde surety of honest behaviour towards her . . . '[32]

The legal rights of women *within* marriage were considerable, and reflect the practical equality existing in the relationship between husband and wife. In particular, the legal status of the seventeenth-century married woman marks the fullness of her participation in her husband's business affairs, which was then a normal aspect of the marriage relationship. The names of married women appear frequently in records of contemporary money transactions, their receipt being valid for debts due to their husbands. The wife was habitually appointed executrix of a man's will – often the sole executrix, with responsibility for the final management of a complicated business or estate. During the husband's lifetime, the wife commonly acted as his business lieutenant, and the records of the Civil War contain many examples of assertive women acting in their husbands' absence to defend the family property. In their role as business partners, these upper-class wives were in no way hampered by the role of mother and its attendant duties; indeed one of the most famous – Ann, Lady Fanshawe – bore twenty-one children in twenty-three years of a married life actively devoted to the defence of her husband's name and property.

Not surprisingly, the rights of a widow were also extensive. It was customary for the widow of a tenant to remain in occupation of his land until she married again or died. In some of the other types of inheritance which occurred in seventeenth-century society, women had prior rights over men – a custom apparently dating back to Anglo-Saxon times when the system of inheritance was generally bilateral.

Married women whose husbands were in trades, inherited the trade from them on their death and usually continued it, a custom which the seventeenth-century guilds allowed for by assigning the husband's trade privileges to his widow (and not to his son). According to the regulations of some guilds, women retained such rights in the event of a subsequent marriage, and could share them with the husband of that marriage.

In pre-industrial Britain, then, a woman's role in adult life was always the role of productive worker – whether in the home, or outside it, on the land, or in the urban workplace. With only one or two exceptions, the laws relating to labour did not differentiate between the sexes: there was no special legislation for women, and women were not prevented from entering any occupation by reason of their sex. The wording of a fourteenth-century Act convincingly illustrates the pre-industrial concept of women as productive workers: in this Act, it was stated that:

the intent of the King, and of his council, is that women, *that is to say*, brewers, bakers, carders and spinners, and workers as well as of wool as of linen-cloth and of silk, brawdesters and breakers of wool . . . may freely use and work as they have done before this time [italics added].33

Such women were not called upon to choose between work and domesticity as alternative vocations. As well as economic changes, industrialization profoundly altered women's family roles. In the first place, the child now occupies a central place in the family, which it did not in the seventeenth century, and modern standards and ideals of childcare reflect the modern view of the child as an infinitely precious and important being. In the second place, the concept of private, home-centred family life is now a primary social value, while it had hardly begun to be so in the seventeenth century. For these changes to take place, the 'privatization' and 'domestication' of women had first to be established.

Three

Women and Industrialization

The most important and enduring consequence of industrialization for women has been the emergence of the modern role of housewife as 'the dominant mature feminine role'.[1] Industrialization affected the roles of men as well as the roles of women. But while for men it enlarged the world outside the home, chiefly by expanding the range of occupations available to them, for women it has meant an involution of the world into the space of the home: 'Our window on the world is looked through with our hands in the sink.'[2] The metaphor of the hands in the sink expresses the captivity of women within the home, that is the dominance of the housewife role in the lives of women, and its separation from other roles and other worlds beyond the home.

Although called a revolution, industrialization in Britain was a gradual process: an unfolding sequence of events. Capitalism, the cause rather than the result of this so-called revolution, had its origins long before 1760, and attained its full development long after 1830. Under the old domestic system of wool production, for instance, the different labour intensities of weaving and spinning provided the basis for a capitalistic role. Since one loom needed four or five spinners, the weaver would often take his raw materials to other families, paying them piece wages for the work they did. The finished cloth was sold in local markets and from there exported abroad, providing another essentially capitalistic role – that of the trader, the merchant clothier. Beginning as a middleman, the merchant clothier increasingly came to control all the processes of manufacture, by owning capital and employing labour

In the seventeenth and early eighteenth centuries, many cottage-based industries were run by elaborate networks of middlemen, whose control over manufacture grew with the increased demand and supply of industrial products. The change to large-scale factory production under the control of these emergent capitalists came under the impetus of three forces: firstly, new inventions in textile machinery made possible a great expansion in the production of textiles; secondly, the discovery of how to smelt iron with coal instead of charcoal, freed the iron industry from its dependence on the forests, and let it expand as a world supplier; thirdly, improvements in the steam engine supplanted water power with steam. Power-driven machinery became possible and profitable, and the factory was necessary to house it.

The 'industrial revolution' began about 1750 and was substantially complete by 1850, at which time about half the population lived in urban centres. In the period between 1760 and 1830, the basic structure of industrialism was established. The population grew and became more mobile, work became more specialized, communications expanded and improved: 'A civilization based on the plough and the pasture perished – in its place stood a new order . . . '[3]

In the new order, work was separate from family life: an activity performed away from the home for its monetary return and not for itself: a labour, not of love or family affection, but of impersonal efficiency. Separation from family relationships, values and considerations was entailed by the rationality of the modern industrial enterprise. Or, as one modern sociology textbook describes it, 'Industrial society is characterised by the existence of specific institutions set up to perform economic activities. From this it follows that in such societies the family cannot . . . be a productive economic unit . . .' Consequently, 'there is only one occupation holder in the family and all the members share the same amount of prestige and economic power – that which derives from his position.'[4]

This kind of situation obtains ideally in the normal

middle-class urban family. The differentiation of the family from the economy, necessitated by the changeover to industrial production, was followed eventually by a differentiation of roles within the family. The woman became the non-employed, economically dependent housewife, and the man became the sole wage- or salary-earner, supporting by his labour his wife – the housewife – and her children. This division of gender roles was incorporated into the ideals of the middle class in the first decades of the nineteenth century, and was increasingly put into practice among middle-class families until after the Second World War. The ideal only became part of working-class culture at the beginning of this century. Even then, economic conditions prevented many working-class families from practising it.

From the viewpoint of the changes in women's situation, the two centuries between the beginnings of industrialization and the present time divide into three rough periods: (1) from 1750 until the early 1840s, when the family was increasingly displaced by the factory as the place of production, but women followed their traditional work out of the home; (2) from the 1840s until 1914, when a decline in the employment of married women outside the home was associated with the rising popularity of a belief in women's natural domesticity; (3) from 1914 until the 1950s, when there is a discernible, though uneven, tendency towards the growing employment of women, coupled with a retention of housewifery as the primary role expected of all women.

Stage 1: From 1750 to 1841

The first impact of the industrial revolution was felt in textile production, since it was in textiles that the first inventions made the factory not the home the more appropriate place of work. Women's work was important to the domestic system of textile production: one writer, referring to the woollen industry in 1714, put the figure at about eight women and children to every man employed. Although they worked at home, the majority were already working as wage-earners, being given material by middlemen who subsequently marketed the thread. From the start of industrialization therefore, the position of women workers was directly affected.

The effect of the first mechanization of textile production was, paradoxically, an increase in the amount of employment available to women, and a rise in their wages. Hargreaves' Spinning Jenny, invented in 1764, multiplied the number of spindles that could be worked by one spinner – a sixteen-spindle model was patented in 1770 and an eighty-spindle model in 1784. The first small Jennies were used by women and children in their cottages, enormously increasing their productivity. (One Jenny produced as much as twenty or thirty people working on the wheel.) They were thus able to command higher wages. Increased production meant that more raw material had to be prepared, so that opportunities for female employment were expanded in this area too.

The other two important inventions, Arkwright's water frame and Crompton's mule, initially provided more opportunities for female employment. The former established the method of spinning by rollers and was driven by water power, but the earliest models left the preliminary operations of carding and roving to be done by women at home. Crompton's mule, which combined features of the Jenny and the frame, was also at first a domestic machine.

Until about 1775, women's work in cotton production increased and improved. Contemporary observers did not emphasize the benefit to women of these changes, but the benefit to the whole family:

What a prodigious difference have our machines made in the gains of the females in a family! Formerly, the chief support of a poor family arose from the loom. A wife could get comparatively little on her single spindle. But, for some years, a good spinner has been able to get as much, or more, than a weaver . . . If it were true that the weaver gets less, yet, as his wife gets more, his family does not suffer. But the fact is that the gains of an industrious family have been, upon an average, much greater than they were before these inventions.[5]

This situation was shortlived. The early machines were improved, enlarged and adapted to water and later to steam power. Cottages could no longer house them. By 1788, Jenny spinning at home was over: 'Thus,' says Ivy Pinchbeck in her study of *Women Workers and the Industrial Revolution*, 'within the space of one generation, what had been women's hereditary occupation was radically changed, and the only class of women spinners left were the unskilled workers in the new factories . . . '[6]

From 1780 on wages fell noticeably as the growth of the new machines created unemployment. The first textile workers' riots occurred. Much of the protest was focused on the changed situation of women workers as contributors to the family wage. From the viewpoint of the men, it is striking that even their own increased wages

did not reconcile them to the economic dependence of their women and children who remained unemployed at home. So accustomed were they to the idea of a family wage, and the financial contribution of women and children, that the substitution of an individual wage and the responsibility of the father for the entire support of his family were changes which at first were neither welcomed nor understood.[7]

During the last decades of the eighteenth century, many factories employed outworkers to clean and wind cotton. Some women were still able to get work, though their wages were much lower than they had been before the introduction of the factory system. By 1830 virtually all the processes involved in cotton production had been removed to the factory. (On the other hand, wool continued to be worked at home until after 1850.) In the early decades of the nineteenth century, the wives of skilled spinners who commanded high wages in the factory were able to retire from industrial work. But the mass of women workers who still had to earn their own living had no alternative but the factory.

At the beginning of the factory system, the majority of the workers were children, usually paupers, sent up in large numbers from workhouses in London and elsewhere. As steam power developed, the superior strength of adult labour was increasingly needed, and in the early years of the nineteenth century more and more women were employed. The earliest female factory workers came from agriculture, from domestic service and the unskilled trades. Women textile workers made redundant by the collapse of the domestic system at first shunned the factories, expressing their antipathy to the new machines. But the factories needed workers with some experience of textile production, and manufacturers began to advertise for 'healthy strong girls'. In the 1830s and 1840s the typical female factory worker was the wife or daughter of a handloom weaver, himself forced to enter the factory. Under the government scheme for the migration of those dependent on the Poor Law, the majority of those migrating to the textile areas were women and children (nearly 5,000 between 1835 and 1837).

The first figures available for the factory employment of women date from 1835. They show that, out of a total of 288,700 workers occupied in textile production, 46 per cent were women, and a further 15 per cent were children of both sexes under the age of thirteen. In the United States at about the same time, textile production appears to have been an even more strongly feminine occupation.

The conditions of the women's employment in the early factories did not necessarily disrupt the unity of the family. In the first textile mills, the tradition of family labour was honoured; whole families would be hired, with the husband–father allocated to one job, and the women and children to another. Parental authority could still be exercised, and children could be trained by, and apprenticed to, their parents, as under the old domestic system. Indeed, this was the main reason why workers themselves approved of child labour in the factories. The failure 'to bring his children up under his own eye' was said to be the 'one great grievance of a moral man'.[8]

From the 1820s on, technological change and the growth of protective labour legislation reduced the factory labour of children. At the close of the eighteenth century, child labour in the factory system was not ancillary to the labour of adults, but the foundation of industry; in the early years of the nineteenth century, the right of children to work in the factories, even in appalling conditions, was publicly defended. In 1784 an epidemic of disease in a cotton mill had first drawn attention to the conditions of factory children. The first Factory Act affecting child labour (in 1802) was concerned only with the improvement of the conditions under which children worked, not with the principle of child labour. Later Acts in 1819, 1825, 1833, 1844, 1847 and 1850 effectively reduced the labour of children, but even these restrictions were not based on the idea that the factory labour of children was wrong in itself. The grounds most often cited were the detriment to health and the low standard of morality obtaining among factory children.

This legislation eventually resulted in a differentiation of adult and child roles. The child assumed its modern role of dependant, and the function of socialization was taken over exclusively by the home. But the child's role and status were only gradually transformed. Despite protective labour legislation, children in poor families continued to work because their wages were essential to the survival of the family. Parish relief was refused to a worker if he had children he could send to the mill. But there was an overall reduction in the number of children employed: between 1835 and 1847 the percentage of children employed in the cotton industry dropped by 7·4 per cent. The percentage of females over thirteen employed rose by roughly the same amount so that a direct effect of the decrease in child labour was an increase in the employment of women.

How did the revolution in production affect women workers

as a whole? The unmarried girl who took factory employment undoubtedly gained in independence: she had her own wage. The same could be said of the married childless woman. Two groups in particular suffered from the changeover to factory production: married women with children, and women who lived in areas where factory employment was not available.

As factories were introduced, industry became concentrated in particular areas. Many thousands of women in scattered rural parishes who had earned money from piecework spinning had their source of income abruptly cut off. The decline in out-work brought much distress, especially in the south-eastern counties, where no alternative work replaced the worsted spinning traditionally done by women in their homes. Returns made to the Poor Law Commissioners in 1833, show the sudden rise in poor rates due to the contraction in the earning opportunities of women and children: in some places there was no work of any kind available to them, whereas 'formerly all the Women and Children had spinning to do, and they brought in as much as the Man did'.[9]

Many of the women affected by unemployment had to support themselves and their children without any aid from a man. That women and children should, in any case, support themselves through their labour was the general working-class view at this time. Indeed, factory work was seen as an improvement in women's situation, though perhaps more by the upper-class paternalist than by the working-class family itself. As a Government Commissioner explained in 1840:

One of the greatest advantages resulting from the progress of manufacturing industry . . . is its tendency to raise the condition of women. Education only is wanting to place the women of Lancashire higher in the social scale than in any other part of the world. *The great drawback to female happiness among the middle and working class is their complete dependence and almost helplessness in securing the means of subsistence* [italics added].[10]

As factories rapidly ceased to employ the labour of whole families, the employed mother (and father) came to face the modern problem of how to care for children in a world which spatially divided home and work. From the employment figures it is impossible to tell how many wives and mothers (or husbands and fathers) were employed in the early factories. But by the mid nineteenth century the married woman was certainly in a minority: estimates suggest that in the late 1840s about one in five of all female operatives was married. Of all married women operatives in the Lancashire area in 1851 about one in five had children under one year old.

Factory work was not the only or even chief occupation of women in the early nineteenth century. The 1841 Census Returns for England and Wales give the main occupations followed by women as domestic service (712,493), cotton manufacture (115,425), dressmaking and millinery (89,079), agriculture (50,654), laundry work (45,019), teaching (29,253).

Domestic service, which employed more than twice as many women as the other occupations put together, was primarily an occupation for the unmarried woman: so was 'teaching', a category which included both the governess and the schoolmistress. Many of the women classified as 'teachers' in the 1841 Census were probably governesses. With industrialization, the rising middle class of manufacturers preferred to follow the example set by the aristocracy and the clergy, employing a governess, a 'superior servant', to teach their daughters at home (their sons being sent away to school).

Agricultural work, like domestic service and teaching, was also a traditional female role. By 1841 it was in decline, as new developments in machinery dispensed with female labour in heavy agricultural work. 'I remember formerly,' said one observer in 1843, 'when girls turned out regularly with the boys to plough, etc., and were up to the knees in dirt, and in the middle of winter, in all kinds of employment. Now you never see a girl about in the fields.'[11]

Of the six main women's occupations in 1841, factory workers were by far the best off: they worked the shortest hours, and received the same rate of wages as men where they were employed in the same work. In other occupations, low wages and bad conditions were common. Factory work was much more attractive then domestic service or agricultural labour. Women themselves appeared to prefer the factory, with its regular companionship, to the more socially isolated conditions of other work. Married women particularly were accused at the time of having 'an extended taste' for factory work, and one contemporary writer observed: 'I must admit that . . . some women prefer the crowded factory to the quiet home because they have a hatred of the solitary housework . . . '[12] The attractions of factory work were frequently mentioned in complaints about the growing scarcity of domestic servants, and the shortage of female labour for the farms.

Certainly factory work was in many cases preferable to the 'sweated' outwork trades with their poor conditions. 'Dressmaking and millinery', the third category of workers listed in the 1841 Census, are examples of the smaller domestic industries which had traditionally occupied women and children. Workers in these trades were dependent on middlemen who frequently cheated them of their proper wages. Working conditions were bad – as one writer exclaimed in 1786, labourers' cottages seemed 'to be built as discouragements to industry' and were 'fit for nothing but eating and sleeping places'.[13] Like laundry work, these occupations were mostly followed by those for whom it was a case of 'domestic industry or nothing' – in other words, married women with small children. Some also chose home-based work since it gave them freedom from discipline imposed by others and freedom to organize their own time. 'We have our liberty at home, and get our meals comfortable, such as they are.'[14]

How were other women's occupations affected by industrialization? The activities of craftswomen and businesswomen decreased markedly during the century of industrial revolution. The separation of the home from business premises made it more difficult for women to share in their husbands' work, and the development of large-scale business, necessitating a greater amount of capital, further reduced women's opportunities. By the end of the eighteenth century it had become impossible for a woman to set up in business on her own account, particularly in London, where wealth increased most rapidly. In the organized guild trades, the separation of home and workshop again reduced female employment, and by the early nineteenth century women's apprenticeship in the guild trades had ceased altogether. Even if apprenticed, women could not get hold of the necessary capital to begin their own business or trade.

The occupations of retail shopkeeping, provisioning and street trading remained open to them. It was Poor Law policy to give assistance to women with children in order that they should be able to enter these occupations. This was a recognition of women's traditional role as productive workers, supporting by their labour themselves and their children.

In the eighteenth century women practised with success and fame as surgeons, dentists and oculists, and in allied fields. Changes accompanying industrialization ended the work of women in these occupations. With the growth of scientific knowledge and the emergence of the hospital movement, women were excluded from all branches of the medical profession: 'As the study of medicine became more scientific, the position of women became more difficult.'[15] The most seriously affected at first were women midwives, but here the changes of the late eighteenth century further advanced a process of 'masculinization' begun two centuries before. Queen Victoria was the first sovereign to employ a male midwife. In the 1870s, the Obstetrical Society of London (the predecessor of the Royal College of Obstetricians and Gynaecologists) declared midwifery to be the branch of medicine for which women were least fitted.

Surveying the whole field of women's work activity from 1750 to 1841, it is clear that the foundations of modern women's situation were laid in the changes associated with industrialization. The separation of the workplace from the home was established: the tradition of family labour and the family wage was abolished. The increasing differentiation of child and adult roles, with the child's growing dependence, heralded the dependence of women in marriage and their restriction to the home. It only remained for the conservatism of the Victorian era to formulate a doctrine of feminine domesticity whereby women could more effectively be tied to their family roles, and the role of housewife could emerge in its modern form.

Stage 2: From 1841 to 1914

Until the early 1840s, the ideology of married women's economic dependence on men, and their restriction to household work and childcare, existed only in embryonic form. The daughters and wives of upper- and middle-class men had not been expected to work for some time. Productive work was denied them, as were the duties of household work and childcare. 'The practice of female idleness spread through the middle class until work for women became a misfortune and a disgrace.'[16] Working-class women were not restricted in this way. Although opportunities for women's productive work had diminished, there was as yet no generally accepted ideology of women's situation to justify the contraction of their roles as productive workers on moral, social, economic or political grounds.

The first clear signs of this ideology emerged in 1841, when factory reformers enlarged their frame of reference to include not only the work of children, but the work of women as well. In 1841, committees of male factory workers called for the 'gradual withdrawal of all female labour from the factory', an appeal which apparently gained some political support. In 1842, the Report of the Royal Commission on the Mines, with its description of the working conditions of women and children in the collieries, 'shocked and horrified the whole of England'. 'Chained, belted, harnessed, like dogs in a go-cart,' said one Commissioner about women colliery workers, 'black, saturated with wet, and more than half-naked, crawling upon their hands and their feet, and dragging their heavy loads behind them – they present an appearance indescribably disgusting and unnatural.'[17] This dramatic report – coloured by the upper-class idea that women's proper place was in the home – made it appear that the employment of women outside the home was an evil in itself.

The 1842 Mines Act – the first Act of protective labour legislation for women – excluded women from colliery employment. Two years later, the 1844 Factory Act took the radical and unprecedented step of classing women of all ages with children and 'protected persons'. Their hours of labour were restricted to twelve a day in the textile trades. In 1847, a further Act limited labour to fifty-eight hours a week for women and young people over thirteen, and an Act of 1850 made the ten-hour day for 'protected persons' effective by abolishing the shift or relay system. Much later, in 1891, an Act was passed prohibiting the employment of women four weeks before and four weeks after childbirth, and the 1895 Factories and Workshops Act prohibited overtime for women.

This protective legislation was both a cause and an effect of industrialization's most important legacy to women: the creation of the modern housewife role. Over the period from 1841 to 1914 the greatest change in women's occupations was the rising incidence of housewifery as the sole occupation for married women. In 1851, one in four married women (with husbands alive) was employed. By 1911, the figure was one in ten.

The increase in the proportion of women occupied solely as housewives is associated with the rise of the belief that woman's place is, or should be, exclusively the home. As one historian has remarked, 'The doctrine that woman's place is in the home is peculiarly the product of a period in which man had been lately displaced from the home as his workplace.'[18] Victorian attempts to get women out of the factories and mills and into the home were motivated largely by the anxiety of men whose own situation had been radically transformed by the change to factory production. The loss of traditional work roles and the new restrictions on the labour of children caused a major crisis in the life and unity of the family. The child's increasing dependence upon adults and the continuing limitations imposed by women's reproductive role came to entail a division of labour between husband and wife, whereby the husband became the main breadwinner, and the wife the main childrearer, living off, and providing for her children out of, the earnings of the man. In this situation the woman factory worker posed the threat of competition. The fear of this threat seems to have been the force behind the early legislation affecting women's employment. At this time, the case for restricting women to unpaid work within the home first began to be argued publicly.

Four main reasons appear in contemporary documents as grounds for restricting or preventing the employment of women outside the home (and encouraging them to busy themselves solely with housewifery). Female employment was condemned on moral grounds, on grounds of damage to physical health, on grounds of neglect of home and family, and, lastly, simply on the grounds that it contravened the 'natural' division of labour between the sexes.

'In the male,' said Lord Shaftesbury, taking up the issue of 'moral' damage,

the moral effects of the [factory] system are very bad; but in the female they are infinitely worse, not alone upon themselves, but upon their families, upon society; and, I may add, upon the country itself. It is bad enough if you corrupt the man, but if you corrupt the woman, you poison the waters of life at the very fountain.[19]

Though the tone of the outcry against the conditions of female employment might suggest otherwise, it was the 'immorality' of female workers to which the strongest objections were raised. 'They are to be found alike vulgar in manner and obscene in language,' said one observer.[20] For the female, factories are 'perfect gates of hell', said Engels in his *The Condition of the Working Class in England in 1844.* 'The collecting of persons of both sexes . . . in a single workroom . . . is not calculated for the favourable development of the female character.'[21]

These protests about the so-called immorality of the female worker were made in the context of the Victorian view of women as persons ideally devoid of sexuality. This view emphasized women's irresponsibility and vulnerability. Women were seen primarily in their role as mothers. Protests about the damage to health consequent upon female employment inevitably stressed the possible impairment of the reproductive function. To quote Engels again:

The influence of factory work upon the female physique also is marked and peculiar . . . Protracted work frequently causes deformities of the pelvis . . . That factory operatives undergo more difficult confinements than other women is testified to by several midwives and accoucheurs, and also that they are more liable to miscarriage.[22]

A book published in 1844 by Charlotte Tonna, entitled *The Wrongs of Women*, was the first of many volumes extolling the virtues of feminine domesticity and attacking 'the monstrous abuse of forcing the female to forsake her proper sphere'. Men, in the form of factory workers and factory commissioners, had already complained lengthily about the fate of men married to employed females, who had 'no home but the beer shop'. Before the fight for the protection of women's labour had begun factory commissioners had observed that the factory employment of female children was in itself a bad thing because it 'prevents them from forming the domestic habits usually acquired by women'.[23] The 1833 Factory Bill had been objected to on the grounds that it might lead to an increase in the employment of married women (which in fact happened).

Charlotte Tonna, as many others after her, criticized the employment of women because it 'reversed the order of nature' as one of her authorities expressed it. Many women, she said, were employed while their husbands stayed at home to look after the children. As one witness described it, the young children awaited their mothers' return from the factories 'crying with cold and hunger, the father having left them to take care of themselves'. 'How, indeed,' this witness went on to observe, 'can the man be expected to perform the housewife's part as the woman ought to do; or even as, with all her faults, she does . . . ?'[24] Either the employment of the wife was seen as dissolving the family 'utterly and of necessity' or else it was thought to bring about an 'insane state of things' which 'unsexes the man and takes from the woman all woman-liness'.[25]

In understanding how the ideology of feminine domesticity was created and maintained in mid-nineteenth century Britain, it is essential to see just what foundations contemporary objections to women's employment had in fact. The doctrine that women belong in the home never carries more conviction than when it is allied with 'proof' that women's activities outside the home are detrimental to the health and welfare of themselves, their families and the country as a whole.

Not surprisingly, the moral effects of factory employment are impossible to ascertain. We do not know if female chastity was impaired or if the illegitimacy rate rose. Neither do we know whether the incidence of reproductive casualty (still-births, prematurity, and post-natal infant mortality) was any higher among employed females than among their unemployed sisters. Fertility among Lancashire cotton operatives did appear to be low, but, although construed at the time as a direct result of factory employment, it seems probable that all working women by this time had some rudimentary knowledge of birth control.

Contemporary claims that infant mortality among factory workers was high had some validity, but a more sophisticated interpretation of the data shows that infant mortality tended to be higher wherever mothers were employed away from the home – whether in factory or field. Where women's employment was associated with poverty and a low standard of living, these factors, rather than employment itself, put the infants of work-ing mothers at risk.[26] The breakup of the family as the unit of labour, and the removal of work from the home, were re-sponsible for one cause of infant mortality directly associated with industrialization. This was the death of babies through artificial feeding.

Conditions of work in industrializing Britain separated the breastfeeding mother from her baby, and at this time human milk was the only safe food for babies. While upper-class mothers had for centuries relieved themselves of the ties of infant care by putting out their children to wet nurses, working-class mothers, in order to achieve any degree of freedom, had to resort to substitute care which involved artificial feeding. 'There can be no doubt,' says Margaret Hewitt in her study of *Wives and Mothers in Victorian Industry*, 'that throughout Victoria's reign, insofar as babies had to be artificially fed because of their mother's absence at work, their lives were imperilled.'[27] Cows' milk was heavily contaminated with bacteria, and it was not until the 1890s that boiling was dis-covered to be some protection against the threat of disease.

The death rate of babies who were wet nursed was about 30 per cent in the mid nineteenth century, probably no higher than the incidence of death among babies fed by their own mothers. Among those 'reared by hand' the death rate ranged from 50 to 80 per cent. Apart from (contaminated) milk, which was rarely bought because of its great expense, bread and water sweetened with sugar and treacle was the food given to these infants. Drugging with syrups containing narcotics – opium, laudanum and morphia – was a common means of quieting crying babies. Though bearing euphemistic names like 'Mother's Blessing' and 'Infant's Preservative', these syrups were in themselves a main cause of infant mortality.*

That increased infant mortality was associated with women's

---

* The modern descendant of these syrups (in Britain at least) is gripe water, available over the counter at any chemist. Its active content is 1 per cent alcohol.

employment in this period is indisputable. That women's employment contravened the 'natural' or 'proper' division of labour between men and women is a contention with no basis in historical fact. Women's economically productive work was not created by the industrial revolution – only changed by it. The factory inherited both women's labour and children's labour from an immemorial past. To the Victorians belongs, not the discovery of the woman worker, but the discovery of the woman worker as an object of pity.

As the productive work of women was in evidence long before the coming of industrialization, so was women's 'neglect' of home and family. Under the old system of domestic industry, women had no more time for housework and childcare than they did in the days of factory work. Industrialization actually led to some improvement in the conditions of home life. When the home housed the tools of work, 'dust and oil and offensive smells' were features of the working world from which no escape could be had, and the old domestic machines were as likely to cause accidental injury and death as the new factory ones.

In the period from 1841 to 1914 the roles of working-class and middle-class women were, on the whole, increasingly differentiated. For the middle-class woman, the doctrine of feminine domesticity was well-established by the mid nineteenth century: marriage had become a fulltime occupation. It was, moreover, an occupation in which women could play the role of 'leisured lady'. Though evident among the aristocracy in the eighteenth century, the idle dependence of the married woman became a practicable ideal for the rising middle classes with industrialization. The idleness of a man's female dependants at home became a mark of prosperity for the Victorian middle-class male: 'The successful business man delighted to show off his wife and daughters expensively clad, living a life of ease and elegance.'[28] At a time when adult females substantially outnumbered males, marriage conferred status on a woman. As a nineteenth-century suffragette remarked to a married woman who was defending the right of wives to the franchise: 'My dear friend, a really good husband is worth all the votes in the world.'[29]

In the second half of the nineteenth century, the doctrine of feminine domesticity began to permeate downwards to the working classes. For working-class women, this doctrine challenged the economic facts of life: one parent's income could not cover the costs of childrearing, and many women had to work. One survey, carried out in 1904, uncovered the following reasons for the employment of married women: death or unemployment of the husband, or insufficiency of the husband's wage; desertion by the husband, preference for factory work as opposed to housework. This survey found that four out of five married women worked because of financial necessity. A similar study carried out in the United States in 1908 showed that less than 5 per cent of employed married women had husbands alive whose wages could be expected to keep the whole family.

The idea that work outside the home for married women was a 'misfortune and a disgrace' became acceptable to the working classes only in the last decades of the nineteenth century. In the early years of the twentieth century working-class married women were increasingly likely to follow the middle-class pattern, choosing the role of non-employed housewife even in cases where their employment would have improved the family's standard of living. From the perspective of women's situation, this change to housewifery among working-class women is the most dramatic result of the industrial revolution.

An account of the lives of working-class women in south London, written in 1913, gives some idea of the degree to which the housewife role was by this time accepted as the norm for all women. Entitled *Round About a Pound a Week*, and published by the Fabian Women's Committee, this account totally accepts the relegation of women to the domestic role and does not question the possibility that the working-class wife might attempt to improve her economic situation by taking paid employment outside the home. The term 'the working mother' as used in this account of women's situation means not 'the employed mother', but the mother occupied solely with house-wifery and motherhood.

At marriage, says this report, young women's lives are far more changed than those of the men. The women

> tell you that . . . they . . . miss the companionship of the factory life and the money of their own to spend, and are rather frightened at the swift approach of motherhood . . . The separation of interests [between husband and wife] soon begins to show itself. The husband goes to the same work – hard, long and monotonous – but at least a change from the growing discomfort of the home. He gets accustomed to seeing his wife slave, and she gets accustomed to seeing him appear and disappear on his daily round of work, which gradually appeals less and less to her imagination, till, at thirty, she hardly knows what his duties are, so overwhelmed is she in the flood of her most absorbing duties and economies . . . [30]

This picture is a very different one from that given in the previous chapter of married women's work activity before industrialization. Then marriage did not mark an abrupt change in the roles of women, though, as with men, it was a sign of the transition to adult status.

The working-class wife's retirement into domesticity was not paralleled by a life of idleness among the unmarried: the un-married working-class girl continued to work outside the home. (Employment for the single *middle*-class girl was a later development.)

Middle-class wives chose housewifery as an occupation long before their working-class sisters partly because they did not actually have to *do* housework. 'The main distinguishing mark between the middle-class woman and those who are considered socially inferior was the attitude of mind which demanded that she should have at least one servant to wait on her.'[31] As Mrs Ellis, the middle-class housewife's mentor, warned her readers in a volume entitled *Wives of England*: 'It can never be said that the atmosphere of a kitchen is an element in which a refined and intellectual woman ought to live; though the department itself is one which no sensible woman would think it a degradation to overlook.' Or as her successor, Mrs Beeton, described it: 'As with the commander of an army, or the leader of any enterprise, so it is with the mistress of a house.'[32] The vast success of Mrs Beeton's *Book of Household Management* and of its American counterpart, Catherine Beecher's *The American Woman's Home*, bear witness to the relevance of this approach for many middle-class housewives.

In 1857, an income of £1,000 a year would support a family and at least five servants: an income of £500, a family and three servants. The wages of a 'maid of all work' were then between £6 10s. and £10 a year 'with allowances for tea, sugar and beer'. From the mid century on, a large proportion of the rising number of females in the population was taken into domestic employment, which in 1881 accounted for one in seven of the total working population.

Nevertheless, from the 1870s on, domestic servants became harder to get, both because of the growing number of middle-class housewives who wanted them, and because girls who were potential recruits for domestic service began to move into the expanding feminine occupations of sales work, clerical work, and teaching. By 1900, there was a 'servant problem', and the possibility of conflict between the housewife and mother roles for the middle-class woman was widely recognized. It was argued that: 'the middle-class mother must perforce be provided with domestic assistance, not that she might indulge in indolence, but that she might be free to devote all her energies to the proper upbringing of her children.'[33]

The servant shortage made the domestic roles of middle-class and working-class women more and more alike. The combination of the maternal role with the housewife/house-worker role, until then a feature of working-class life only, became the norm. Where the middle-class wife had been idle she now worked, and in this transition lies perhaps one explanation of housework's modern status as non-work. The mid-nineteenth-century role of housewife–supervisor became the twentieth-century role of housewife–worker. The working-class woman had long been in this situation, but this fact was concealed beneath her role as productive worker. At the point in history when working-class women began to turn to house-wifery as a fulltime occupation in significant numbers, the middle-class woman began to take part in the actual work required by it.

Other changes in the roles of women in the family during the later part of this period followed the same trend towards casting both middle- and working-class married women in the modern role of housewife. First and foremost, a revolution was occur-ring in the role and status of the child in society. General mortality declined from the middle of the nineteenth century, and infant mortality – deaths in the first year of life – fell signi-ficantly around the turn of the century. The increasing likeli-hood that a child would survive into adulthood altered the attitude to children: the individual child came to be seen as irreplaceable. Whilst, in the seventeenth century, childhood ceased at seven or eight, the evolution of the modern school system removed children from the adult world for a much longer time, thus lengthening their period of dependence on adults. In 1833 the first allocation of money for educational purposes was made by the central government; by 1856, the state's expenditure on education had become so large that a Department of Education was set up; in 1870 an Education Act provided compulsory elementary education for all children. Thirty-two years later came an Act which established a state system of secondary education.

The growth of the state educational system proceeded directly from the needs of an industrialized society. The specialization of work roles called for a more literate and know-ledgeable population. The differentiation of adult and child roles brought about by the factory system established the child as an economic liability rather than an asset, a status recognized by the school system:

> The world of the school is the world of the child, dependent on a wider, adult society, but apart from it; a world which by its very existence asserts the difference in the natures of the child and the man ... The abiding importance of the school is that, in providing a separate institution for children, it gives to childhood an independent and recognisable status.[34]

But if industrialization caused the removal of the child from society by the school, then it caused a similar change in the structure of the family. With the separation of the family from the economy came the withdrawal of the family from society, the domesticity of women, and the idea of the home as a private place – a refuge from the public world of work and sociability. The modern ideal of family life had its origins in the aristocratic household. From medieval times until the first half of the nineteenth century, family life in the working classes followed an essentially pre-industrial pattern. Only from this time did the working-class family acquire the idea of the dwelling place as a home, composed of different rooms with different functions, and the idea of family life as a private and basically child-centred affair. The improvements in the working-class dwelling which made these developments possible did not really begin until the twentieth century, and so belong with the changes of the last period. But in this middle period the working-class housewife had already inherited one important middle-class tradition: the Victorian household which included servants was two homes within one; the kitchen – for servants – and the living room – for the family. The two remained, and still remain, differentiated spaces. The housewife has an identity in the kitchen which is separate from the identity of the family gathered in the living room. The modern tendency to small cubicle-like kitchens stresses this separation.

Before 1914, the housewife's work was affected little by technological advance. The public health movement, dating from the 1830s, had brought about improvements in sanitation, water supplies and so on. Some lightening of the burden came from an increased provision of food and clothes by the factory. Tinned food became available from about 1880, and diet was generally improving, but the invention of the vacuum cleaner in 1901 was one of a few hints of the new era of domestic machinery to come.

The transformation of the housewife's role from manufacture to service had begun before the end of the century. Significantly, it was women, not men, who took over the factory manufacture of domestic products. By 1911, there were many new preserving food factories, producing such goods as chocolate, jam and biscuits. Factories and laundries expanded, making and washing clothes – activities that would formerly have taken place at home. In all these areas, women workers played a major role.

A comparison of the employment occupations of women over the whole period from 1841 to 1914 reveals few changes. A greater number of women workers were engaged in food production; women's employment expanded in 'light' metal industries. The most striking change was the emergence of the office as a place of work for women: 'The male clerk who pushed a pen was in retreat before the girl who could use a typewriter.'[35] From 19 in 1851, the number of female clerks rose to 146,000 in 1911. The expansion in clerical work for women was second in importance only to the rise of housewifery as the sole occupation for married women.

These changes occurred mostly in the last few years of the nineteenth century. In 1851, 1881 and 1891, the majority of wage-earning women were still in the same occupations as in 1841, with domestic service and the textile industries taking first and second place respectively. Women's work in agriculture declined significantly after the late 1860s, as the demand for agricultural labour generally declined after the invention of new machinery, and as arable land was gradually converted to pasture. By 1900 (according to the Census) women's agricultural work had virtually disappeared. In 1911, more than twice as many women were employed in domestic service as in textile manufacture, jobs which, together with dressmaking, accounted for two thirds of all employed women. But the movement of women away from domestic service and textile work into other industries (most of them with strong traditional domestic connotations) was already observable.

Professional work for women at the beginning of this century remained as restricted as it had been throughout the Victorian period. Three hundred and forty seven thousand professional women were returned in the 1911 Census, 75 per cent of whom were teachers or nurses. Medicine officially opened its doors to women in 1878, but in 1911 there were only 477 women doctors.

With the rise of feminism in the later part of the period – a movement born, not in the factory, but in the middle-class drawing room – protests about the legal merging of the woman's identity with the man's on marriage achieved a measure of legal independence for the married woman. The economic dependence of the housewife persisted, and the idea of motherhood as a fulltime occupation for all women came into fashion, thus reinforcing the ties of women to the home.

Stage 3 : From 1914 to 1950

In this third period, the changes in women's situation brought about by industrialization have been consolidated. With the notable exception of the war years, woman's role as housewife has been continuously affirmed as the proper use for female energy. Her dependence on men is an accepted fact.

One facet of women's situation has seen some improvement: the area of their legal and political rights. Another distinctly modern trend has been the growing tendency for women to combine the roles of housewife and productive worker. The experience of the First World War activated both these changes. The war had a corrosive effect on Victorian attitudes to women: it 'brought to women a dramatic opportunity to function *directly*

– rather than through the medium of the family – in vocational, sexual and political-community roles. It was as Mary Doe and Susie Roe, rather than as Mrs John Doe or Mrs Susie Roe, that women were called into service.'[36]

At the outbreak of war in 1914, about three and a quarter million women were employed as wage- or salary-earners. Women made up just under a third of the total labour force: about one in four females in the population were employed: one in ten of all married women. The sudden rise in the demand for female labour occasioned by the war drew an additional 1·7 million women into the labour force. At the peak of this demand between January 1916 and July 1918, the percentage of females employed rose 22·5 per cent.

The women were recruited into many fields. Nearly 200,000 women entered government departments; 500,000 took over clerical work in private offices; 250,000 returned to the land. Eight hundred thousand women were recruited into the engineering industry, one of the most strongly masculine occupations. Women became munitions workers, car drivers, tram conductors, bakers: 'In fact everything except miners and builders.'[37]

Middle-class women were particularly affected by this sudden rise in the valuation of female labour. They threw off the restraints of respectability with legitimate patriotic relish.

Women who had been quiet mothers of families were suddenly transformed into efficient plumbers, chimney sweeps or gravediggers; flighty and giggling young girls turned into housepainters and electricians; ladies whose lives had been spent in the hunting-field turned into canal boatmen and ploughmen, and through their steady work and toil the life of the country was carried on.[38]

Most significantly, the doctrine of feminine domesticity was challenged: 'There are still,' said Walter Long, a staunch Conservative, 'places where women believe their place is in the home; that idea must be met and combated.'[39] Women's domesticity had for the time being ceased to be a masculine convenience.

These radical changes in women's employment receded in the years following the end of the war (although they picked up again later). By 1921, the proportion of women in paid employment was actually smaller than before the war. Women's magazines of the period faithfully mirrored the shifts in women's situation:

Victorian magazines which catered to a female sex virtually in domestic bondage rarely betrayed the existence of a world outside the home . . . But as soon as war drew women into the forefront of social action, the women's press quickly developed a commensurate degree of social awareness. However, this lasted only as long as women's freedom to participate in non-domestic activities outside the home, a freedom which narrowed considerably with the return to peace.[40]

The return to the home was not entirely voluntary, since, by the Pre-War Practices Act, men had a legal right to claim back their former jobs. But women had 'earned' one prize – and that was the vote, promised them in 1918, and obtained a decade later. In 1919, an Act was passed allowing women to be elected to Parliament, and by the Sex Disqualification Removal Act of the same year many legal barriers to women's participation in educational and occupational life were theoretically removed. The era of legislation towards sex-equality, begun in the last decades of the nineteenth century, had truly arrived.

From the early 1920s on, the combination of the two roles – housewife and paid worker – was a developing feature of women's situation. The Second World War, like the first, called for more female labour. Every kind of pressure and appeal was brought to bear on women, and especially on married women, to take work of some kind. Employers introduced special measures to facilitate the employment of married women with domestic responsibilities, and in January 1945, at the height of the war effort, there were 1,535 day nurseries for two-to-five-year-olds. Between 1939 and 1943 the percentage of women employed in industry and the services doubled.

In the first war, many women brought into employment –
both married and unmarried – had exchanged idleness for
productive work. By the time the second war began, employment for the unmarried female in all class groups was established as the normal practice. In the second war, therefore,
married women constituted the chief reserve of labour. During
the six years of the war, an additional two million married
women learnt to combine the role of housewife with the role
of productive worker.

From 27 per cent in 1939, the percentage of the labour force
made up of female workers rose to 39 per cent in 1945. Today
38 per cent of the labour force is made up of women, and
around three quarters of the women employed are also housewives.

These changes in the sex-distribution of employment
certainly represent changes in women's roles, but the extent of
the change is often overestimated. As the next chapter shows,
a closer look at women's situation – both in the occupational
world and in the family – reveals the persistence of traditional
ideas about 'woman's place'.

Industrialization has had these lasting consequences: the
separation of the man from the intimate daily routines of
domestic life; the economic dependence of women and
children on men; the isolation of housework and childcare from
other work. Hence, through the allocation to women of housework and childcare, through modern definitions of the role of
housewife and the role of mother, industrialization has meant
the restriction of the woman–housewife to the home. The restriction is psychological more than physical. Today's housewife
can, and does, leave the four walls of home for factory, office,
school, hospital or shop, but her world is permanently divided
from the world of men. The institutionalization of the housewife role as the primary role for all women means that an
expansion of their world outside the home is retarded by the
metaphor, and the reality, of the world looked at through the
window over the kitchen sink.

Four

The Situation of Women Today

The two themes which underlie the continuing social differentiation of women from men (women's situation) are (1) *domesticity* as a defining feature of women's situation, and (2) *ambivalence* in the cultural values applied to women's roles. Since the social stereotype of women portrays them as domesticated, a view of women as people is always mixed with a perception of their social difference from men: they are housewives.

1 Domesticity: Within the Family

As a consequence of industrialization, the home means 'family' rather than 'work'. Our language contains the phrase 'a family man', but there is no corresponding phrase for women. It would be socially redundant: the family *means* women. Women bear children, women rear children, women are in the home as housewives: if the home means the family, then the family *is* women.

What kind of family is this?

Compared with other family systems throughout history and in different cultures, it is small, mobile and non-productive. On one level it is functionless: it has no broad economic or political or social significance. But on another level, its functions are crucial:

The functions of the family in a highly differentiated society are not to be interpreted as functions directly on behalf of the society, but on behalf of personality . . . It is because the *human* personality is not 'born' but must be 'made' through the socialization process that in the first instance families are necessary. They are 'factories' which produce human personalities.[1]

The family produces people. It does this in two ways – by socializing children, and by stabilizing adult personalities in the socially approved moulds of wife–mother–housewife and husband–father. The production of people is not a new function for 'the' family as such, but its significance in the case of the modern family is enlarged through the family's loss of its other, pre-industrial functions. Because women are the childbearers, the modern emphasis on people-production also affects women directly. This connection is clarified when the importance of gender – femininity and masculinity – in the structure of the modern family is understood.

Gender differentiation between the roles of female and male is the axis of the modern family's structure. 'Marriage is rooted in the family rather than the family in marriage.'[2] Husband and wife are not the same sort of role, nor are father and mother, nor are housewife and non-housewife. The modern family stresses two sorts of bond: a cross-sex bond (marriage) and a cross-generational bond (the parent–child relationship). They share the same pattern of gender role-differentiation, and a clue to the nature of this differentiation is given by linguistic usage. The following are the conventional couplets: husband and wife, mother and father, man and wife. In each case a reversal sounds odd: wife and husband, father and mother, wife and man. The last couplet has the oddest ring, because a reversal of terms destroys the meaning of the phrase, which is man (person) and wife (female-person-in-the-possession-and-under-the-control-of-man). As it indicates, marriage is a situation of inequality: in marriage, women are not equal with men. This is because marriage defines a woman's place in society as it does not a man's. 'Differentiation' is a neutral word. The contrast between the roles of female and male in the family is not simply one of differentiation but of opposition. The order of terms in the couplet 'husband and wife' indicates a patriarchal structure.

The only couplet in which the female role conventionally takes precedence over the male role is the parental one – 'mother and father'. This is simply because the woman in the family is the childrearing parent.

In *Coal is Our Life*, a description of a British coalmining community written in 1956, there is a very good illustration of how gender differentiation structures marriage and family life. Although the community in question is working-class, although coalmining is a community-based occupation of a type declining in importance in modern society, and although the description was written almost two decades ago, the picture given is valuable because it clearly portrays the structure of female and male roles basic to modern marriage.

In 'Ashton', the man in the family works in the pit, and the woman in the family works at home. The occupational role of the man is 'reinforced by the custom of family life, the division of responsibility and duties in the household . . . and an ideology which accentuates the confinement of the mother to the home. "Woman's place is in the home" is a very definite and firm principle of thought and action . . .' Conversely, 'a man's centres of activity are *outside* the home; it is outside his home that there are located the criteria of success and social acceptance . . . ' Home is 'a haven for a tired man when he returns from work; here he expects to find a meal prepared, a room clean and tidy, a seat comfortable and warm, and a wife ready to give him what he wants . . . ' The wife, for her part, must

in a very consciously accepted division of labour . . . keep in good order the household provided for by the money handed to her each Friday by her husband. While he is at work, she should complete her day's work – washing, ironing, cleaning or whatever it may be . . . The miner feels that he does an extremely difficult day's work; he makes it plain that he thinks it a 'poor do' if his wife cannot carry out her side of the contract.

The rigidity of the separation between husband and wife roles is confirmed by the male's ritual rejection of meals which are not 'proper' meals – those not cooked by the man's own wife: fish and chips bought from a shop fall into this category, but so does any meal not prepared by the wife's own hands. One man threw on the fire a meal cooked by his wife's sister-in-law and told his wife forcibly 'that he had married *her* and he was going to have his meals cooked by *her* alone'.[3]

The domestic role is the only avenue of fulfilment for women in Ashton. Moreover it is a role whose activities 'are of a very limited range and do not allow for much expression of qualities of intellect or personality'. The consequence is that women of 'varying potentialities' are 'moulded to the same shape'; physically, as well as in terms of personality.[4] Interest wanes in affairs outside the home, their vitality is drained by the burden they carry for total responsibility in the home. They lose their individuality.

The role of the male is only tangentially a family role. The shared values and life of the pit form the basis for other exclusively masculine groups and activities: a male 'togetherness' which is fundamentally opposed to participation in family life. The antagonism between a man's wife and children on the one hand, and his 'mates' on the other – an underlying theme of social life – is begun before marriage, when the contradictory demands of the male peer group and the girl friend are reconciled by the commitment to male solidarity:

One young man of twenty-three, even though his holidays coincided with those of his fiancée, booked her accommodation at Blackpool and paid for the whole of her holiday. 'I'm not having her hanging round all week through my holidays!' When the young man married the same girl six months later, he did not tell his friends of the wedding until a few days before the actual ceremony.[5]

'Man and wife' in Ashton are strangers to each other. Their relationship lacks intimacy; they have little to say to each other and sex is rarely satisfactory. Yet (or perhaps therefore) total disintegration of marriage is uncommon: husband and wife have not got close enough to want to be apart. Marriage is a matter simply of 'carrying on' – a goal guaranteed 'so long as the man works and gives his wife and family sufficient, and the woman uses the family's wage "wisely" and gives her husband the few things he demands'.[6]

Through the deep separation between the lives of men and women, tension is built into the structure of marriage. 'It is not an exaggeration to say that the "row" is an institution for the present day family.' The 'row' is the ritual expression of both spouses' discontent, but the wife's frustrations are more often the activating factor. Her dissatisfactions are greater; while the husband, deprived of emotional satisfaction, protests at his exclusion from the supportive intimacy of close family relationships, the wife, deprived of 'personhood', protests against the completeness of her captivity: 'There's nothing I can do . . . Where could I go?'[7]

The Ashton pattern of rigidly segregated marital roles is found mostly in working-class communities today. This is not coincidental. Social recognition as individuals is conferred in Western culture on men and women chiefly through education and training and, to some extent, in the world of paid work. Working-class women lack the access to these areas that middle-class women have, and a dogmatic insistence on the place of women in marriage is therefore less likely to be diluted by a belief (albeit superficial) in sex equality.

An Ashton marriage is a 'normal' marriage. Although the behaviour of husband and wife is extreme in its emphasis on the importance of gender, the man and the woman are both playing their socially approved roles. Idiosyncratic definitions of marital roles are difficult. In their book *Dual-Career Families*, Rhona and Robert Rapoport discuss what they call 'environmental sanctions' on the dual-career pattern. In recent years, negative sanctions on married women's employment have diminished, they say, but in the area of women's domestic roles traditional ideas have shown no corresponding tendency to change. It is not enough for a married couple to say, 'We are not like that: we do things differently,' for the woman to work as an electrical engineer, and for the man to rear children, cook meals, and cite his wife as salary-earner on credit applications. The objection will be raised that they are husband and wife.

The family defines people's identities. It is not merely actual – female and male living together with their children – but ideological. To locate a person as a member of a family is to bestow automatically on that person a socially given identity: man–husband–father, woman–wife–mother–housewife, and child–son/daughter.*

A number of social developments this century have amplified the importance of gender in the family, and thus the importance of domesticity in women. One of these is the increased emotional investment of society in the family, and therefore of *people* in the family. The family has become increasingly the locus of all meaningful personal life. 'Familism', the sociological name for this orientation towards the family, entails a style of life decisively centred on the small family of two parents and children: a major emotional investment in family relationships, which are, for all family members, their chief source of social and psychological support. Although the reduction in family size since industrialization has probably been exaggerated, some narrowing down of family relationships to the nucleus of parents and children has taken place. Certainly it is this unit which now represents the sentimental ideal: the cornflakes-advertisement pattern of father, mother, boy and girl (suggesting a symmetry which contrasts with the actual differentiation between mother and father roles).

If society has grown more 'family-oriented' the family itself has identified more and more squarely with its physical location, the home. 'Home' and 'family' are now virtually interchangeable terms. A central value of the modern family is dedication to the goal of a steadily rising standard of living.

* David Cooper: 'The power of the family resides in its social mediating function' (*The Death of the Family*, p. 6).

The cost of the home has enlarged to absorb an increasing proportion of every family's income.

Before the First World War, the working-class home typically consisted of one or two rooms, crammed together with other homes sharing grossly inadequate sanitary arrangements. Since then, improvements in sanitation, in water supply, in other amenities, and also in the general standard of home building, have led to a visible improvement in the physical aspects of family life. There has been a tendency for the size of the working-class home to increase, and for the decoration and equipment of homes generally to become more elaborate and less differentiated by social class. 'Do it yourself' is the popular phrase which expresses the involvement of family members in the maintenance, decoration and general elaboration of the home. Husband–fathers are called upon to paint walls and make purchasing decisions, wife–mothers to expand the amount of physical and emotional energy invested in the activity of housework. The size of the family may have decreased, but a raised involvement in home life has demanded more of women's time. 'Consumerism', the involvement of society in the family, the involvement of the family in the physical aspects of living, has elevated the importance of housewifery. New domestic equipment constantly requires the acquisition of yet more equipment, for technical as well as status reasons. The fitted carpet demands the carpet sweeper and the carpet shampooer; highly polished furniture demands the polish that will effortlessly and effectively maintain its immaculate gloss. All demand 'more' and 'better' housework.

Women's roles as mothers have also been subject to amplification. Childhood is not what it used to be – and still is in many societies – a short, rather little-valued prelude to the all-important business of adulthood. Modern industrial society is demonstrably child-oriented: childhood is prolonged well past puberty, rather than attenuated well before it: startling discontinuities separate child role from adult role; children are, throughout their years of dependence, and in contrast to adults, inviolable, innocent, precious creatures. The intrinsic worth of every human being is epitomized, if not always exemplified, in the state of childhood: children are good.[8]

This view of the child accords with the high value ostensibly placed on individuality in Western society. It also owes much to the development of child psychology as a separate scientific discipline. 'With the publication of Darwin's *Descent of Man* in 1871,' says one author, 'the child became a unique part of scientific endeavour.'[9] 'He' was studied in the interests of understanding evolution. By 1900 the study of children was established as an independent discipline. The emergence of psychoanalysis in the first decades of this century gave to childhood a lasting importance.

These developments have two main implications for women as childrearers. Firstly, knowledge about childhood as a critical period in the formation of adult character makes 'successful' performance of the maternal role crucial. 'Parenthood,' said the anthropologist Margaret Mead of American society in 1952, 'is a responsible anxious matter . . . Within the family, children are given an extraordinary amount of attention, when judged by the standards of most other societies. Their needs, their wishes and their performances are regarded as central and worthy of adult attention.'[10] The consequence of this for the mother, given modern family structure, is that she becomes the principal disciplining and character-moulding parent.

The second important implication is the need for women as childrearers to be in touch with the standards of childcare – and the needs of children – specified by the experts. Until late in Western history the only experts in childcare and child behaviour outside the family were the midwife and the teacher. Now the world is full of experts. The basic structure for the dissemination to women of knowledge about childcare includes antenatal, postnatal and child-welfare clinics and classes, health visitors, maternity hospitals, and child-health specialists. This structure began to emerge at the turn of the century. In Britain the prototype of the modern infant-welfare clinic was opened in 1899. But information about childcare standards is also spread in more popular form by the media, which hold up, for women's imitation rather than inspection, the image of the ideal mother, beautiful, patient, coping and utterly bound up with the world of her small child's needs.

The discovery of the child's importance has affected women more than it has men. Child psychology, not at the beginning, but later on, insisted that children needed their mothers rather than their fathers. (This 'myth of motherhood' is examined in Chapter 8.) A second source of the modern stress on maternity is a more diffuse one, what Kate Millett has called 'the reaction in ideology' of the post-war years: a general reaction against the move towards sex equality in favour of a reaffirmation of traditional gender roles. In the modern family, the terms 'mother' and 'father' denote roles which are qualitatively different. A child's two parents are not interchangeable: the mother is the caretaker of the child, and the father its breadwinner.

'The husband's work is his chief role in life.'[11] The father's role towards children derives directly from his occupational role, with the child's material welfare depending, in the first instance, on the father's willingness to neglect it. The physical aspects of childcare are not emphasized; and when the father does take over these duties, he is said to be acting as a 'substitute mother' or as 'mother's helper'. 'The father is needed at home to help mother feel well in her body and happy in her mind . . . father is needed to give mother moral support, to be the backing for her authority, to be the human being who stands for the law and order which the mother plants in the life of the child.'[12] Implicit in this differentiation of parental roles is the command, for the male parent, 'Self first, child second.' In the case of the female parent, the formula is reversed to read, 'Child first, self second.' Women abdicate their personhood for the sake of their maternity.

A study of *Motherless Families* in Britain, carried out by Victor George and Paul Wilding, illustrates the popularity of the belief that mothers and fathers cannot (and should not) care for children in the same way. Despite the generally poorer economic situation of women in modern society, more people interviewed for this study believed that single mothers, as opposed to single fathers, could provide adequately for their children. 'The two main reasons, comment the authors, 'given for the father's inability to provide adequately for his children were a general belief that he cannot replace the mother and that he cannot provide for the emotional needs of children.' A second indication of the sharp distinction between mother and father roles is given by the replies to the question asked in this study, 'Should a father or mother (in a single-parent family) with children below school age go to work?' While the vast majority of responses indicated that a father in this situation would be expected to go out to work, opinions were reversed in the case of mothers: mothers, it was felt, should stay at home.[13]

The treatment of single-parent families by the social-security system reflects this assymetry. Mostly single mothers are encouraged to stay at home and single fathers to take employment. In the George and Wilding study, one father of a three-and-a-half-year-old and a two-year-old said, 'I try to explain the situation to them [Supplementary Benefit Officers] but they're always trying to get you to work.' Another father of seven children said, 'One of them told me . . . that it was time I got a housekeeper and went out to work, and stopped living off the community . . . '[14] But even when employed, the single father's responsibility for his children remains. Employers do not tolerate the domestic involvement of men in their children, as they expect it of women: men are sacked for 'too much' childcare.[15]

In the family role of women 'mothering' is thus seen as an essential ingredient, its absence pathogenic, threatening the whole purpose of the family – the production of healthy children. The same aura of pathogenicity is attached to women's deviation from conventional wife and mother roles. 'One can draw up . . . an ascending scale of more or less unconscious masculine identifications in the woman,' says one psychiatrist, putting forward the traditional view: 'At their fullest, I suppose these would manifest as a consistent rejection of the passive feminine role and thus of marriage.' Correspondingly, a 'normal' woman 'can best fulfil her role as a woman when she can be the wife to a man "who is somebody" – one sure of his sexual identity and worth . . . Then she is prepared to surrender her self-containment, her own masculine instrumentality and detachment.'[16]

The family as an institution is a prescription for gender-role normalcy: one woman, one man, and one or more children. Families with adopted children count, but single-parent families do not. They represent a social situation full of ambiguities, and are stigmatized and ostracized. There are strong economic, childcare, and social pressures for the normalization of the family unit. Within the gender-role structure of the family, women are reduced to a common social type: the housewife–wife–mother. The woman doctor, shop assistant, professional engineer, primary schoolteacher, ballet dancer, factory worker, all become Mrs X, the mother of Mr Y's children, the supporter of Mr Y's career/job, the washer of his clothes, the caretaker and creator of his home, the centre and symbol of his family life.

2 Domesticity: Outside the Family

The emotional and social importance of the family as people-producer in modern society has the consequence that its pattern of gender roles radiates out to many other areas of social and economic life.

One particularly invidious example of this process is the British practice of denying social-security benefits to the single – unmarried, deserted, divorced, widowed – woman if she is found to be cohabiting with a male. 'Special investigators' are employed by the Department of Health and Social Security to investigate the validity of benefit claims. In 1970 allowances to 4,388 women were withdrawn after investigation for cohabitation or 'fictitious desertion'.

The criterion set out in the rules for the special investigators of these cases is 'not whether the woman and her children are in need . . . but whether she is living with a man who can be said to have a liability to maintain her'.[17] This procedure is backed by law, being statutorily derived from Paragraph 3 of the 2nd Schedule to the 1966 Ministry of Social Security Act, which provides that: 'Where a husband and wife are members of the same household their requirements and resources shall be aggregated and *shall be treated as the husband's and similarly . . . as regards two persons cohabiting as man and wife*' [italics added].[18]

One woman, whose case was investigated under this rule, was accused of cohabiting with her lodger, and hence of drawing her widow's pension under false pretences. 'I think I have the right to have anyone I want to live in my own house,' she said in an appeal against a demand for the repayment of pension money amounting to £321: 'There is nothing to stop a landlady sleeping with a lodger if she wants to. My husband worked hard and paid insurance stamps to cover anything that might happen to us.'[19]

The inequity of this situation is clear. Within marriage, the role of the female is assumed to be a financially dependent one. Outside marriage the interpretation of dependence on a man is imposed. It may have no basis in truth, and, indeed, its truth or falsity is strictly irrelevant. This is because the issue is not whether the man is actually supporting the woman but whether he is having regular sexual intercourse with her. 'Regular sexual intercourse' is held to constitute marriage because marriage is *ideally* the context for adult sexual satisfaction in modern society. This moral idealism, as the cohabitation example shows, is more binding on women than men. Not all echoes, moreover, of the old adage, 'Marriage is legalized prostitution', have been removed from the institution of modern marriage: a woman who charged her husband for sexual intercourse was recently held to have provided him with legal grounds for divorce.[20]

The cohabitation example demonstrates especially clearly just how the place of women in marriage and in society continues to be defined by their sex-status – with the expectation of domesticity and dependence on men being of utmost importance – in direct opposition to the modern ideology of sex-equality. This example reveals women's persisting social and economic differentiation from men.

In the world of education and work outside the home, divisions between the sexes endure and show signs of becoming more pronounced. The crucial factor is women's domesticity.

Assertions of increasing equality between the sexes are often based on employment statistics. A closing gap in the proportion of the labour force made up of males and females, together with an apparently rising similarity in the jobs they do, are adduced as evidence for the convergence in gender roles. In fact the impression of convergence is illusory.

The greatest increase this century in the proportion of female workers employed outside the home in Britain has taken place since 1950. While one in four of all adult females was employed in 1951, the figure is now one in two: while one in five married women was employed in 1951, the current figure is nearer one in two; of all women employed, two out of three are now married, compared with a 1951 figure of less than half. The combination of marriage (and thus of housewifery) with employment is the change most often commented on. As Richard Titmuss observes, in the decade from 1950 to 1960 the total labour force of Great Britain expanded by $1\frac{1}{2}$ million, and the addition of married female workers accounted for $1\frac{1}{4}$ million of this total increase.

But a main reason for this development is the increased popularity, and the falling age, of marriage. In 1931, 59 per cent of women aged 25–9 in England and Wales were married; in 1966, 87 per cent. The mean age of marriage for women is now 22 years, and for men, 25 years. Spinsterhood as a lifetime status is fast disappearing. Compared with the position in 1950, women are now more likely to be married, to be married young, and to be both married (housewives) and employed.

Against this must be set the relative stability in the proportion of female workers who combine employment with motherhood. About a quarter of all female workers have also been mothers over the period from 1949 to 1966 (though recent figures suggest that this combination of employment and motherhood may be gaining in popularity).

These statistics in themselves hardly suggest that a revolution has taken place. Married women, it has been said, have been recapturing the economic functions they had once, but lost during industrialization. The image is one of an old tradition re-established. Yet, behind these statistics of employment, the traditional differentiation between women's and men's roles endures still. In terms of the work they do, in terms of the patterns of their work-careers, in terms of the financial benefits which accrue to them as a result of work, the roles of men and women in the world of work remain differentiated. Women's defining role is a domestic one.

The bulk of women's work has been, and still is, concentrated in the domestic sector. Teaching, nursing, factory work producing domestic products, and retail sales work are the occupations of most employed women in most industrialized countries. The rise of 'white-collar' occupations has added low-grade clerical and secretarial work to this list of feminine occupations (and the growth of feminine clerical work is the main change in women's employment in recent years). Although office work is not domestic, it has other qualities which account for its easy assimilation to the feminine employment role: 'Today's secretary,' says Mary Kathleen Benet in *Secretary: An Enquiry into the Female Ghetto*,

also acts as wife, mother, mistress and maid . . . Office work is . . . the business equivalent of housekeeping . . . Both jobs are custodial, concerned with tidying up, putting away, and restoring order rather than with producing anything . . . Filing is like washing the dishes, and induces the same sense of frustration. Typing a perfect letter is as transient as achievement as cooking an egg . . . [21]

Most professional women are either teachers or nurses. In 1970, women made up 52 per cent of all schoolteachers in England and Wales, but 75 per cent of all primary schoolteachers. Similar figures hold for the United States and other countries. Nursing is a 90 per cent feminine occupation in virtually all Western countries. The role of nurse is especially congruent with the traditional role of the female in Western culture.

In the United States, the nurse is referred to as 'she'; in England, a nurse is referred to as 'sister', be the individual male or female . . . The announcement of a man's status as a nurse will come as a revelation and a surprise . . . They [the patients] want to call us 'Doctor'. We say we are a nurse. They say, 'you are a Doctor as far as we're concerned.'

Moreover, for the male nurse, 'it is more than his professional role that is questioned. It is his entire sexual identity. There is a set of mental equations which go: Female + Nursing Role = Nurse, Male + Nursing Role = Homosexual.'[22]

In the United States, Britain, Belgium, Denmark, Germany, Italy, the Netherlands, Norway and Sweden, employed women are concentrated in the same five occupations of nursing, teaching, unskilled or semi-skilled factory work, domestic work and clerical work. Women are relatively scarce in 'masculine' occupations: dentistry, engineering, medicine and the law. There is a pronounced tendency for women entering 'masculine' occupations to take up traditional feminine interests within these occupations. Women lawyers take up matrimonial work: women doctors take up obstetrics, gynaecology and pediatrics. One 1971 study of a group of female medical students showed the popularity of these specialisms, and it also demonstrated the acceptance of the conventional stereotype of woman's role in society by these 'intelligent and highly selected' women. They believed, for example, that women make more sympathetic doctors than men, are better at working with women and children, and are less good at science than men. The latter belief 'is not borne out by examination results' comment the researchers who carried out the study.[23]

One computation of sex segregation in occupations over the period from 1900 to 1960 in the United States shows almost no change in the degree to which occupations are sex-differentiated, and there is no suggestion of change since 1960. In Britain in 1971, just over half the female work force was concentrated in three industries (out of a possible twenty-four in the Standard Industrial Classification): distributive trades, miscellaneous services (laundries, dry cleaning and so on), and professional/scientific services – which, so far as women are concerned, means teaching and nursing. This was a heavier concentration than in 1959. The popular impression of gender interchangeability in occupational role may be due to the fast growth of employed women in some sectors: but these sectors – for instance white-collar work – are those in which the tendency to discriminate by gender has always been strong. What has been happening is that the rapid growth in women's employment has 'feminized' low-skill occupations. According to a British Labour Party Report, *Discrimination Against Women*, over the five-year period 1961–6, male employment fell in twenty out of thirty-eight less skilled occupations, but female employment rose in nineteen out of twenty-four such occupations.

The constancy of gender-differentiation patterns in occupations within Western culture is demonstrated by a comparison between the United States in 1950 and Sweden in 1962. In the former, seven tenths of all women in the labour force were found in a mere twenty different occupations. In the latter – Sweden being a country with a very different history – the proportion was exactly the same. Furthermore, in these occupations in the United States, only 12 per cent of working men were found, and in Sweden, twelve years later, only 11·7 per cent. In both countries, two fifths of all working women were in the five basic occupations already mentioned.

Higher education does not make as much difference to the jobs women take as it does in the case of men. The majority of all women university graduates take up teaching as a career. Three out of five of an American sample of employed graduates studied in 1952 worked as schoolteachers; so did two out of three of employed graduates in West Germany in 1961; so did half of all employed female graduates in Great Britain in 1966. A recent study of British graduates by R. K. Kelsall, Anne Poole and Annette Kuhn demonstrates that for graduate men of low social-class origins, schoolteaching represents an attractive career because it is seen as a channel of upward social mobility. But 'women graduates of whatever social class found schoolteaching very attractive . . . ' While a third of the male graduates took up teaching, two thirds of the female graduates chose this profession. 'In fact the proportion of women who took up schoolteaching exceeded the proportion (55 per cent) who had expressed a desire to teach after hearing their finals results. As a result, few women were engaged in any other sectors of employment and were especially unlikely to be in industry or the professions.'[24]

Higher education does not substantially increase the chances that women will in fact be employed. Fifty-one per cent of married women who had completed their education at the age of 19 or older were employed in Great Britain in 1965, but so were 43 per cent of married women who had left school at 15 or earlier. Kelsall, Poole and Kuhn comment on the graduates in their sample: 'Married women graduates . . . were much less likely than women as a whole to be in employment. These data . . . show just how ascriptive sex roles would appear to influence considerably both the chances of women being in employment and the type of work they actually undertake.'[25]

Not only do women on the whole take up different jobs, but the level of their jobs in terms of pay, skill, prestige and responsibility also remains significantly lower than that of men. According to a survey of male and female graduates published by the British Institute of Management in 1972, 40 per cent of employed women graduates earn £1,750 a year or less – but only 14 per cent of the men do so. (And 5 per cent of the women, but 25 per cent of the men, earn £2,500 a year or more). In 1970, the average hourly earnings of female manual workers in Great Britain were 40 per cent lower than men's. The average weekly earnings of administrative, technical and clerical employees were 45 per cent lower than men's. Almost half of all employed women, but only a quarter of employed men were in unskilled or semi-skilled manual work. Only 13 per cent of all managers of 'large establishments' were women in 1966, a percentage which varies according to the 'gender' of the occupation in question: 16 per cent of all managers in the clothing and footwear industries were female, but only 3·6 per cent of those in the engineering and electrical goods industries.

The domesticity of women's jobs is reinforced by the omission of one job from the employment statistics: that of housewife. One in two housewives still does not hold a job outside the home. Even in the Soviet Union, where employment work is, in terms of official ideology, a component of the feminine role, eleven million women are neither studying nor out at work. Some of these women are mothers. According to a national survey of women's employment in Britain, only one in three of all adult women who have responsibility for children are employed – two out of three are not. The proportion of women with children who are not employed is highest when the children are small: 85 per cent of those with children aged 0–2 years are not working outside the home. But as children become less dependent, the proportion of women employed to not-employed becomes more equal, so that 44 per cent of those with children between five and fifteen years are employed outside the home.

The discrepancy between the situations of men and women here is not due to women's biological role in childbearing, but to their cultural role in childrearing. Maternity in this sense is, like domesticity, an essential component of femininity, and it is the interaction of the two which distinguishes the situation of the female (housewife–wife–mother) from that of the male (husband–father).

Most part-time workers are women, and most part-time women workers choose this work because of their domestic responsibilities. According to the 1966 British Census, 88 per cent of part-time workers are female. The proportion of women working part-time is generally lower among more highly educated women, and among women in professional jobs. For example, the analysis by Michael Fogarty and his colleagues in *Sex, Career and Family* shows that only about one in ten women with Advanced Level General Certificate of Education worked part-time in Britain in 1965, and only one in ten women engineers in 1967 was engaged in part-time work. But this also reflects the lower likelihood of marriage and motherhood in this group. According to the 1968 survey of women's employment in Britain, 34 per cent of the employed women were in part-time work and four out of five of these attributed their decision to work part-time to 'responsibility for husband', 'responsibility for children' or 'other domestic duties'.

In the words of one social scientist committed to the ideal of sex-equality, this situation reflects the fact that:

Part-time employment is this generation's false panacea for avoiding a more basic change in the relations between men and women, a means whereby, with practically no change in the man's role and minimal change in the woman's, she can continue the same wife and mother she has been in the past, with a minor appendage to these roles as an intermittent professional or clerical worker.[26]

The typical pattern for women has three phases: employment, followed by fulltime domesticity, followed by a job again. Among women marrying in the 1930s and 1940s, the usual practice was to give up work at marriage: now the birth of the first child is the usual occasion for the withdrawal of women into housewifery. A related development is the return to employment of older married women, when the ties of childrearing no longer bind them so firmly to the home. Few women manage to be what has been termed 'continuous-in' workers. Few even of the highly educated achieve this degree of commitment: through the expectations traditionally held about women, most retire from work when motherhood is imminent. The 'dual-career' family is a 'statistically minor variant'.

Compared to men, women are then (1) concentrated in occupations which reflect the domesticity of the conventional feminine role, and (2) likely to be less consistently involved in a job or career. Supporting these sex differences as relatively stable features of women's situation are statistics which show no decrease in recent years in the extent to which occupations are differentiated by gender.

In Britain, an analysis of the Census data over the last half century (carried out in the P.E.P. study *Sex, Career and Family*) gives an interesting picture. When women first achieved entry into previously masculine professions between the census years of 1921 and 1931, the numbers of women in these professions rose dramatically – twice as fast as the number of men (by 3 per cent a year as opposed to 0·8 per cent). This was the 'classic decade of breakthrough'. In the following two decades, from 1931 to 1951, the two rates of growth became much closer together, though women still had a slight edge over men with an annual growth rate of 3·6 per cent against 3 per cent. But from 1951 to 1961 the number of men went on growing at 4·5 per cent a year while the number of women actually fell by nearly 1 per cent a year. The professions affected in this way included science, medicine, engineering, surveying and accountancy. For the 1960s the trend is no further fall in women's share of these professions, but on the other hand, no resumption of the earlier advance.

This sequence is one of breakthrough to acceptance followed by stagnation. Marriage, and housewifery, are basic impediments to occupational sex-equality. The female professional worker is likely to differ in one important respect from the male professional worker: she is between three and four times more

likely to be unmarried. While the employment of male professional workers is associated with marriage (marriage en-
hancing the male's career commitment) the employment of
female professional workers is associated with the unmarried
state (marriage acting as an obstacle to the female career role).

3 Ambivalence

The perpetuation of women's domesticity within and outside
the family demonstrates the structural ambivalence in their
situation.

On the one hand, society sees women as members of a sex
category, a fact which results in the allocation to them of
traditional feminine roles: ' . . . the primary status-carrying
role is, in a sense, that of housewife. The woman's fundamental
status is that of her husband's wife, the mother of his children . . . '[27] These values are traditional, and overtly sex-
discriminatory. On the other hand, society perceives women
as human beings, endowed with the potentiality for individual
fulfilment: 'All human beings are born free and equal in dignity
and rights.'[28] Liberal–democratic values theoretically apply to
all human beings regardless of sex. In these values, it is the
intrinsic worth of every human personality which is stressed:
'to be a person is to be independent, responsible, and self-
respected, and thereby to be worthy of concern and respect in
one's own right.'[29]

The tension between these two sets of values for the individual women is illustrated in a study of 'Cultural Contradictions
and Sex Roles' carried out by the American sociologist, Mirra
Komarovsky, some years ago. Komarovsky found college
women to be aware of the expectation that they should play
two sorts of roles. While being pressured towards intellectual
achievement in their role as individuals, they also felt pressured
to underachievement in their role as women. 'When a girl asks
me what marks I got last semester, I answer, "Not so good –
only one A," ' said one of Komarovsky's students: 'but when

a boy asks the same question, I say very brightly, with a note of surprise, "Imagine, I got an A!"' Komarovsky termed the two roles prescribed by these opposing values 'the modern role' and 'the feminine role' respectively. The modern role, she observed, 'is, in a sense, no sex role at all, because it partly obliterates the differentiation in sex. It demands of the woman much the same virtues, patterns of behaviour and attitudes that it does of the man of a corresponding age.'[30] Conversely, the feminine role prescribes behaviour which is neither dominant nor aggressive but emotional and sympathetic: behaviour which is exclusively feminine. Marriage and motherhood represent the goal of the feminine role, while a career is the goal to which the modern role is oriented.*

These goals are mutually exclusive, because the achievement of both calls for more time, energy, and commitment than one person can reasonably supply, and because 'the fundamental personality traits each evokes are at points diametrically opposed, so that what are assets for one become liabilities for the other, and the full realization of one role threatens defeat in the other.'[31]

This is a situation of 'structural ambivalence' for women. Ambivalence is 'the social state in which a person in any of his [sic] statuses . . . faces contradictory normative expectations of attitudes, beliefs, and behaviour, which specify how any of these statuses should be defined'. An important point is that 'each of the contradictory expectations is often as legitimate as the next'.[32]

Women confront a contradiction between alternatives of apparently equal legitimacy. During education, supposedly the route to self-realization, they are expected to act out a more traditional role: that of looking attractive to and being deferential towards men. Two opposing definitions of women's adult

---

*According to Epstein (*Woman's Place*, p. 65) this situation has not changed since Komarovsky first studied it: 'College women's plans for the future are highly contingent and subject to modification because of spouses or future spouses.'

identity arise from these expectations. In one a woman 'strives to fulfil herself directly by realizing her own potentialities . . . Her distinguishing feature is that she seeks fulfilment through her own accomplishments.' In the other, a woman is 'the counterpart of the man and children in her life. She realizes herself indirectly by fostering their fulfilment.'[33]

Since traditional concepts of femininity are built around the housewife–wife–mother roles, it would appear that the conflict women today face is a conflict between the domestic role and a role as an individual human being. Yet if this were so, it would not be possible to explain women's relative failure to make use of the opportunities available to them outside the home, and the frequency with which they choose to define themselves as housewives, wives and mothers, rather than as individuals. A more convincing answer is that the conflict to which women are exposed is a conflict between *alternative gender roles*.

A 'gender role' is a role assigned on the basis of biological sex, which defines specific personality traits and behavioural responses as appropriate to a person of that sex. Biologically, people are male or female; culturally, they are pressured to be masculine or feminine. The definition of masculinity and femininity varies between different societies and also historically within each society. Modern industrial society has created opportunities for the equality of male and female but has retained, and even heightened, the differentiation between masculinity and femininity.[34]

Men are people: women are women. Men have careers, women look after the house and children (and men).

While the virtues of domesticity are upheld on a verbal level, social practice confers all the prestige upon the man's achievement-oriented role. The role of wife and mother, with very few exceptions, is incompatible with an occupational role, and does not allow the individual woman to realise the dominant goal set by our culture.[35]

Two questions arise: how did this gender-role conflict emerge; and what are its consequences for women today?

Modern women, so it is often pointed out, are emancipated. But the fact of emancipation is entirely compatible with the assertion that women's central conflict today poses a choice between traditional feminine and masculine behaviour. The key lies in the meaning of the word 'emancipation': its literal meaning is 'led out of the state of slavery'. The verb 'to emancipate' makes the object of emancipation a passive object: women do not emancipate themselves, they *are* emancipated. The state from which people are emancipated is by definition a state of slavery, but the state to which they are emancipated is not necessarily one of liberation.

A parallel to women's situation is the emancipation of Negroes in the American south. From slavery they moved to a state of 'segregation' – the 'Jim Crow' system – in which their situation continued to be radically differentiated from that of the white man, though their status was, ostensibly, 'free'. Along with the white man's exploitation of the Negro in the slavery period grew up 'the old assumptions of Anglo-Saxon superiority and innate African inferiority, white supremacy and Negro subordination'. In so far therefore as 'segregation is based on these assumptions, it is based on the old pro-slavery argument and has its remote ideological roots in the slavery period'.[36]

The same is true of women. The ideology of women's innate difference from men, their domesticity, their inferiority, has been carried over into the era of 'women's equality'. Equality for women in effect has meant the same as segregation for Negroes: both are a recognition of 'free' status, but neither grant the conditions necessary for liberation.

The history of women's emancipation is the (as yet uncompleted) history of women's piecemeal admission to rights and responsibilities previously defined as masculine prerogatives. The right to higher education, the right to vote, the right to hold professional jobs, the right to retain legally one's personal identity in marriage – all these (and many more) were exclusively masculine privileges conferred by men on women in the course of women's long and continuing struggle for sex-equality. Because these privileges were originally masculine, and because the society which conceded them to women was, and is, a society in which men, not women, hold the major share of effective power and prestige, the standard of individual achievement and self-realization they represent has remained a masculine standard. It is men who constitute the norm, with which women, members of an 'inferior' sex, are compared: 'The man comes forward as a representative of the universal, he may be defined without reference to a complementary female role . . . he is less sex-determined.'[37]

So far as education is concerned: 'The fact that homemaking is woman's most important role has never been seriously questioned either by those arguing in favour of college education for women or by those opposing it.'[38] Historically, the fight for women's education had to contend with the masculine argument that the education of women would sterilize them and thus render them unfit for the childbearing role: that 'too much thinking . . . interferes with the punctual discharge of household duties'[39]; that if women were literate, they might learn the advantages of forging their husbands' signatures. 'Educate women and you educate the teachers of men,' was the argument which finally won the day:[40] the convenience of sex-discrimination became the convenience (to men) of sex equality.*

Today, the education of women remains a specific subject, set apart from the topic of education in general. In library catalogues 'women's education' has several hundred entries, but 'men's education' is not listed. Democratic ideals may suggest that higher education is non-discriminatory but it is actually continuous with social definitions of masculinity. A

---

* Jessie Bernard (*Women and the Public Interest*, p. 255) notes that the convenience argument is extended to women's liberation today: 'One young husband was won over to his wife's point of view when she convinced him of the servility of traditional role prescriptions. *He* did not want an inferior wife.'

recent lecture by an eminent social scientist given at Bedford College – the first institution for women's higher education to be founded in Britain – began with the following statement: 'The *particular oddity* which I want to discuss this evening is the higher education of women.'[4]

With higher education stereotyped as masculine women will tend to reject educational opportunity because they see it as threatening their femininity. In a gender-differentiated society, one of the most important ways of conforming as an adult involves conformity with the standards of one's gender role. Criminal behaviour is socially perceived as 'deviant': so also is cross-gender behaviour. 'Feminine' behaviour on the part of men and 'masculine' behaviour on the part of women is frequently the subject of social ridicule – and ridicule is one of the most effective means there is of expressing social disapproval. Motivated largely by fear, this ridicule reflects the threat cross-gender behaviour poses to people's learnt identities as masculine and feminine: for women it means that equality may be deferred because 'acting feminine' appears a more rational and safer choice than 'becoming masculine'.

In education and employment, progress towards sex equality is hampered through women's choice of traditional feminine alternatives. As Komarovsky demonstrated in her study of contradictory expectations felt by college girls, educational equality is perceived as a threat to the conventional relationship between the sexes – a relationship based on the *opposition* of masculinity and femininity – as in the phrase the 'opposite' (not merely the 'other') sex.

In Sweden since 1968, the eradication of gender differentiation has been the declared policy of all public bodies including the central government. The aim is not (as in other countries) the more vaguely specified goal of women's equality with men, but the abolition of all barriers to the non-differentiation of gender roles. Despite this, the education and employment fields show a continuing, marked and traditional differentiation by gender. During secondary education, girls persist in choosing to prepare themselves for typically feminine vocations – primary-school teaching, nursing, hairdressing, retail sales work, etc. – and boys select masculine vocations –mostly technical, scientific and mechanical work. 'Especially for young people,' one commentator observes, 'the fear of going too far in behaviour not typical for one's own sex is very great.' Hence the real obstacles to greater equality are not easily abolished by governmental policy-directive; they are obstacles 'having to do with deeply-rooted ideas, role-expectations, role-ideals, values and habits . . . obstacles based on conventions in the pattern of social relations itself.'[42]

The Swedish example is illuminating precisely because the battle to abolish social differentiation between gender roles has been fought so purposively there. The persistence of the dichotomy between masculine and feminine roles suggests that the roots of this conflict are very deep indeed (even allowing for the conformist traditions of that society).

In Britain and the United States, the same distinctions between feminine and masculine educational subjects and employment work roles are to be found, and the same reasons for their continuation dilute the effect of an official commitment to sex equality. As in Sweden, it is not only the women themselves who perceive education – and certain sorts of education – as 'masculine', but parents, teachers, and indeed the whole fabric of a gender-differentiated culture.

If higher education particularly is seen as masculine, then a lower value is attached to education in general in the case of girls than in the case of boys. Numerous studies of attitudes towards children support the remark of one American mother: 'I feel that my son is more important than my daughters. So we spend much more time on his education . . . my girls [will] probably get married . . . '[43] The lower value placed on education for girls was one reason why the 1961–3 Committee on Higher Education in Britain rejected the introduction of a loan system for the financing of higher education. 'Where women are concerned,' the Report states, the effect might well be either that British parents would be strengthened in their age-long disinclination to consider their daughters to be as deserving of higher education as their sons, or that the eligibility for marriage of the more educated would be diminished by the addition to their charms of what would be in effect a negative dowry.[44]

The first effect of a situation in which education is more highly valued for males than for females is the simple under-representation of females in school, college and university populations. In England and Wales in 1970, 21 per cent of all boys aged seventeen were at school compared with 19 per cent of girls. At age eighteen, the figures were 8 per cent (boys) and 5 per cent (girls). The proportion of females to males in education declines increasingly from minimum school-leaving age on. In the United States in 1966, 50·6 per cent of all high-school graduates were female, but of college graduates, the female percentage was 40·7 per cent. In the *Sex, Career and Family* analysis of education data, 8·8 per cent of all British males in the appropriate age group entered university in 1967, but only 3·8 per cent of females did so. Of British first-degree graduates in 1970, 33·4 per cent were female. A third of the British university undergraduate population was female in 1970, but under a quarter of postgraduates were women, and only one in ten of all higher degrees were obtained by women in that year.

The second effect is a sex-specialization in subjects studied, evident from secondary-school level on: in the last years of school, boys form the majority of those taking technical, mathematical and science subjects: girls specialize in arts subjects, in social studies and in domestic science. In England and Wales in 1966, 17 per cent of girls taking first year Advanced Level General Certificate of Education courses took mathematics and science subjects only: 47 per cent of the boys did so.

Differentiation by sex in subjects studied continues as one ascends the educational ladder. In 1970, six in a hundred of all women undergraduates, but one in five male undergraduates,

in Great Britain took applied science. Whereas men outnumbered women in universities by about three to one, women
outnumbered men in colleges of education by more or less the
same ratio. The subjects taken by higher-degree graduates also
divide by sex: while one in ten of postgraduate students in pure
and applied science were women in 1970, nearly half of those
taking arts subjects were women. Three quarters of all women
taking higher degrees chose arts or social studies; more than
half of the men chose science. The same pattern is also found
in the United States and in many other Western countries.

From education, the theme of opposition between masculine
and feminine roles continues into employment.

Women's 'rejection' of the masculine role is most evident in
the professions. The consensus of opinion among participants
in a British conference discussion on 'Reasons for Women's
Lack of Advancement' was that 'Women's prejudice [against
women] was nearly as strong as men's: frequently they
bolstered the man-made stereotype and repeated that "a woman
must remain feminine". They also showed a complete lack of
confidence in those bold enough to attempt to break the ties of
prejudice.'[45]

It is the 'career' which is particularly equated with masculinity. To quote another study:

Conflict faces the would-be career woman, for the core of attri-
butes found in most professional and occupational roles is considered to be masculine ... persistence and drive, personal dedication, aggressiveness, emotional detachment, and a kind of sexless
matter-of-factness equated with intellectual performance ...
Women who work in male-dominated occupations ... are often
thought to be sexless. The woman who takes her work seriously –
the career-woman – traditionally has been viewed as the antithesis
of the feminine woman.[46]

While to call a man 'ambitious' is to complement him, to call
a woman 'ambitious' may be to insult her. Ambition itself is a
masculine attribute.

The career women whose work requires assertive character-istics may meet disapproval from other women as well as from men, who consider her 'sexless' or 'unfeminine'. Fear of such an outcome discourages many women from pursuing 'mascu-line' careers, and is one of the main reasons why occupational equality shows as yet no signs of being achieved.

A sample of university graduates interviewed in the British study of *Sex, Career and Family* gave, as reasons why women did not enter 'masculine' professions (pure and applied science, engineering, industrial management), either 'Men in this field resent women colleagues,' 'Most parents discourage their daughters from training for such a field' or 'Women are afraid they will be considered unfeminine.' This latter explanation was offered most frequently in the case of engineering, where more than half the reasons placed at the top of the list cited this objection. A similar study of graduates in the United States reports the same finding. The major reasons given by women for women's low entry into the engineering profession is that women would be considered unfeminine if they entered it, and that parents discourage their daughters from training for such work. A survey of *Women in Top Jobs* shows that even women who have achieved and persisted in high-level professional careers tend to side-step the confrontation with a man's world. They carve out for themselves specifically feminine roles which do not compete directly with those of their male colleagues.

The consequences of this conflict between masculine and feminine alternatives take the form of a new emphasis on femininity: an induced abrogation of 'personhood', through the equation of self-realizing opportunities with the social image of masculinity. The values attached to women's situation may be ambivalent, but the outcome is unequivocal: the conservation of traditional forms of behaviour, rather than the initiation of change. The stress on sex-equality appears self-delusory. Can women be equal to men outside the home when they are not equal within it? The opening of the professions to women, the right of access they theoretically have to all forms of higher education and training, the opportunities which are now available to them for public political and business careers: these are, for the vast majority of women in our society, mere visions. They represent what R. H. Tawney once described as 'the impertinent courtesy of an invitation offered to unwelcome guests in the certainty that circumstances will prevent them from accepting it'.[47]

Five

Housewives and Their Work Today

Behind the structural ambivalence of women's situation, with its emphasis on femininity and domesticity, stands the woman-as-housewife. Everybody in a sense knows what being a housewife is like; but in another sense, nobody knows. The social trivialization of housework and women has meant that the behaviour and feelings of women as housewives (rather than as wives and mothers) is an unresearched area. Housework is not a respectable subject for study.

In this chapter some findings from a study of housewives are briefly presented and discussed: the chapter forms a prelude to the case-studies of four housewives which follow. The study from which this material is taken is a survey of women's attitudes to, and satisfaction with, housework, based on interviews with a random sample of forty housewives, which I carried out in 1971.[1]

The modern housewife has a dual personality: she is both acting out a feminine role, and she is a worker involved in an occupation which has all the characteristics of other work roles except one – it is unpaid. In the current debate about the position of women, sometimes one of these two aspects is stressed, sometimes the other. While the women's liberationist maintains that housewifery is domestic servitude – labour-exploitation – the defenders of traditional femininity argue that the housewife role is a freely chosen occupation offering scope for individual creative skill. While one says that housewives are oppressed, the other says that housewives are free from the oppression of most workers – restrictions of personality and freedom consequent on the imposition of repetitive industrial work routines and work rhythms.

In fact housewives do value the theoretical autonomy their role offers. Of the forty housewives I interviewed in suburban London in 1971, twenty-eight said that the 'best thing' about being a housewife is that you're your own boss, you don't have to go to work and you have free time:

The thing that's nice about being a housewife is you have your own time, there's nobody behind you with a punch card. You're your own boss [ex-hotel chambermaid married to a painter and decorator].

On the other hand, the autonomy conferred by the housewife role has a tendency to be fictional rather than real. Being one's own boss implies the necessity to supervise one's own work: to see that housework gets done, in other words.

The worst thing is I suppose that you've got to do the work because you *are* at home. Even though I've got the option of not doing it, I don't really feel I *could* not do it, because I feel I *ought* to do it [ex-computer programmer married to an advertising manager].

The housewife is 'free from' rather than 'free to'; the absence of external supervision is not balanced by the liberty to use time for one's own ends. The taking of leisure is self-defeating:

It's not that anyone's going to whip me if I don't do it – but I know there's going to be double the quantity tomorrow, so really I'm just beating my own brow [ex-shop assistant, married to a lorry driver].

Housewives are sharply aware of the fact that, however much or little husbands may share domestic tasks with them, the responsibility for getting the work done remains theirs. This is one area of separation between husband and wife which persists, despite the twentieth-century emphasis on companionate and child-involved marital roles. From what housewives say about their husbands' participation in domestic work, it is clear that one factor responsible is the continuing belief in 'natural' differences between the sexes:

> I don't agree with men doing housework – I don't think it's a man's job . . . I certainly wouldn't like to see my husband cleaning a room up. I don't think it's mannish for a man to stay at home. I like a man to be a man [ex-bookkeeper married to a journalist].

> I don't mind if husbands do their share, but not too much. They should help – but not all the time. Like there's a chappie here who goes out on a Sunday with a pinafore on him. I don't like that, I don't think they should broadcast it – it's not genuine [ex-hotel chambermaid married to a painter and decorator].

There are husbands who will not go in shops, husbands who will go in shops but who will not carry the shopping bag for fear of being labelled 'effeminate'; husbands who – in the complementary area of childcare – will not push prams or change nappies:

> Now, he will not take the baby out in the pram – he'll carry him . . . He says he'll wait till he's in a pushchair . . . I don't know why, he won't tell me [ex-audio typist married to a food wholesaler].

> [Does your husband ever change a dirty nappy?] No! He absolutely refuses. He says, 'no thank you, goodbye, I'm going out!' If I'm changing a nappy, he runs out of the room, it makes him sick. He thinks it's my duty [ex-fashion model, married to a retail chemist].

The net effect of this insistence on traditional stereotypes of feminine and masculine roles, together with social-structural factors which maintain women's domesticity (inequality in the job world, lack of institutional childcare facilities) is a tremendous pressure on women to become psychologically involved with housework. One of the most striking aspects of these forty interviews is the investment of women in their housework standards and routines. Every housewife was able to say what her standards were and how she organized (or aimed to organize) her day, and most gave the impression that once specified, these ways of behaving attained an objective air which compelled obedience from the housewife as worker. On this dimension of housework behaviour, as on many others, class differences were minimal. Working-class and middle-class housewives may talk about their experiences differently, but linguistic distinctions do not necessarily denote a diversity of experience.

Janet Gallagher, an ex-factory worker, and the wife of a driver's mate, describes her approach to housework:

Some people that I know start at the bottom of the house and then clean up – but I must start at the top of the house: I've always done it from the top. I start cleaning in the morning after I've got Mary [the eldest of her four children] to school. I do the upstairs rooms, then I polish the stairs, and the hall and the front room. I go right through – every single day I'm on my knees polishing, from top to bottom.

I often get days when I kill myself cleaning and polishing and then the place doesn't look clean when I've finished it. I'll go and do it all over again. I must get it right, because sometimes it doesn't turn out the way I want it. What really gets me in a bad temper is when I've killed myself cleaning it up, and the children come along and start throwing everything about . . . When I clean a house up, I expect it to stay clean, but it don't.

In the evenings if I can't find anything to do, I'll clean out the cupboards or something. I get very bored and irritable if I haven't got nothing to do, and I take it out on the children. I must find something to do, I must be going all the time. I can't sit down and read the paper or anything like that, I get really bored then, I must keep going because I do like housework.

This is the 'houseproud' housewife: the woman with an 'obsessive' interest in keeping a perfectly clean, tidy house. The terms 'houseproud' and 'obsessive' are in quotation marks advisedly. They describe not so much the facts of the situation, but a set of social values pertaining to them: the stereotype of housework as trivial and inferior work, the view of women as neurotically preoccupied with unimportant matters, and the low social esteem in which women's traditional pursuits are held.

In fact Janet Gallagher and others like her are pursuing a very rational course indeed. Faced with housework as their job, they devise rules which give the work the kind of structure most employed workers automatically find in their job situation. Having defined the rules they then attempt to adhere to them, and to derive reward from carrying them out. Since housework is not paid and husbands are by and large uncritical appraisers of their wives' work in the home, self-reward for housework activity is virtually the only kind housewives can hope to experience. Extreme concern with the physical appearance and cleanliness of the home is, thus, a possibility inherent in the situation of women as housewives: a logical consequence of the 'successful' performance of the housewife role.

The specification of high standards and repetitive routines has the function of job enlargement, and explains an observation many people have made about the modern housewife. While automation and the improvement in living conditions generally decreases the amount of housework to be done, housewives today do not seem to be spending less time doing housework than their mothers or grandmothers. There is, apparently, an inbuilt tendency to raise standards and elaborate routines; those made redundant by machines, or by the factory production of domestic commodities, are replaced by new, more intricate, more sophisticated patterns of behaviour.

The source of this tendency lies in one unusual feature of the housewife role. Among work roles it is unique, in that it is prefaced by an extremely long period of apprenticeship. The apprenticeship is not subject to voluntary contract. Since sex – being born female – is the relevant criterion for admittance, a woman's apprenticeship to housewifery is part of her overall socialization for the feminine role. During childhood, an identification with the mother or other female adult who cares for the housewife-to-be instills a sense of housework as a feminine responsibility. The mother is not only a female child's role-model for feminine behaviour, but for housework behaviour also. The daughter watches, imitates and later actively helps. Through this process of identification, women are perpetually assigned to the housewife role: the motivation to be a housewife, and to do housework, is developed as an integral personality function.[2] But the process has a much more specific effect. Ways of doing housework – standards to be achieved, and routines to be followed – are passed on from mother to daughter.

[Would you say you have particular ways of doing housework?] I have the same standards as my mother. If anything needs doing, she does it. You don't have to look round and say 'that needs doing', because it's done. *I always try to model myself on her* [ex-audio typist married to a food wholesaler].

The mother's influence may be recalled with respect to particular work tasks:

I like washing. I like to see washing on the line – especially sheets, and the boys' shirts. I think this is a bit of my mother: she's extremely particular, my mother [ex-nurse, married to a local authority inspector].

There may also be a direct rebellion against maternal housework standards, a response different in kind from simple imitation, but with the same significance:

I think I'm like I am because my mother was untidy. I think it made me go the other way. I can't stand things untidy [ex-manicurist, married to a sales representative].

The specification of standards and routines is a process intimately linked with the housewife's antecedent socialization. While the technical/physical conditions of housewifery may have altered substantially in the last half century or so, the tendency for housework activity to proliferate has deeper origins. Lack of change in the processes of feminine-role learning is at least partly responsible for the modern housewife's continuing psychological involvement with her work.

These forty housewives exhibit two differing approaches to housework. In one, the housewife seeks satisfaction in housework: the housewife role is part of her self-image. In the other, the motivation is instead to acknowledge the possibility of dissatisfaction, and to accord more priority to the roles of wife and mother than to the role of housewife. These different approaches are indicated by the answers women gave to a 'test' of self-concepts, in which they were asked to answer the question 'Who am I?' ten times over. Janet Gallagher's self-image is strongly domestic:

> I am a housewife.
> I am going to the shop.
> I am a mother.
> I am a good housewife.
> I am a mother of four children.
> I am a hard worker.
> I am a wife.
> I am a good cleaner.
> I am a good washer.
> I am always working.

In contrast to this list, Catherine Prince's ten self-descriptions tell the reader something about her personality; they give evidence of non-domestic interests, and omit any direct mention of housewifery:

> I am Catherine Prince.
> I am a woman.
> I am a wife.
> I am a mother.
> I am a socialist.
> I am interested in the world at large.
> I am involved with other people.
> I am lazy.
> I am reasonably contented.
> I am unambitious.

For women with the first orientation, in which the housewife role is intrinsic to the self-concept, housework is done for itself, and the rewards obtained from housewifery are quite narrowly restricted to the performance of housework itself. This orientation could be called 'traditional', in that it tends to be characteristic of close-knit working-class communities where the accent is on sex segregation and the restriction of women's non-domestic opportunities.[3] In the second orientation, housework is seen in a rather more detached way, as an 'instrumental' activity, to be performed for ulterior goals, in which a self-conscious commitment to motherhood and a belief in companionate marriage are all-important. The paradox here is that a marriage in which leisure interests and decision-making are shared between husband and wife becomes a somewhat segregated marriage in the housework and childcare areas, through the man's involvement in the career world. This outcome is contingent on beliefs about the proper roles of men and women, and on institutional forces which effectively maintain gender differentiation – particularly those in the career/job world.

More working-class than middle-class housewives have a traditional orientation to housework, and more middle-class housewives have an instrumental orientation. Length of education is a factor of primary importance here. An education prolonged beyond minimum school-leaving age produces some degree of detachment from the image of oneself as a housewife, and engenders a self-consciously disparaging attitude to housework. In the words of one graduate housewife:

I don't like saying I'm a housewife because I think being a housewife isn't a very satisfactory occupation . . . Being a housewife is only going to be a small part of my life. I shall have two children and as soon as I can get them off to school I shall get a job again [ex-computer programmer, married to an advertising manager].

Despite these differences in approach to their work, all housewives have to contend with a shared fate: the daily experience of doing housework. Two further paradoxes are encountered at this point. Firstly an instrumental approach to housework, by admitting the probability of dissatisfaction, establishes a sufficiently relaxed context for some satisfaction to be felt. On the other hand, the traditional motivation to be satisfied as a housewife is a condition of extreme vulnerability to housework's inherent deprivations.

In answer to a question about the 'worst' aspects of being a housewife, twenty-eight housewives named housework as the most disliked aspect. Thirteen further responses (out of a total of forty-eight – some housewives gave more than one answer) mentioned constant domestic responsibility, isolation, loneliness and having to get housework done. When asked about work tasks – cleaning, shopping, cooking, washing up, washing and ironing – many of these qualities are mentioned again. Attitudes to these tasks are not merely idiosyncratic, reflecting differences in personality and temperament between housewives. The same disliked characteristics of particular work tasks are referred to constantly by different housewives. On an overall assessment of work satisfaction/dissatisfaction, twenty-eight of the housewives come out as dissatisfied or very dissatisfied with housework.

In reply to another question, inviting a comparison between the roles of the sexes in marriage, housewives say that housework is hard, dissatisfying work:

[Do you think women work as hard, harder or not so hard as their husbands?] I always say housework is hard, but my husband doesn't say that at all. I think he's wrong, because I'm going all the time. When his job's finished, it's finished . . . Sunday he can lie in bed till twelve, get up, get dressed, and go for a drink, but my job never changes [ex-factory worker married to a driver's mate].

The defensive tones in which many of these remarks are made locate the debate about the nature of housework as an item in a constant marital dialogue: *I* say I work hard, but *he* doesn't say that at all. While the housewife is saying she works harder than her husband, she is at the same time protesting about the low status of housework. She has to overstate her case, because housework is not socially counted as work – the implication of this image being that the housewife herself is an uninteresting, worthless person; a cabbage:

When I think of a housewife it is of something not very nice to be – somebody who's got no interests outside the home [ex-office worker married to a cinema manager].

A perception of the low status of housework is almost universal in this sample, and leads to great resentment on the part of some housewives:

I'm not married to a house. I hate the word 'housewife'. They say, 'What are you?' and you say, 'I've got a baby ... I'm a mother and a wife,' and they say, 'Oh just a housewife.' Just a housewife! The hardest job in the world. You're *never* just a housewife. Into that category comes everything ... [ex-shop assistant married to a lorry driver].

Along with the low status of housewifery as a dissatisfying quality go its monotony, inherent time limits, fragmentation and social isolation. Thirty out of forty housewives experience monotony in housework, and thirty-six, fragmentation – work as a series of unconnected tasks, none of which require the worker's full attention. Half of the forty say they have too much to get done during the day, but most housewives mention frequent time limits as sources of dissatisfaction with particular work tasks. Cooking, for instance, recognized as a potentially creative activity by the majority of housewives, often is not, because husbands and children demand certain sorts of meals at particular times during the day, and the housewife also has to meet a mass of other demands on her time.

Monotony, fragmentation and excessive speed (a category which includes frequent time limits) are often cited as sources of job dissatisfaction for industrial workers. In the table below, the incidences of these experiences in the case of housewives and in the case of factory workers is compared:

The Experience of Monotony, Fragmentation and Speed in Work Activity: Housewives and Factory Workers Compared

| Workers | Percentage Experiencing: | | |
	Monotony	Fragmentation	Speed
Housewives	75	90	50
Factory Workers[4]	41	70	31
Assembly-Line Workers[4]	67	86	36

Housewives experience more monotony, fragmentation and social isolation in their work than do workers in the factory. Somewhat predictably, perhaps, they have more in common with assembly-line workers than with those whose jobs involve less repetition and more skill.

Like the repetitive tasks which make up housework, the isolation of the housewife as worker is a feature of her situation which few women can escape, and which for many is a cause for complaint. A pattern of restricted social contacts is linked with work dissatisfaction. From a housewife on a new housing estate:

I could be murdered here and no one would know. When the milkman comes, it's an event [ex-shop assistant married to a lorry driver].

Or, as another woman puts it:

You feel, 'I wish I could talk to somebody' . . . Not knowing anybody else you tend to get this feeling that unless you got out and talk to someone, you'll go stark raving mad [ex-machine operator, married to a shop manager].

To counterbalance the dissatisfaction of housewifery it could be argued that many women have the delights of motherhood.

All the forty women in this survey were mothers, but from the information they gave, it would seem that the combination of the housewife and mother roles is far from an unmixed blessing. Children are directly antithetical to the demands of the housewife role: they are neither tidy nor clean in their 'natural' state. Their demands are not necessarily timed to integrate with housework routines, and may positively frustrate the mother in her role as housewife. (Women may actually receive less help from their husbands during the childrearing stage of marriage than before: studies show that a husband's willingness to help during the dual employment pre-child period diminishes markedly when children tie his wife to the home.)

Being a 'good' mother does not call for the same qualities as being a 'good' housewife, and the pressure to be both at the same time may be an insupportable burden. Children may suffer, because the goals of housework may become the goals of childcare, and a dedication to keeping children clean and tidy may override an interest in their separate development as individuals. This possibility is illustrated in the following reply to the question, 'Do you like looking after the child (or children)?'

Yes. The only thing is with her nappies. I get so disappointed if they don't look so white when I do them by hand. I think to myself, 'Don't they look awful?' I used to boil them at his Mum's on the stove, but I can't do it here, I've got an electric one . . . I started boiling them in one of me saucepans, but it looked so awful I stopped . . . I'm trying to train her now, and I get so disappointed when she keeps messing . . . sometimes she does it beside the pot when the pot's right there, and I don't like that [ex-factory machinist, married to a painter and decorator].

For this housewife 'looking after the child' means the work involved in keeping the child and her clothes clean. The single word 'yes' expresses her enjoyment of childcare.

All these characteristics of the housewife's situation present a formidable obstacle to the achievement of work satisfaction.

Because this is the case, a housewife's declaration to the effect that she likes housework has to be suspected. This is the second paradox embedded in the issue of different approaches to housework and patterns of satisfaction/dissatisfaction with it.

Many housewives who begin their interviews by saying they like or love housework show later on that they actually derive a great deal of dissatisfaction from task performance. This contradiction can be explained by taking the statement, 'I like (or love) housework,' as an assertion of a basic identification with the housewife role, a commitment to the traditional value of feminine domesticity. For a woman who feels herself to be a housewife an open declaration of dislike in relation to housework may very well be experienced as threatening: if I am my work, I can only dislike it by disliking myself. The condition of intense psychological involvement in housework is one of great insecurity, especially in times when the position of women is subject to change. The tone of much contemporary discussion on the theme of women's roles appears to denigrate housewifery, to hold up only the career-woman image as worthy of emulation. This other norm of dissatisfaction is referred to implicitly by some educated middle-class housewives, whose statement, 'I hate housework,' thus may also have symbolic value, designating acceptance of the image of the woman-emancipated-from-her-traditional-role.

The moral is therefore: listen carefully to what women say. Because housework is such a personal subject for most women, clues to satisfaction and dissatisfaction may be offered only indirectly.

In the next chapter, four housewives talk about their situation. These four interviews have been selected from the forty which make up the survey discussed above and reported in more detail elsewhere.[5] They are representative of the larger sample, although each was chosen because it highlights specific aspects of the housewife situation. A short introduction prefaces each interview drawing attention to these particular points.

None of the four housewives whose case-histories are quoted make statements in which tremendous dissatisfaction with housework is given priority, and none totally reject the house-wife role. A great deal of dissatisfaction with housework may exist in a concealed form. In fact overall assessments of satis-faction/dissatisfaction made on the basis of these interviews rate three of the four housewives as dissatisfied with housework – two of them (Juliet Warren and Sally Jordan) as very dis-satisfied. Of the four, only Margaret Nicholson is classed as satisfied.

The interviews were tape-recorded, and have been edited so that much of the original data on housework attitudes and routines is omitted. Names, and other identifying details, have, of course, been changed. The resulting accounts are brief portraits not only of women's lives as housewives, but also of women's situation generally – the situation of young married women in modern industrial society.

Six

Four Housewives

1 Patricia Andrews

Patricia Andrews is twenty-four: a lively, articulate redhead interviewed in curlers and an immaculate nylon overall. Her home is an unfurnished flat consisting of three rooms, kitchen and bathroom, on the second floor of a terraced house of the 1930s era. The flat is spotless, although as she points out, this effect is achieved with difficulty, because the structure and exterior maintenance of the house is poor. In terms of the tools of her trade, and her work environment, she is not especially well-off: she has no vacuum cleaner, and her washing machine is an erratic, secondhand appliance which washes but does not dry the clothes. The wet clothes have to be transferred to a separate spin drier. Heating is by means of free-standing paraffin fires, and the bathroom leads directly off the kitchen, which is hardly convenient.

Patricia Andrews's attitude to housework is that she likes it but doesn't know why. However, she is able to trace her approach to housework back to her mother, from whom she has also acquired a tendency to specify repetitive routines and high, inflexible standards, which are very important to her. In these respects Patricia is typical of many of the other forty housewives.

Her interview is also interesting because it gives prominence to the segregation of sex roles associated with a 'traditional' orientation to housework. The division between husband's and wife's interests and responsibilities labels not only housework, but everything domestic as the wife's domain, including children and the management of the household income. In Patricia Andrews's case, an alliance with the housewife in the flat below mirrors the informal 'housewives' associations' of close-knit working-class communities, and ranges women against men in the wider context of leisure activities. The question, 'Do you go out on your own?' was interpreted as a question about Patricia and her friend downstairs, and not about Patricia on her own; a question about whether she would like to go out on her own more received the reply that she went out enough with her husband (about once a month) but would like more time away from the house with her friend.

The two women share an interest in flirtatious relationships with men, and for Patricia Andrews 'getting drunk' is a pastime mentioned in association with this. Yet she is neither an adulteress nor an alcoholic: the significance of these two topics is symbolic. On the one hand, they are diversionary interests: they liven up an otherwise routine and boring life. On the other, they serve as taunts to her husband, as ways of 'getting back' at him for the injustices she perceives he inflicts on her.

The version of the interview reproduced here begins with some details about Patricia Andrews's background, which includes an early-completed education, an early marriage, and a paid-employment life consisting of uninteresting, unchallenging, and low-skill jobs. In these ways, her case-history reflects the restricted experiences which characterize the pre-housewife period of many women's lives, and which also feature in the interview with Sally Jordan.

This one'll be two in the summer, and the other one'll be five: she goes to school all day. I was eighteen when we got married. My parents didn't want me to get married – they thought I was too young. But my sister was eighteen when she got married, and so was my mother, so they didn't have a leg to stand on, really. We were going to wait seven years for a baby. Three months after we got married I fell for Karen.

I left school at fifteen. I wanted to be a nurse or an air hostess, but I didn't do any of those things because I left school and I hadn't done any 'O'-levels or anything; all I did was this course in typing. My first job was as a telephonist and typist – it was a junior post really: junior clerk it was called. I didn't like that job. I was washing up, and making toast more than anything. 'Pat, get this, get that, get us another cup of coffee' – it was like that all the time. I left there and went into a factory to get my money to get engaged – to save up for getting married, because the money wasn't good enough. I enjoyed the work in the factory, though I thought I'd never get it at first; I was wiring up fluorescent signs – you know, the ones that hang outside shops. It took about a fortnight to learn. Yes, I quite enjoyed the factory, although I'd never wanted to go into one: it was something different. The atmosphere was good, nobody posh, everybody having a laugh – we had a record player on all day.

After about two years I got enough money from that job and we got married, and I went temporary. That was a copy-typing job – secretary's work. It was a nice boss and nice girls. I was temporary, and this other girl had this postion and she kept having time off, and they put me in her position and made me permanent. That made me feel good. He made me permanent, that's right: and then just a month after he made me permanent, I got pregnant, and had to leave anyway.

I didn't want to give up work – well, I wanted to give up for the reason that I was having a baby – but otherwise I didn't. I missed it, not at first, because there was a lot to do with the baby, but afterwards. I've often felt I'd like to be back at work since.

That was the four years between leaving school and having Karen. I haven't worked properly since then, although I've tried to do typing at home. It was ridiculous what you had to do to make up the money, and there was a lot of rushing about getting the work. I wouldn't work at the moment: I wouldn't put Stephen anywhere, I'd wait until he was at school. Two years to go! I wouldn't want anyone else bringing them up, because I've seen too many children put out. I just don't believe in it.

My husband does deliveries for a building firm. His day starts early, sometimes at half six, sometimes at half five. He's back at half five in the afternoon, except for when he does overtime, and then he isn't back till nine. Saturday it's eight till one thirty: it *is* supposed to be eight in the week, but that's all overtime. He has to do that to make up his money to live – and for this place!

When he gets up he puts the alarm on for me for eight. Sometimes I turn it off and lay there: usually I get up. I come out here, go to the toilet, have a wash, and get the breakfast. They won't eat a cooked breakfast; she has cornflakes and he has weetabix. Karen dresses herself while I get the breakfast and she has breakfast while I'm doing my hair. Some days before I go up to the school if I get up earlier, I do the beds. Then I take her to school – it's just two doors down. Stephen stays asleep while I go; I leave the catch on the door, and my friend downstairs listens. Then I come back, and get Stephen out of his cot, and give him breakfast.

I wash up. Then I wash these two floors first. Then I dress him. Then I do the bedroom, the front room and the children's bedroom. Then I get on to the washing. I do the washing Monday and Friday: it takes about an hour and a half. I aim to finish by twelve, so I can meet Karen from school and she can come home and have some lunch. We have soup or scrambled eggs or something dinner time, and a dinner at night. I never sit down in the morning; I never even have breakfast. I don't sit down till half past four when I watch *Crossroads*. In the afternoon I usually go shopping, if I didn't I might sit down with him, but I'd rather go out. I just go down the lane getting bits of dinner; I know near enough everybody round here. I go with either the friend downstairs, or a friend up the road. Or I go to the clinic; in the summer we walk to the Broadway and have dinner in Miller's department store.

I do see people most days; more so since Karen went to school because I meet the girls up there. I've just met another friend and I've been round to hers twice this week, she's just had a baby, and she was a bit fed up. Other days I just meet Karen from school, come back, wash the net curtains, do the ironing or something.

Karen comes home at half past three. She has juice and a biscuit and they watch the children's programmes on T.V. Then my friend comes up or we go down there and have coffee and watch *Crossroads*. I start dinner at five. Then I get cleared up in here till about seven o'clock. Then I wash the children; I put Stephen to bed first. Karen has to stay up because I daren't put them down together. She goes to bed about half past seven or eight, when Stephen's asleep. That's every day, really. I do the same things in the same order every day. Stupid, isn't it?

I do housework the same on Saturday and Sunday, I'm a fanatic for housework. I dust, go round with the carpet sweeper, and wash these two floors every day. The only thing I don't do the same is I don't do the stairs and I don't polish properly on a Saturday and a Sunday, because he's home and he don't like it. He can't bear me doing housework: he goes potty with me – he gets in a temper. When he's here I try to leave it but I do keep looking at it and wishing I could get up and do it.

[Do you like housework?]

I don't mind housework, really. It all depends how I feel. Sometimes I really like doing housework – I mean *enjoy* doing housework – and other times, if he's carrying on, I hate doing it. I mind doing it when I'm pregnant. I thought I was pregnant this week, and I didn't want to do anything. But I'm alright, so I'm enjoying it! I must say I hate rushing housework. My husband might come home – say now – and want egg and bacon and I get in a temper because I've got to stop doing my work. I don't like being interrupted. Most mornings he comes in for breakfast like that.* He'll come up in his big hob-nailed boots when I'm washing the floors.

I like shopping if I've got plenty of money. That isn't very often. If I've got to go round and look for cheap stuff, I don't like it. I like cooking: my friend and I try new recipes off the Jimmy Young show, and have a laugh. We don't do it together, but we do it the same day and see what it turns out like. I get fed up with the same old things. I don't like washing up, and I always try to get my husband to wash up, but he won't, most of the time. Washing I hate: this machine has a nasty habit of emptying onto the floor and there's water all over the floor by the time I've finished, so I have to wash the floor again. Stephen puts things in the water too. I don't like ironing; well, I don't mind if I'm talking to someone while I'm doing it, but I don't like ironing when I'm just standing there doing it.

But generally I don't really know whether I like housework. I just do it. I can't say I *like* washing floors: kneeling on the floors, washing them, no, not really. I do it to keep it clean. Stephen's all over the floor, and if they're not done, he's going to get filthy. These

*Because her husband works locally, he is able to have most of his meals at home.

floors are terrible, they show every mark. It's just routine, I suppose; it's just a habit. I know my Mum always used to wash her floors every day. It's just a thing I've always done since I've been married. I don't know why. I feel it *ought* to be done. I've never been able to go out and leave anything. I could never leave washing up in the sink, or anything like that. My mother's *exactly* the same.

She's like it, and my sisters are like it: when we were little we had to help in the home. We weren't allowed out if we didn't. I used to change the beds and hoover; we always washed up. I didn't enjoy it – I always used to try and get out of it! That was when I was ten or eleven. Before I got married, I didn't mind doing it, because I knew I'd have to do it anyway.

[Do you like looking after the children?]

Yes, I like looking after them, but I'd rather be at work. [Why?] Because of this [child crying] – whining all the time. I'd like to go to work because I'd like my own place. I'd like to put my money away; I don't like the thought of living here for the rest of my life paying this money for this place. That's one thing I'm always thinking about: it's all we row about – because he's not bothered; nobody in his family's ever bought their own place.

My mum worked to buy her own house. She did night work at London airport, catering for the planes so that she didn't have to leave the children. She did it to get out of the prefab; they bought a house, we got out, and then she packed up work. She's working now not for the money, but because there's no one at home. If I worked it wouldn't be for myself, it'd be for *all* of us.

[Are there any things you particularly like doing for the children?]

I like taking them out. Every Saturday we go to my mother's, and then we stay at my mother's for tea one week and his mother's the next. They love going out. Karen's always saying, 'Is it Nanny day today?' Karen likes doing yoga. We watch it on television and do it together; the only trouble is, she does it much better than I do. And she likes me drawing for her, making things with Lego, reading to her.

I'll tell you one thing I *don't* like: I don't like training them. I'm trying to potty train him now. One day it lasted – Sunday – and then Monday, my God! I'm screaming and stiff with temper to get him on the potty, and you get him on it and he's on there about an hour before he does anything. The other day we were watching television, and he done a wee wee in the potty, I brought it out here, emptied it, and took it back for the next one, and he done one – another one, within seconds – on the floor.

[Does your husband help in the house?]

He makes the tea every night while I do the children. Sunday dinnertime he washes up, and sometimes in the week. If I'm ill, he'll do cleaning, but otherwise I'd rather do it myself, because they don't do it properly anyway. I look at it and think, 'Oh my God!'

He doesn't go shopping for me now, but he used to when he had a different job. Now he's always at work; and when he does come home, he's really tired.

He takes them out every Sunday morning up the park while I get the dinner on. He got a bike for Karen – a two-wheeler one – and painted it all up different colours. He buys them clothes and toys – hammers and things, all the wrong toys that I wouldn't buy. He changes nappies, though he doesn't like it when they're dirty. I phone my Mum once a week, and when I come back he's done Stephen, he's all ready for bed. He fed them when they were babies – well, I breast fed for three months, both of them, so he couldn't do that, but he gave them the bottle.

We don't fight as much now we've got children. Except over money and sex – normal things. Especially sex. He always wants it. He'd do it if he came home now and you were here. He thinks you should never have a stomach ache, and I have them quite often. He sulks and I get pushed on the edge of the bed. So does Sandra downstairs; you can hear every movement down there and they can hear every movement up here and any time our bed squeaks they bang on the ceiling with a broom. The other night they were rowing and you could hear everything they were saying, and of course we were having a row about it too, and we just lay there and laughed. We thought it was so funny – exactly the same thing going on upstairs and downstairs.

We don't go out very much. Sundays in the summer we might go to my sister's in Sussex – places like that. Sometimes we go to parties. Or his sister comes over and we go to the pictures or visit friends.

[Do you ever go out on your own?]

Sometimes I go to the pictures with my friend downstairs, if I'm lucky, and we're not rowing – me and my husband, that is. We used to go once a week, but now it's only occasionally. We'd like to go once a week – they go to the pub once a week. They're jealous, you see. We went to the pictures once and two blokes followed us home and stood outside shouting up creating a fuss, so we're not allowed out any more! They go out – they go and play darts. If they're out we feel we should be able to go out. They don't feel we should, but we do!

[But you don't go out on your own?]

No. Well, yes I do. I go out and see my friend sometimes. Last Friday I went because she was moving, and I got drunk. He wasn't very pleased about that. I'm a flirt, my husband says – only because he's jealous. When I have been drinking – I've never touched a drink until this Christmas, and ever since then I've been drinking – I can feel myself relaxing; my friend's the same – we do go after the blokes. But he's the same, he goes after the girls. He's always kissing my friend, so I've started kissing her husband!

I've been feeling fed up recently because we used to go out once a week and we don't do that any more.

[You'd like to go out more with your husband?]

No, with my friend. I go out enough with him! It's so nice just to get on a bus without screaming children. I tell you, me and my friend get on that bus and we thoroughly enjoy just the ride. A bit of peace: you just feel relaxed. We liked going out once a week, because it was something to look forward to each week. You can work better when you've got something to look forward to.

[Do you ever feel you'd rather be doing anything else at the moment, apart from being a housewife?]

Earning some money. He gives me his wage slip every week; he never gives me less than £20; he has to really, because it wouldn't cover the bills. On a good week, he still only has £3 for himself I pay all the bills, I pay the rent and I put money for all the bills away and whatever's left out of that I just put in an envelope and that goes on things we need. I take the family allowance out in the week whenever I get short. But I can't *save* anything towards a home.

It's not a bad flat, I suppose, but it's very damp. It's so damp, we have to redecorate it more than once a year. If he didn't work at a building place and get cheap paint and wallpaper, we'd never be able to afford to keep it up. The children's room is very damp. That's mainly why I want a house – for them. Their own garden, a back door they can go out of. Here, I've got back stairs going down there which you could break your neck on. I wish we'd saved up for a house before we got married. Otherwise I don't regret anything: the main thing was to get married and have children.

[What would you say are the best things about being a housewife?] You're your own boss. [And the worst?] Being taken for granted. He never says anything about the way I keep the flat. If I say that to him, he says it always looks nice. Housework is a waste of time, really. My friend and I are always saying that. You do it, your husband comes home and it all gets mucked up again. I mean I went out yesterday and I left it so nice up here, and I came back and I knew my husband had been in: there was all splashings on the sink.

[Do you think that women work as hard as their husbands?] I do. He doesn't. He thinks we have a lovely life. He usually comes home and says, 'You've got a cushy life.' Housewives have always got the children, you're with them all day – if they wake up in the night you've got to see to them – well not got to, but more women than men get up in the middle of the night. You've got to watch them all the time – especially at this age.

[Do you ever envy your husband?] I often say to him, 'I wish I was the bloke.' Just getting out every day – the different places he drives to every day. But not always. When I think of the dirty side of it, I don't fancy it.

[What would you think of a marriage in which the wife went out to work and the husband stayed at home to do housework and look after the children?] I wouldn't like that. I don't think men can look after the children and do the housework and everything like we do. It's not the same. I'd think the man was a bit funny, wouldn't you? Lazy sod.

[Do you think there are any ways in which women are treated unfairly?] To be quite honest, I've never really thought about it. I don't really know much about what goes on except around the home. [In the home?] Yes, because if a man wants to go out for a drink he can just get up and go, we can't, can we – we can't just get up and go, they'd have a lot to say about that, wouldn't they? Same as in the daytime – we can't just get up and go and leave the children on their own.

2 Juliet Warren

Juliet Warren's account of life as a housewife portrays what has come to be thought of as the typical dilemma of the middle-class wife: the frustration of moving from a challenging career to fulltime housewifery and motherhood. In fact this dilemma is almost certainly less typical than is commonly thought. The problems of highly educated women with the housewife role have been studied more closely than those of any other group, and the conclusions drawn from these studies are not applicable to the mass of both middle-class and working-class women whose education and job experiences are more restricted.

Nonetheless, Juliet Warren's interview is particularly valuable as an account of a life crisis – the passage from one style of life to another. Today, as opposed to fifty or a hundred years ago (among the middle and upper classes, that is), the birth of the first child, and not marriage itself, is the major transforming event in a woman's life. After nearly a year of motherhood, Juliet has still not 'adjusted' to her situation, and her memories of pre-motherhood life are made daily more vivid by the contacts her husband still has with the world in which she worked: television. Compulsive biscuit-eating, excessive anxiety over the baby's welfare, and general depression and disorganization are the 'symptoms' of her lack of adjustment. Doing housework all the time is, as she points out, quite different from doing it some of the time.

This interview includes quite a number of comments on the influence of the social environment on the formation of attitudes to housework and childcare. Especially interesting is Juliet Warren's revised opinion of her mother's 'terrible' housework behaviour, now she detects the same tendencies in herself. The label 'terrible' is interesting too, because as applied to a housewife the term can mean one of two things: either a very 'good' housewife (i.e. one with very high standards) or a very 'bad' housewife (one with very low standards). In the conventional wisdom about housework, both extremes are deplored.

This edited version of Juliet Warren's interview contains a great deal of material on the mother–child relationship, and on the experience of childbirth, particularly in the context of an 'egalitarian' marriage. Although not of direct relevance to housework attitudes, this material is fascinating from another, connected viewpoint. Juliet Warren's observations about her husband's maternal role towards their child in relation to the attitudes of other men in their social circle illustrate how a sharing of responsibility here – in the area of childcare – is still viewed as deviant masculine behaviour in Western culture. Her recollections of childbirth highlight some of the aspects of this process which may be medically mismanaged with consequences for the mother–child relationship: a general sense of disappointment and a tendency to be overimpressed with the problems of looking after a baby. The comments about sentimental ideals of motherhood are partly motivated by the experience of trying to combine childcare with housework, but are also protests about the general mystification to which women's roles are still subject. It is interesting to note that although aware of this process, Juliet Warren has not successfully detached herself from its influence. Her feeling that she *ought* to cook for the baby, rather than use tins, parallels the advice of many babycare books: a 'good' mother will prepare home-cooked food for her baby, even though canned food may be nutritionally and bacteriologically superior. Her attempts to cook interesting meals for her husband demonstrate her striving after the image of a good housewife – again, an image of which she is certainly aware.

In technical, environmental terms, Juliet Warren's situation is better than that of many housewives. A fully automatic washing machine 'liberates' her from the burden of washing, and the car, at least in theory, offers a promise of escape. She lives in a flat: three spacious rooms, kitchen and bathroom, decorated in a recognizably middle-class manner, with sisal carpets, dried grasses and William Morris print curtains.

Sara is eleven months old. My husband's a director of documentary films for television, and he's away a lot. He's in Rome at the moment. Since Christmas he's been filming in Germany, and then he did a film about an artist in Tuscany, and then he did a thing about the Common Market which was half in England and half in France. He gets about two weeks off inbetween jobs. That means it fluctuates very much – sometimes he's here all day, and sometimes we don't see him for weeks on end.

[Do you have a job?]

Not now. I did before I had her. I used to work in television as well. I was a producer's assistant for a programme called *Review of the Day*. That was irregular hours too; you see, we both worked irregular hours. It was enjoyable in a way, because we were very used to it, and we'd been doing it together for years. When I became pregnant and had her and gave up work it was no fun any more, inasmuch as I realize now how much away he is.

It's difficult to describe my daily routine, because it varies according to when he's here and when he isn't. I get up as late as possible, which usually means about eight o'clock. Sara can sit up in her cot now, so probably the only reason she cries in the morning is because it's dark. She wakes up about half past seven—eight o'clock, and periodically during the night as well. She sleeps in her own room, and when you go in you find she's just sitting there having a little cry, because she's all alone, and she doesn't know quite what she's doing. I feel I've got to go to her, although some people probably wouldn't bother. This morning I didn't get up until nine, actually, because she'd been up a few times in the night and I was too tired.

First I make her breakfast and I usually have something myself. Then I wash up and sort of potter around doing things. I endeavour to get the place straight – not *cleaning* really, just straightening it – tidying it. I come in and pick up everything and just run the thing over to pick up crumbs – you know, that sort of thing. We've got lots of wood and lots of antiques which desperately need a lot of polishing, and I do polish them, but I don't do them as much as I used to before I had the baby. It depends if we're having people to dinner – the table gets a good clean that day. I tend to do the bare necessities.

Mostly the day consists of repetitive things like sorting out the baby's clothes, doing the washing. I try to do the washing every day, though sometimes I don't manage to. With a machine it's not too bad, because if it does mount up after two or three days I can just shove it all in and do it. Ideally I like to do it every day because it minimizes it all. I sometimes go to the launderette, just to dry things off. I don't need to really; it's just an extra walk, so I feel justified in doing it. I do a bit of shopping every day. This is the first day for ages I haven't been out and I planned it this way; I bought food yesterday to enable me to stay in and do my bedroom out. I do more shopping on Friday – getting the food for the weekend. I mostly go out every day because of Sara, that's why I do bits of shopping every day instead of doing one big load. When we change our car I might do it once or twice a week, and still go out for walks and things, but not to be loaded down with shopping. I don't use the car we've got now because it's such an awkward car to park.

I don't sit down in the morning. Sara has her lunch about half past twelve. I don't always cook for her – just occasionally I do a casserole. I feel very good about that – something super to eat for a change! Actually I cooked one today, you can smell it can't you? She ate it, thank God! Mostly I use tins, but I'm gradually trying to change over. When I know Tom's away for two weeks, I think I must try and organize myself so I can cook a meal for her every day. I don't cook for myself at lunchtime. I've put on lots of weight; I'm still a stone overweight. I find it very difficult to cook for myself properly and eat the right things. I tend to eat things I shouldn't eat; I'm a great biscuit fan. When you say do I sit down, it's not true to say I don't sit down all day because at lunchtime after feeding her I might sit down with a cup of coffee and some biscuits and something like a cheese sandwich – things like that. Which is awful, because I must slim, but it's very difficult at the moment.

Usually I go out in the afternoons, I suppose two or three days a week I see people. I've made quite a few friends round here who have babies, and that's rather nice. There's a girl I know who lives down on the green, and she's got a daughter the same age, and she brings her baby to me on Thursdays while she goes off for a couple of hours, and I do the same to her on Tuesdays. She goes off to a class – she's doing a course in Dutch – or she goes to a class in flower arranging. [What do *you* do?] Well, I haven't really come to terms with it all yet. I feel I should be doing something important, but in fact I have a quick slurp round the shops on my own. We've only had this arrangement for a few weeks. I may try and do something much more interesting on Tuesday afternoons.

Father Joseph from the church also comes to see me quite often – I'm not a Catholic, but my husband is. He knows I've finished work and he tries to encourage me to do things with the church. He doesn't talk about religion or anything – he's a marvellous person, very outgoing.

Just before Christmas all these things started to happen, and I got invited to things called 'coffee mornings' which I really loathe the idea of, but in fact they turned out not too badly at all. It was an opportunity to say, 'On Wednesday morning I have got to get out and go somewhere.' The people I've met through those things have kept on a relationship.

There's a girl round the corner, she's quite young, she's become very friendly with me, and it's marvellous – she's got a car, and she's always wanting to help. She desperately wants a baby and she's at home because she's given up work. She was told to rest, she's had a couple of miscarriages. She's quite keen on getting me in on lots of things connected with the church. They have a bookshop and she wants me to go and help with that.

Those sorts of things happen, but nothing more exciting than that!

I think if I sat down and made a schedule of all the things one should do in the day, it would turn out to be quite a lot. Going out in the afternoons, I hardly ever finish everything, because I can't bear to work in the evenings, I never have been one for doing things in the evening. Like washing: I've got friends who say 'Oh no, I must wash out the baby's things in the evening,' and I think, 'Well, good luck,' because I just couldn't.

I feed Sara about half past five, but she doesn't go down straight away. She's got this funny thing now, where she gets hold of the rungs of the cot and she turns herself over which is very annoying. I can't tuck her in, so I just leave her to sort herself out and when I come back her bottom's up in the air and she's sucking her thumb, and she's not in the bedclothes. That can go on for an hour and a half; sheer exhaustion gets her in the end.

After I've put her to bed I make myself a cup of coffee and get myself some biscuits and I come in here and I stay, and that's it. I don't know what I'd do without television. I suppose because I've been in the business I can look at it with a more critical eye, and I do try to select things rather than just sit down and switch it on. [Do you like housework?]

No. When I was working I used to have days off, and I used to come back here and I used to get a tremendous kick out of doing everything – all the housework. But now I'm doing it every day it really is the biggest bore of my life. I used to be very methodical – I still am, I suppose, a bit – I can't bear to have mess around me. I do find it very boring now every day.

My standards have definitely dropped since I've been doing housework all the time. I suppose it's because I really cannot do anything uninterrupted and I still can't get used to that. It takes a lot of effort – like today, I woke up with a feeling, 'I'm going to clean this place up.' I always have great intentions at the beginning of the day, but by the end of it, just doing the routine things, I'm so fagged out I just collapse. Anyone listening to that recorder will probably think the place is a pigsty which, as you can see, it isn't. I'm very aware that there are little jobs I ought to do. I used to be pretty thorough and there are things where I think, 'Oh I haven't got time to do that.'

My trouble is I'm just not organized. For instance, I find it so exhausting just trying to think of what to eat: that's why I get so fed up with cooking. It's not the actual cooking itself. To make things work out well, one needs to plan ahead and be very organized really, and I suppose I haven't done my groundwork sufficiently. Probably my trouble is that I'm trying to be better at it than I need be. Tom's home so little that when he is home – even if it's for a fortnight – I feel I've got to cook something interesting, and the effort that goes into that every night is a bit much, really. If I were to provide him with just some chops and vegetables, he wouldn't think much of that. He's not a very critical person, but he's appreciative of good cooking – any man is. It's silly really, because he's out all the time filming and eating in good restaurants, and I try to keep the standards up by doing it at home. Perhaps it would be better just to have ordinary food.

I suppose really I don't *mind* doing any of it. It's just that en masse it's a bit formidable. That feeling's only built up over the past year, and I hope it'll be different in another year. It's the *combination* of the baby and the housework that's so difficult. I mean she's super, but there are times when she does need a lot of attention, and I just have to adapt and not worry too much about not doing the housework . . . But I do worry, simply because it's there again tomorrow: it's not removed.

I used to read all the literature available about having a baby, and really there is a tremendous halo of enjoyment about it. No one ever tells you about the hard work. You know you've got to do bottles and nappies and all the rest of it, but no one ever tells you how shattering it is to be doing it all the time, seven days a week. There are no books anywhere that are realistic. In fact I was thinking the other day, I'd really like to write a paper on it – on having a baby and how it's not all a super enviable state. It sounds awful, because one has a child, and she's absolutely beautiful and perfect and gorgeous – I couldn't live without her either – but to suddenly change from working – and I left it late, well, I'm thirty now – and then to find yourself doing housework all the time.

We were married on the tenth of March one year and she was born on the seventh of March the year after. We'd been living together for a long time, and we decided to settle down, get married and have babies.

When I had her we didn't have either of our mothers up. He did it: he had three weeks off, and he and I managed the baby together. He was absolutely fabulous. I was feeding her for two months, so he wasn't able to do that, but there were lots of other things he could do. I was giving her a bottle as well – that's why I only fed her for two months, because I had to give her a supplement in a bottle. I didn't get much co-operation from the nurses in the hospital. The awful thing was I never really thought about feeding by bottle, I didn't have any bottles, I had to get bottles on the way home from the hospital. She was forceps born; she was forty-eight hours cotnursed, and I didn't actually see her: it was agonizing, and I was very worried about this feeding thing as well, because I'd read that you had to feed your baby pretty soon, for it to be successful. And I kept saying to the sister, 'What about feeding?' and she kept saying, 'Don't worry, it'll be alright.' Of course it was pretty hopeless. I kept on asking advice, and they really weren't for it at all. They had this awful pump thing so that after you'd fed the baby, you had to go on the pump to see how much milk you'd got left. There was this coloured nurse who was really against it, and she said, 'You haven't got enough milk and that's that.' She made me start giving little bottles every feed. Oh it was awful. I felt frustrated; disappointed, I suppose. It only added to the disappointment of not seeing her born as well, because she was born under an anaesthetic in the end. The labour was induced because I was putting on weight and they said they would have me in. Her head wasn't turning properly and it was very important that she should be born quickly or something, so they just clamped me under an anaesthetic and that was it. The whole thing was a big disappointment. Tom was with me right until she was born, and he would have been there for the actual birth too. He saw her before I did. He kept doing little drawings of her, and bringing them down, because she was in this special ward.

He was very keen to learn and he'll do absolutely anything you have to do for a baby. Nappies, bottles – anything. And he enjoys it. It's very much 'our' baby. Tom and Sara have a marvellous relationship: he has a special way of talking to her. He's very thrilled and proud of her, and it's very nice to see them together. I think sometimes when talking to other people if he realized that other men aren't so keen – some friends of ours, the husband wouldn't ever touch the baby, apart from seeing it all clean and nice – and the producer he's working with now, he doesn't have anything to do with his new baby, and the baby is sort of isolated upstairs – and I know Tom when he heard about that was sort of slightly, 'Well, is he right?'

I think a large part of it is environment. His mother is an incredible woman: very well organized, beautifully run home, beautifully clean, and beautifully arranged flowers everywhere. He's very untidy: his mother was always running after him with white shirts, all this sort of thing, but I think there's still a little bit of his mother in him, in that if he sees there are so many things to do, he can pick out the important things and do them, and he *cares* about them. The only trouble is that with the baby, the involvement goes to the extent that it's like a dual mother. He's the mother as well as me. He might come home for a week after being away filming, and he's giving her a drink while I'm cooking the meal, and he says, 'Haven't you bought her any new teats – she hasn't had any for weeks!' That makes me angry because maybe I have bought some. There is criticism on that level. He gets very angry with me sometimes if I'm disorganized. Such silly things, as maybe I've bathed her but I haven't got her feed hotted up which is stupid, because then I've got a crying baby on my hands, or the bottle's too hot, and I haven't got any cold water to cool it down. It makes me angry too: it's terrible, all this unnecessary feeling.

[Do you like looking after the baby?]

I always worry about her: whether she's got enough clothes on, whether she's warm enough, or too cold, should I be potty training her, or is it too soon – all the time. When Tom used to go away first of all when I had her I used to creep into the room and our floors are very creaky, and I always landed up on the creakiest floor board and she'd wake up and then she'd cry, and it'd be my fault. I used to be ridiculous: I was so strung up about it all. I used to have the television very quiet . . . I'm tending to get over that a little bit now: I realize that she's not quite so vulnerable. She fell off the bed the day before yesterday for the first time ever – and I read somewhere that if a baby at a year old hasn't fallen off anything it's overprotected, and she's eleven months, so I thought that wasn't bad! Spock, that was, actually.

Something that particularly gives me pleasure now is taking her out for walks in the park. She's recognizing animals now. She doesn't talk, but she seems to be trying very hard. She points at things when I say the names – like 'clock'. My sister-in-law says I'm ridiculous, because she'll never say things like 'clock'. She says you have to say things like 'tick tock'. When we're in the park and there's masses of dogs racing around and I say, 'Look Sara, there's a dog,' she adores it, and I think she'll just say 'dog' one day, but my sister-in-law says, no she won't. Perhaps she's right.

There's very little I don't enjoy about the baby. I can't think of anything – except perhaps I get a bit fed up when I'm trying to feed her and she makes a mess, and every time I try to give her some milk out of a cup it goes all over the place. I get fed up with that. It isn't that she doesn't want to drink it, she just wants to put her fingers in it too.

Tom and I had a long time to build a good relationship together before we got married, before we said, 'Right, let's make this legal and get married and have a baby,' and we did it in that order. I think all that backlog of relationship and doing things together helped us tremendously over those first few months, because I'm sure that's where a lot of marriages begin to break down. I keep thinking it must be so hard on someone young getting married and then finding herself pregnant and having a baby, because it's very tough. It's much tougher than anything else previous to that. Actually having the responsibility of a baby to look after, and the work involved, it really is quite something.

That's another thing, if I ever get round to writing that article. All women are potential mothers: by the very fact that they are women they should be able to conceive and have children, but I think it depends very much on your environment when young as to your attitude to having a baby. I was brought up as the youngest of four – the others were boys anyway – and I had very little contact with babies. When my brothers got married and had children they moved away from home, and on their rare annual visits I wouldn't even pick up the babies. I didn't want to know. I'm sure a lot of that is why a first child is such a worry.

My mother had to work when I was a child. She had a little job cleaning, or whatever she could find to fit in the hours, because I had an invalid brother. My father wasn't much use – they're separated now. She used to take cleaning jobs because she could get up at five in the morning and be back by half past seven. She worked very hard actually, that's why I feel so miserable when I think about it – that living amongst it, I was too close to be able to see. It's very sad, really. It's very sad also that there are people who still do it, although things are meant to be so much easier now, and everyone's supposed to be able to have a car and so on. And the knowledge of it doesn't prevent oneself from saying, 'Oh God, there isn't enough room here, I want a house,' and so on. I've got past the stage where I used to feel guilty about it. It's no good: it's human nature to want something else.

My mother's a terrible housewife. Very muddly, very disorganized, and I can see so clearly where she falls wrong in the way she does things. The cupboards are always in a mess: she's quite erratic and mad in the way she keeps house. I'm not like her. I'm the opposite. I like things in neat compartments. When I lived at home it was always a bit of a nightmare because I was always trying to get things straight and it was a very frustrating business. When I moved away I used to go home for weekends, and I used to spend a lot of the weekend trying to sort out my mother's cupboards. I don't see her so often now, and certainly I've changed completely in my reaction to her and the way she keeps house. When I go down there I just accept it and think, 'Well, poor woman she works,' and I realize what it's all about now perhaps – it's an insight into the way she was, having a baby myself. How she coped, I do not know. When I think of the terrible things one felt about one's own mother! I can see how it all makes sense now, because I find I'm slackening *my* standards.

[When you were a child what did your mother want you to do?] Be a secretary, I suppose. She never really said whether she wanted me to get married and have babies. But it was just an accepted pattern of life. She got married when she was eighteen; she was probably quite relieved to find I got married when I was twenty-nine.

I left school after O-levels – at sixteen, sixteen and a half. Then I worked in a lawyer's office for about a year and a half, doing a secretarial job. Then I joined the B.B.C., I didn't do a proper training: I seemed just to fall into the right place at the right time. I started in Manchester – my home town – and after about two years there I wanted a transfer to London, so I came here and I got put in a job I didn't like very much – to do with children's programmes. I then asked to change it, and something came up and I knew people and they seemed to like me and I got into this programme called *Review of the Day*. Because it was a late-night programme, I used to get in at ten in the morning and then not be home again till the middle of the night – half past one or two. I couldn't do it when I was pregnant. I just got too tired.

[What did you enjoy about your work?] Meeting people, and because it was very much doing research into items for programmes. I had to collate a lot of information about a person who was being interviewed, or perhaps a subject that was being done. Just contact with people.

I'd like to go back to work. I think it's a very good idea for mothers to work, if you can be organized enough, simply for the stimulus it would give. You see, being at home you've got no deadline anymore. Getting up in the morning to look after a baby and do housework is different from getting up and going to work, and perhaps dressing up to go somewhere special. I'd enjoy it just to dress up and think, 'I've got to be in by ten,' and getting in and meeting people for those few hours, and then coming home again.

I don't think children suffer. What I'd like to do is buy a house, so we've got more room, and go to work perhaps mornings, or something like that, and with my salary I'd have a girl in – an au pair perhaps – just for the company it'd afford me while Tom's away, and also to look after the baby mornings so I can go to work and at least be doing something other than chores. I don't think Sara would suffer under that sort of arrangement. She certainly doesn't care when I leave her with this other mother in the afternoon; she's a very friendly little thing.

If I was asked to put my occupation on a form I wouldn't put 'housewife', I'd put 'mother'. I would hate to think of myself just being a housewife. I think that's why I'm so frustrated: I really cannot come to terms with the fact that I am. That's why I'm exploring all these things to do. I think I'm quite lucky to live in this area because the sort of women one's likely to meet with young children who've given up careers and so on are quite interesting and intelligent people. I want to identify with people like that rather than sit back here and say 'Yes, I'm a housewife, and I'm happy,' because I wouldn't be. I'm a wife and mother. 'Housewife' is like 'spinster' and 'spinster' is a terrible label to put on anyone. I think 'housewife' is a terrible label too.

Although I'm on my own a lot, I don't really have enough time *to* myself. Even just a day to go into town would be nice; I miss that very much, going to browse round shops, going to Fenwicks, and things like that. It's a regrettable thing really, when Tom's home sometimes, he's home for a very short time, and I say, 'I'd love to go shopping,' and he says, 'We can't possibly all go – it's absolutely crazy; you go,' and he's shoved me off, and I've gone into town and it's awful, because we used to do that sort of thing together. That's another thing I can't really come to terms with, but I'll have to, especially if we have another baby: that's all gone, that side of my life. Just the ordinary things – of being able to do things together: drifting around, looking at antiques, that kind of thing. That companionship we always had.

I find the need now much greater to go out and see films and things than I did when I first had her. It didn't matter so much then, perhaps because of the newness. I'm glad I left getting married and having a baby so late because I don't think it would have made any difference to my reaction to it had I been ten years younger. I would still have had the same worries. I'm only glad I'm more mature: perhaps I would have been worse. I've quite enjoyed the way things have fallen into place as I've gone along. The only thing is, there were various opportunities available to me over the years which I never took – interesting jobs I could have done. I think I've been a bit too cautious. But the main thing's worked out – getting married and having a baby.

[When you feel really happy these days, what sort of thing makes you feel like that?]

When Tom's here. When we're walking in the country or something. It sounds corny – but it's a very simple thing, very free. [And when you feel fed up?] It's usually prompted by the baby crying in the evening, which I can't stand. That causes utter depression – tears and the lot – especially if I've been on my own. The last few weeks she's been doing that, until about ten, and I really get so strung up and tense and that sends me into a depression, because I feel so fed up with my lot.

[Do you think women work as hard as their husbands?]

Yes, I think so. I can only compare myself with my own husband. He works tremendously hard mentally and physically as well, but I think to a certain extent I'm equal with him because I have all the mental fatigue of looking after her and worrying about her, and of being here and doing things. I would say possibly I don't do my job as well as he does his. Particularly the wife bit – that's rather painful at the moment, because I feel perhaps I'm not doing it all that well, regarding making sure all the shirts are ironed, that side of things. He doesn't mind – well, maybe he does. I'm not that bad, really; if he were here he'd probably say I was bloody good. But I feel I'm not doing things a hundred per cent as well as I ought to.

I think looking after a house and a baby is a job. This feeling of wanting to switch off at six o'clock is saying, 'That's it for the day.' But it's also more than a job: you're totally involved with it: it's your own home and your own flesh and blood.

[Do you ever envy your husband?]

I did on this trip actually, because he was talking about going ski-ing and I thought, 'That sounds rather nice,' and I did go ski-ing with him in Austria when we were both working. The thing that made me envious was that this girl – the secretary on this particular film – rang up and there was a slight chance that they might not be going on that day, and suddenly I was in there again and I remembered how exciting it was, and she was talking about it, and I was commiserating with her, and saying, 'I know, many's the time you go with your bag packed to go off filming somewhere and all the arrangements are changed.' She was talking about it and I thought, 'How nice to be going off like that.' When they're filming they work in a group and there's such a lot of companionship within it, just through the situation of being there together – and I sort of envied that part, having known it, you see. I know what he's doing, which is good in a way because it gives us something to talk about, but on the other hand I do get fed up because I'm not sharing in it any more. I said all this to Tom and he said, 'Of course this girl isn't all that popular with the men' – that's part of a secretary/production assistant's job – and he said, 'She'd love to be in your place, to be married and have a baby,' which of course she would. Then I could remain sane about it, by thinking, 'Well, perhaps I have got the best world.'

3 Margaret Nicholson

Margaret Nicholson gives the impression of being a very satisfied housewife. This is not altogether untrue. Over the years she has developed her own mode of coping with the deprivations of housewifery, a mode in which the determined pursuit of social interaction – chiefly with other young housewife–mothers – occupies an important place. Added to this is a tremendous investment in children as a source of satisfaction. Margaret Nicholson's three daughters are offered experiences which their mother feels she missed out on in her childhood – clean clothes every day, nice clothes and so on. They have their hair styled in a fashion which she wishes she could adopt but feels unable to – her hair is curly and she feels it would not look nice worn in the long-blonde-hair-and-fringe image to which her daughters are now successfully assimilated. She buys the children fashionable clothes and forgoes buying them for herself, obtaining pleasure from *their* pleasure.

Her daily life very much revolves around the three themes of childcare, home-keeping and husband-servicing. Her husband's devotion to his career has reached the point where he is simply not at home most of the time: his progressive withdrawal from domestic concerns is described by her as a sign of 'maturity'. (In other words mature masculinity implies non-domesticity, whereas the opposite is true of femininity.) Margaret Nicholson is not wholly successful in adapting to this deprivation of her husband's company, though she is thoroughly persuaded that it is up to her to adapt and not up to him to change. The marriage, egalitarian in ideology, is effectively patriarchal in practice.

Beneath the surface of the interview one detects a rather insecure and dependent person. Experiences mentioned by Margaret Nicholson locate this dependence and insecurity partly in her educational background. An academic failure which seriously eroded her self-confidence led to the perception that the future opportunities left to her consisted of working in a shop or factory or office. Such an insight into women's condition is unusual at the age of eleven. The subsequent progression of experiences – through a typing course and a secretarial job to an early marriage, another secretarial job and then full-time housewifery – hardly gave her a chance to gain confidence in herself as an independent person.

To some extent, Margaret Nicholson is taking refuge in her femininity, a quality which she explains is very important to her. Femininity can be a pseudonym for many forms of chronic insecurity and lack of trust of oneself. It is not a question of criticizing women for a retreat into femininity, but rather one of understanding how social pressures make this an attractive escape. In this respect, Margaret Nicholson's situation illustrates one outcome for women of their gender-role conditioning. For such women the role of housewife is an unparalleled haven.

Housework has a crucial value as an index of femininity. Margaret Nicholson is just as involved in housework as Patricia Andrews, although her standards and routines – or rather lack of routines – are different: it is almost as though she is asserting her individuality in the way she does housework.

In material terms the Nicholsons are well-off. They are in the process of buying the very large and expensive house in which they have rented a seven-room flat for the past ten years. The house is in what estate agents describe as a 'desirable neighbourhood': it is an area of high-priced houses, near several new privately developed housing estates, and in the catchment area of the state primary school which middle-class parents regard as being the best in the district.

Lucy is six: Kate is just four and Rebecca will be two in June: three girls. The plan was four in eight years but I chickened out last summer – four is a lot to cope with. Anyway, I'd be bound to have another girl; people say 'leave a bigger gap, and you'll change the sex!'

Peter is the director of a publishing firm. He used to be a journalist, but then he was offered the chance of a stake in this firm – it's a new company – and he'd always wanted something of his own. Journalism is such a rat race. It's only a small stake, but it was what he wanted. I don't really know that much about his job, I suppose.

I get up at seven, and I'm afraid some days the first thing I do is I have to iron a shirt for Peter and a blouse for Lucy. Then I usually run the bath for the children. If they want their breakfast first I give them their breakfast. They usually refuse a cooked breakfast; they love weetabix, they have two or three weetabix and then they like toast and jam afterwards. I feel a bit guilty about this; I have cooked breakfast in the past but it's just been played around with. Peter usually gets up at half past eight to leave here at half past nine, and if I'm very busy he will get himself something. If he got up when the others did, I would naturally cook for him every day. It's very busy here in the morning. I have to get Lucy ready for school, take her, come back, get Kate ready for playgroup, take her, come back, and then take Peter to the station. Sometimes I walk to the school and the playgroup, but if Peter's in a hurry and is waiting here, I have to take the car, so I can get him to the station on time.

On some days I have to go straight out again for a dental appointment – that kind of thing. One day a week I help at Kate's playgroup. Otherwise I come back, make the beds and wash up: I must admit I rarely wipe up at that point – I just leave it to drain. I tidy up in the sitting room which is a mess because the children like to dress in front of the fire in the morning, so there are towels and dressing gowns and nightdresses everywhere.

Making up beds and washing up are the two things I really don't like. But I do have a domestic help – two days a week. That was Mrs James you saw yesterday. I thought it was rather funny, you came in and you said, 'I've come to do a survey of what housewives think about housework,' and of course she stood in the kitchen and said, 'It's rather apt, coming today'; naturally I would have to say, 'No, I don't like doing housework too much.' Mrs James is very nice and every Monday she makes up all the beds for me with clean sheets, and I really appreciate that. I hate making beds; it's a real effort to do that. I suppose partly with the children's beds it's because they have all their toys in there and if they have friends in they play doctors and nurses in the bunks and they open them all up again and that's frustrating. [Why don't you like washing up?] I just find it very tiresome, because it crops up all day long. I don't feel justified in asking Peter for a dishwasher because I don't have enough washing up.

If there's some washing to do I might do that next. I don't really *enjoy* washing clothes but I couldn't put them in a washing machine! I haven't got a washing machine because I don't want one. I send sheets to the laundry and I go to the launderette once a week for towels and pillowcases, and I pay them to do it and they do it for me. But I couldn't put the children's dresses in a machine: babystretch suits especially are ruined. I feel if you just wash the clothes by hand, gently, and rinse them thoroughly and don't tumble dry them, they are nicer – they *look* nicer. For instance, one or two dresses that Lucy had, Rebecca is wearing, and I'm sure it's because I've looked after them. I wash all Peter's shirts by hand, and that's from choice as well. I must admit, I get satisfaction out of washing when I see, after I've washed, dried and ironed the clothes, that they *are* still nice.

But that's just me, you see: I make hard work for myself but I don't mind.

I do the washing twice a week. I fill the bath with detergent and put them in there to soak. The children have clean clothes every day, so they don't seem to get really dirty. Doing them that way most of the dirt soaks off. I put them in the bath in the morning and then take them out later on. I've still got a pile in there now, and sometime tonight I'll have to rinse them out and put them through the spin drier and then I'll have to iron a shirt for Peter because he wants a special shirt tomorrow.

I've got a spin drier and an airer, and I do have a clothes horse in the bathroom. When we've got a garden, I would like one of those rotary washing lines, so you can take it in. I don't really like to see a linen line across the garden all the time. I suppose it's been instilled in us because when we came here we were told no one really has a linen line across the back, and no one wants to start it, but I notice one or two people have recently.

I haven't got a set day for washing: I haven't got a set routine for anything I'm afraid. I'm a bit impulsive, I like to do housework when I want to do it – and I enjoy the feeling when it's all done. But I would hate to have fixed days for things and feel I *had* to do them then. I do take the car to one of the big supermarkets every Friday for the weekend shopping, but that's because I take an elderly neighbour to do *her* shopping, and I've done that for quite a few years now. I do it because she relies on me.

I must shop every day for something, even if it isn't every day for food. I can usually think of something I want, and I think this is partly brought about by having the car. It's also because I like to think each day what I want to eat, and not buy for two or three days at a time. [Do you like shopping?] I quite enjoy going round a supermarket if I've got the time, and lots of money, and I know I can choose all these lovely foods. I hate being rushed over shopping. If I've got someone coming to lunch and I haven't thought what to eat I go out and I buy foolishly and in that way I don't like shopping. If I know what I want and I go down and I can buy it and I don't have to keep hunting around, that's alright.

Quite often I go out to lunch or have someone here – say two or three times a week – and then I see someone for tea with the children. I think there's only about one afternoon a week I'm *not* seeing someone. Monday afternoon I try to take Mrs James home: Friday afternoon Lucy's got a dancing lesson – ballet and tap.

I cook at lunchtime for Rebecca and myself and usually I do a high tea: fish fingers or sausages or spaghetti bolognese – for all the children if I've got a friend in – and if we go out we quite often have a similar sort of tea. If they want something to eat before they go to bed, they'll have it. I never mind cooking for the children because I know I love food and I never mind cooking for me! It's never any trouble cooking for them because I understand that they love food as well, I suppose.

I try to get them in bed by seven. I find it impossible to get them there any earlier. They all go together; Lucy is quite content to go with the other two, although she's older. There is an awful lot of clearing up to do at that end of the day, especially if I've had a friend to tea. Today I had a friend with three children, so there were six children to clear up after!

Many evenings I spend on my own, because Peter's never in before eight or nine and quite often it's eleven or twelve, and when he has to go to his club with someone it's two or three in the morning. I think this is partly because he is very enthusiastic about his work – if he does come home at eight, he brings work with him!

In the evening I read the paper, or I watch television – I watch a fair bit of television. I take time to make phone calls to friends, to my parents, to my brother – without the children rushing round screaming. I also use the time to finish off odd bits of housework I haven't done in the day.

Some evenings I've stood and I've ironed eleven shirts and it hasn't worried me at all. I like to iron in here, with the television on, and when I've done them I hang them along the picture rail, and I get a great sense of satisfaction seeing them hanging all the way round the room! Silly, isn't it?

I know the way I organize housework is peculiar; I make extra work for myself, and I'm not at all a methodical person. I don't have terribly high standards, except perhaps for keeping the loo and the basin clean. I'd rather do things with Vim than dust and polish, and I suppose that's part of the same hygiene thing. It does worry me underneath about the kitchen if the gas cooker top is dirty and if the sink's dirty, and the fridge. It makes me feel guilty in that it should be done. But I still wouldn't put off going out for the day or seeing a friend or taking the children out. When we were first married Peter used to complain that the place was too tidy and neat, that I was too fussy, and he said, 'You want just to relax a bit more and don't worry if it's untidy,' and now when he comes in he says sometimes, 'When I said that, I didn't mean you to go completely the other way!'

If my parents or my sister-in-law are coming, I really make an effort, because my mother's house is always quite spotless. Whereas, if Peter's mother's coming, I know I don't have to worry. My mother washes by hand; she bought a new washing machine and she got rid of it after a few weeks, because she just never used it. She's got one of these huge old gas coppers, which sounds dreadful these days – and she boils a lot – and I know I've always admired her whiteness. I've heard people in her road say, 'Doris's washing always looks so spotless.' I admire hers, but it doesn't particularly worry me. The only thing that did worry me were teatowels, so now I've gone over completely to buying dark purple or black and then I needn't worry.

I had a granny – she was eighty-eight when she died – and she used to say, 'you're the only person, Meg, who I feel completely relaxed with because I know you'll never criticize: I know you're not going to look round and say, "Oh what an untidy granny I've got." ' My grannies were both very understanding, but my mother isn't a sympathetic person. I was born during the war, when my father was away in the Army. They'd only been married a few months, and just before I was born my mother went back to live with her parents. My grandparents really brought me up: we lived with them till I was nine, and I didn't want to leave – I was closer to them than to my parents, really.

After I was born my mother went to work in a bakery. She had to actually, because she needed the money. She stopped working when my brother was born, and then when he went to school she started again. Like before, that was partly to earn money, because my father was invalided out of the Army. Her work was always part-time: she was there when we came home from school and she was there when we went in the morning, so as far as we were concerned, she's always been there.

[Did you help your mother around the house?]

Yes, I remember not wanting to make the beds, wash up, that sort of thing. The only thing I took a stand about was that I wanted clean clothes every day and my mother used to moan about that, I suppose understandably. So from the age of about thirteen I said, 'Right, I'll do my own washing and my own ironing.' I suppose this is why with my children they have everything clean on every day.

My mother thought I should leave school at fifteen to earn money and help out, but my grandfather made it possible for me to stay on. My first ambition was to be an opera singer. I loved singing; I knew I could sing in tune, I was in the school choir, and I just enjoyed it. As I got older I realized I could never do that. I went to a secondary modern school because I failed my eleven plus. At the age of eleven, when I knew I'd failed my eleven plus, I said to my mother, 'There's only one thing I can do now, and that's take shorthand and typing,' which I did. At my school one could either do a pre-nursing course or a shorthand and typing course, and although I was very interested in nursing, I just didn't think I had the right temperament. I can remember saying at the age of eleven, 'What else is there? A shop or a factory, and I'm not going in to either of those.' My mother was amazed that at that age I should have such set ideas. One is so limited if one fails the eleven plus. And of course it was such a big thing then: I felt so inferior. I think I have got a chip on my shoulder about education definitely. I haven't formed this opinion myself but so many people have told me I've got an inferiority complex about my education, my upbringing – about what I'm capable of. I've been told that I probably feel inadequate a lot of the time, which is true. After I decided I had to do shorthand and typing I thought it would be quite nice to be a secretary to an author or someone that travelled. Underneath I knew I'd never have the confidence to apply for any of those sorts of jobs.

I left school at sixteen and a half and I went to work in a solicitor's office. I come from a small village in Dorset and there was only one solicitor's there: I worked for him. It was suggested by my tutor because maths was my weakest subject and he said, 'If you can find a job where figures aren't the most important thing, then I would.' I was there for about two years, and then when I was eighteen I left home to come to London, to be with Peter.

I'd met him when I was seventeen – his family lived a few miles away, and he used to visit them at weekends. I met him and I knew he was the person I wanted to marry. I suppose I always wanted to get married and have children, but because I wore glasses, I never thought a boy would ask me out. He tried to get a job down there and settle there but he couldn't, and he had a good offer in London, so he asked me if I'd come back with him. At first we lived in hostels but after a month we wrote home and said could we get married because we wanted the tax rebate. It was my granny, really; she said, 'You're both living in hostels, why don't you get married?' We said, 'We can't really afford it;' she said, 'It doesn't really matter whether you can afford it or not, just get married and live in a furnished flat,' which was exactly what we did.

In London I worked in a solicitor's office again. I worked there for five years: I'm a bit of a sticker I'm afraid. I don't like change of any kind. They were very nice there – they didn't mind if one was late in the morning, or wanted an extra lunch-hour. I never wanted to rush off in the evening because of Peter's late hours, so I was quite prepared to stay and work another hour.

I enjoyed work, but I don't think I'd ever go back to an office. I disliked the actual typing part of it: I was a bit disappointed that I wasn't a fast, accurate typist. Actually, it always amazed me that I could grasp shorthand and look at it and translate it back onto the typewriter. [What else did you enjoy about work?] Being with people and having something to do with something – someone to talk to.

I didn't mind very much when I stopped work: I worked up until a month before Lucy was due, and I just didn't ever want to leave. It wasn't really until Kate was born that I felt completely at ease about not working: that I felt it was really worthwhile giving up work.

I was very unsure about how I would react to children – that's partly why we were married for five years before we had any. Obviously I felt I didn't want children when I was nineteen; we both wanted some time on our own. But after about two and a half years, Peter was keen to start a family and I just wasn't. He didn't press it or anything, but eventually he said we really must start a family, so I agreed, and I was taking the precautions anyway. So we went in for Lucy, and I thought I'd like an August baby, and of course I never dreamed that I'd conceive the first month that I didn't use a precaution. Right up until the time I had her, I wasn't sure whether I would want her. I was even planning to put her in a nursery and go back to work. But the minute I saw her I loved her and I knew I couldn't let anyone else look after her. I just felt, I suppose, luckily for me, my maternal instinct: it came then, just in time. We'd always planned a large family and I said to Peter, 'I know now it'll be alright because I know that I will love having children.' He was quite relieved!

I chickened out on the fourth baby partly because I was ill. I had these bad pains in my tummy. I had to have a barium meal, and a follow-through, and it kept recurring, and I decided then it was a bit silly to become pregnant. The X-ray was clear. They thought it might be a tummy ulcer, or some gland that was playing up, or it might be gall bladder. I'm certain that it is a little tummy ulcer that keeps coming back and playing up. My neighbour says it's because I rush around seeing too many people during the day, but I'm far happier doing that because I do have the evenings on my own.

I get satisfaction out of doing everything for the children. I've never minded anything I've done for them – feeding them, having to get up for them in the night. I know – I hope – they appreciate what I do. Sometimes it's an effort to have friends in if you feel a bit tired, but you do it for the children, because they enjoy seeing friends. Quite often I take them to the park or swimming: I don't really want to go for myself, but I do it. I love seeing their faces when they've got something they want. Kate's just got a midimac from Biba, which she got for her birthday, and she was so thrilled with it. Although I need a new coat I'm going to buy Lucy one as well, and do without myself, because they just are so thrilled with it. They love clothes, actually; I suppose they're a bit young, but they do love clothes. I love watching them draw and play, and I do help them quite a bit. I hate tidying up after them, though. I never mind explaining things to them, and I read them stories at night: as long as I can remember I've read a story at night.

One thing I just couldn't bring myself to do was breastfeed the babies, although I loved them. I've got a thing about it, that it sort of nauseates me in a way: I had a long talk with the doctor about it. It worried me that I should breastfeed for the children's sake, partly because my mother-in-law breastfed six and she said I was denying them their birthright. My mother was quite impartial really: although she breastfed both of us, she'd never even mention the subject. I don't know what it is, because I think of myself as being feminine, but I just couldn't bring myself to do that. The doctor said, 'Don't worry: other women feel like you.' I bottle fed them, and I don't think anyone could pick them out now and say, 'Oh dear, that's a bottle-fed child.' They were very contented babies. The girl downstairs had a baby a couple of months ago, and she just cries and cries, and I'm sure she's hungry because she's breastfed. She says the baby's just cross.

Peter's very good with the children. With Lucy he fed her, changed her, bathed her – he didn't have to be asked: he just offered. Now he's often prepared to have them – perhaps on a Saturday afternoon if I want to go out to the shops, or he'll have Rebecca in the morning, because Kate has a dancing lesson on Saturday, and he's quite willing to listen on the alarm for other people's children as well. He's very willing to babysit at any time, but he's very unreliable about getting home to do it.

[Does he change nappies?]

If she's wet, he'll change her, but if he knows she's dirty I'm afraid he'll leave her. He never used to be like this, but I think it's just sort of grown on him really: he's got out of the way of babies, I suppose. He's had so little time with getting on in business, and he's become more mature, and probably feels less inclined to do it.

It's the same with housework. He doesn't help now, but he did when I was working. Now I would have to ask him to wash up and he probably wouldn't do it. Because he has so little time I would feel very selfish asking him to wash up. If we've had people in to dinner, he'll help me wash up then, and he'll also help me dish up which I find a bit embarrassing.

One thing we do agree about is that it's more important to go out a lot and enjoy ourselves while we're young, rather than spend money on beautiful things for our home – we'd rather sit and admire our beautiful antiques when we're sixty, say, if we're still here. I go out to a young mothers' group every other Thursday – we have speakers on various topics or we go out for a meal, or we just have coffee in each other's homes. I also go to the local theatre, and to the cinema with a friend occasionally. Peter doesn't really go out. If he's out it's usually that he's having a drink with Nigel and Alan – his partners – or he's met friends; there's so many pubs where he works, it's difficult to get home! We go out together a lot; every weekend – Friday or Saturday. Sometimes I go up to meet him and we go to a film.

I don't think the children suffer: after all, they're asleep most of the time we're out. I wouldn't ever go away from them. Peter has said, 'Let's go away for the weekend,' but I've always said no – I wouldn't even go away for the weekend. I just feel I must have them with me, I don't know why. Some friends of ours have gone off for a couple of weeks when their baby's been young, and I wouldn't even do that; I'd feel I was missing that time in the baby's life. They're young so little time. When we went to France last year for three weeks I suppose I could have left Rebecca with my parents or sister-in-law but I just couldn't bear the thought of being without her for three weeks. I don't think it's fair on a child that age either. I feel that when they're very young one should be with them.

[Would you like to work now?]

Peter has jokingly said, 'Mary's a dress designer, Nancy does illustrations for children's books, someone else can do this and that, what can you do?' I say: 'Well, what I can do, I wouldn't do.' I have done typing at home but with the third baby it was just too much. It was slave labour, anyway: very hard work. The only thing is, I wouldn't mind helping Peter out: I wouldn't like actually to work for him, because he is a very efficient person at work, and I think he demands great efficiency from his secretaries. I wouldn't want a lot of responsibility.

I think it's too difficult to work with a child under school age. I wouldn't *condemn* anyone if they feel they've got to, but I feel a child does miss its mother.

[When you feel really happy these days, what sort of thing makes you feel like that?]

I feel happy when I look at the children, because I'm so pleased that they're all normal and happy: I think one is happier when one's had children. It's a different sort of happiness: one feels fulfilled.

Although I'm a very inadequate person I don't *feel* inadequate as a mother. Sometimes I suppose you do stop and think – am I doing the right thing, am I bringing up my children in the right way. It's a frightening thought, really: that more the mother than the father is responsible for moulding that child. I believe children are born as they are, but I don't believe they'll grow up a certain way anyway. I think they're moulded by the mother. When they misbehave badly at the very time when you don't want them to let you down, you wonder if you've done the right thing. Sometimes Kate's terribly awkward, and I think, 'Oh dear, perhaps it's because she's the middle one,' and perhaps I have shown too much attention to Rebecca – although I tried terribly hard not to. I look at other children and think, 'They're perfect – why aren't mine?'

I am satisfied really: we have a good life. The only thing is I do get discontented very easily with material things, and Peter says material things aren't important. It's people that count.

[And when you're fed up?]

When I know the bank manager's been on to Peter and he's down about money. We're both bad about money – we never work out what we spend. For instance, I don't have housekeeping. Peter just brings home money and puts it on the bedroom mantelpiece and we both take it. I haven't got a bank account, and I don't want one because quite honestly I spend everything I have. He gives me blank cheques, but I know I'll only write out for what I've asked him for. Only on one or two occasions have I seen shoes or something and gone in and got them with the Barclaycard, and then I've had to ring him immediately and say, 'I've done this and I shouldn't have done.' In fact he says I have most of his money for one thing or another; for kids' clothes, for playgroup. [Would you like some money of your own?] It doesn't bother me really, because I'm never made to feel that Peter's the breadwinner and I'm totally dependent on him.

[What would you say are the best things about being a housewife?]

I think one of them is not having to work – having some time to oneself. [And the worst?] Having the housework and washing up and making beds. I don't like the word 'housewife' really. I always think it conjures up some dull, cabbage-like woman. I think 'mother' is a much warmer word. The other day Lucy said she wanted to be a nurse when she was grown up, but Kate said, 'I want to be a mummy, so I can drive the car all day!'

I never feel I am a cabbage, and can only talk about the children. I like discussing Peter's business with him. He's the kind of person who likes to come in and talk about his business and perhaps get something off his chest, but I'm always willing to listen, and I'm interested, and we have very fierce discussions on politics and world affairs.

[Do you think women have a better or worse deal in marriage than men?]

A better deal. The men have to support the wives. They're really responsible for the money and the way of life. They're far more prone to horrible illnesses like cancer. I never think I work as hard as Peter. I know it's a different kind of work, but he does work terribly hard. I think it's much easier being a woman: I feel the man should be – not the domineering partner – but the *dominant* partner. I don't think women are inferior, but I think they're different. I don't know how to put it without it sounding as though the male is the superior being, but I'm glad I can look up to my husband and not look down on him.

I'm not really for equality for women totally. Obviously I think women should get a fair deal – equal pay for equal jobs. But I wouldn't want to see it like it is in America – with a complete reversal, and the women in charge of the men.

[What would you think of a marriage in which the wife went out to work and the man stayed at home?]

If it suited that particular couple, I couldn't condemn them. But knowing Peter, I'm sure *he* wouldn't want to do that. And I wouldn't want to, and I think perhaps most couples wouldn't. But you do get cases where perhaps the woman can earn a lot more than her husband and it might be more beneficial for them to have it that way round. I can't really think it's a natural state for the man to stay at home: it goes against the grain really, when you think about it. I would think it was unmasculine in a way. I don't believe it would satisfy a really masculine man to do it all the time, and not to have a job as a responsible person supporting a wife and children.

[Do you ever envy your husband?]

Sometimes I envy him his knowledge. I'm very afraid of getting into a conversation where it's above my head and I just can't hold my own, especially if we're in mixed company, because it would let Peter down. Another thing I suppose is that I envy him his freedom, and I am intolerant of his late hours, which makes me feel guilty, because he's kind, he's gentle, he's so understanding and generous: totally unselfish. He never *intends* to stay out so long, but he's there, and he gets totally engrossed in what he's doing, and he seems to forget here. Most evenings he doesn't phone to say where he is, and when he's coming home. It only worries me in that when I see him I criticize him. I just can't sit here, and not say anything.

[What do you think of the women's liberation movement?]

I think it's all right in moderation, but I'm afraid that what I think is that the people who are now in the forefront of it have gone too far the other way. People like this Yvonne Mitchell* – the blonde-haired girl, is that her name? And another one of them: I think they're what they call feminists, aren't they? They just don't want men at all. They're not really interested in being equal with men; they're just interested in completely domineering men and being absolutely self-sufficient. Well, I think women should be self-sufficient, but they're really taking it to the other extreme, I feel. Those women they usually have on television just put me off completely and utterly: they think men are dirt.

4 Sally Jordan

Sally Jordan lives in a three-bedroom council house on an estate isolated from the rest of the borough by a motorway. The area is bleak, but her house is decorated and furnished with a fastidious attention to detail. The interview took place in the 'front' room. Sally was nervous at first – she chain-smoked – but later became more forthcoming. She is small and dark and sprightly, and looks a great deal older than her years.

Sally's interview is remarkable on a number of scores. As a woman she is extremely oppressed. In her marriage she is subject to the dominance of her husband, who seems unwilling to allow her any freedom as an individual, and who helps very little with the burden of childcare and housework. Her reproductive history is a sad list of casualties. Like one in three of women with school-age children she is employed outside the home – for money she asserts, although she also says she enjoys her work and thinks it does her good. Certainly it is important to her as a source of personal identity. But her job is not a skilled or challenging one and probably its main benefit to her (apart from the value of getting out of the house and meeting people) is that she knows she is more than 'just a housewife'.

These dimensions of oppression are added to her oppression

* Juliet Mitchell.

as a housewife. Her feelings about her home – that it is a prison – are interpreted by her doctor as a neurotic symptom. In this respect, the interview with Sally Jordan illustrates the conventional psychoanalytical interpretation of female disorder – that personal lack of adjustment to a role is all that needs to be corrected. No account is taken by the doctor of the facts of her situation, or the validity inherent in her complaints about it.

Finally, Sally has developed unusual insights into women's situation. She is apparently not simply echoing an article she has read or a television programme she has watched, but has come to this level of awareness on her own. She sees that women are prepared – conditioned – for the housewife role: that she is, indeed, preparing her own daughter for it. She understands the pressures towards conspicuous consumption in the housewife situation, implying that such consumption has a displacement function in that it distracts women's attention from the implications of their role. But despite these insights, Sally believes in the superiority of men, the right of husbands to order their wives' lives, and the fitness of women for domestic duties. She is socially blinded to a vision of her 'disorder' as a rational response to a problematic situation: she herself participates in those traditional myths about women which surreptiously label them as inferior and openly condemn them to a secondary role in society.

I'm twenty-seven – nearly twenty-eight. I've got three children, one of nine, one of eight, and one of four and a half. Two boys and a girl: the youngest's a girl. They all go to school – I got the four-year-old in because at the time I worked in the school kitchens, and they let her in because I worked at the school. My husband's a dustman – a refuse collector, they call them, don't they? His working hours vary: some days seven till three, maybe other days seven till five, or it can even go on seven till seven. He always starts at seven. He works Saturday morning till one.

I've got a part-time job: I'm a shrink wrapper. If I fill in a form and have to put what I am, I put 'shrink wrapper'. I know it sounds ridiculous, but that's what I actually am. I would rather describe myself as a shrink wrapper than as a housewife. I pack tins in cellophane, and the cellophane shrinks – that's what shrink wrapping is. The tins go to cash-and-carrys and supermarkets. My hours are nine till one Monday to Friday; in the school holidays a friend two doors away looks after the children. I normally have time off if they're ill.

You want to know what I do every day?

My husband gets up first. I get a cup of tea and toast in bed, then I get up. I get up with the aggro – the miseries, about ten to seven. I come downstairs like a mad bull and I don't stop till I leave the house at twenty-five past eight. I try to do as much as I can before I go to work. I come down, lay the table for breakfast, get dressed, and then I charge around doing what I can: the children make their own beds. I make my bed, I carpet sweep: if I'm hoovering, I leave that till I come home, I dust, draw curtains, drink tea, smoke a million fags with nerves, and then I make sure the children are all dressed and ready for school. That time goes very quick. My boys go to school on their own, the little girl goes with my friend next door. I don't take her, but I collect her.

I get to work early, so I can have coffee before I start. I get there about twenty to nine, put the kettle on, make myself a cup of coffee, and I'm supposed to start at nine, but by the time I actually get down there it's ten past. We have a tea break, it's supposed to be a quarter of an hour, but we have a half hour. We finish at one o'clock. Then I have to do all my shopping, buy the dinners, and that; Thursdays and Fridays are busy shopping days. Wednesdays I don't do any.

I come in, prepare me dinner – get the vegetables ready – and then I do washing, ironing, have a cup of tea. I do hand washing every day for about an hour; I leave the other things for a machine wash. I've got a washing machine, a twin tub, and in the winter I dry the clothes on a clothes horse, or I lug them down the launderette, and in the summer they hang on my line in the garden. Sometimes I iron of an evening: I do a big load on Saturdays, about two hours, and then maybe an hour and a half on Sundays.

After I've had a cup of tea, it's usually time to go and pick up my little girl. I come back about a quarter to four, change the little girl's school clothes, and then the boys come in at four. I lay the table. And then you hear my mouth, from then till they go to bed! I've got no patience. I used to, but I haven't now.

I cook an evening meal. My children have dinners at school, but they also have dinners of an evening: I don't do tea for them when they come in from school. We have dinner about five usually, unless I'm doing a roast, and that takes a bit longer. I put my husband's in the oven.

After that I wash up, put the dishes away, sweep the floor, wash the floor, and then where the children have been playing I come in here and tidy up. They go to bed at seven. I take them up, but the two boys have their light on for half an hour to read. The light goes off at half past seven, and then I come down, make a cup of coffee, and I sit down!

This is for equality: my husband comes in, he'll have his dinner, he'll have a rest – he'll go to sleep. He'll wake up about half past seven, when I give him a cup of coffee, he'll have a bath – I haven't got an immersion heater, I have to light the boiler for his bath even in the summer – he'll get dressed, then he goes down the pub. Every night. He goes about eight and he comes back when it closes: in the week, about eleven, and at the weekend, at twelve. He's done that ever since we've been married.

Saturdays he finishes work at one. I get up, do breakfast, I get the washing machine out, and that takes me a long time because my machine is rather an awkward thing. One day it'll go, another day it won't. And then I do my place through from top to bottom – polish, hoover everywhere. I finish about one and I do a late dinner, because although my husband finishes work at one, he doesn't come home till half past three; he goes to the pub. Me and the children have ours about two, his goes in the oven, and then it gets thrown out because he never eats on a Saturday. But I still cook from habit. Saturday afternoon he goes asleep, and I sit there. He sleeps till about six, has his bath, gets himself dressed, and then he goes down the pub.

Sundays he gets up and goes to football about half past nine, and he comes in about twenty to three. He has his dinner, goes asleep, wakes up about six, has his dinner, has a wash, gets dressed, and at eight o'clock he goes down the pub. Most Sunday nights I have a babysitter, and I get ready and go down the pub too. I like a game of bingo – one night a week I might pop off for a game. If I win I might go a second time.

[Do you like housework?]

I don't dislike it, but I suppose it's because I'm not at it all day. I go to work, and I'm only on housework half a day. The times when I haven't worked and I've been doing housework all day I've gone mad. I make a point not to do housework all day, because I wouldn't like it. A woman's work is never done; she's on the go all the time. I mean even before you go to bed you've got something to do – emptying ashtrays, wash a few cups; you're still working. Even if you go to bed at twelve o'clock, you've still got something to do before you go up.

I don't like my place looking untidy; I don't like to see a place cluttered. There's a place for everything. When I first came out of hospital I was told not to do any heavy lifting, but I still had to have everything in its place. I don't know why I'm like that. Perhaps it's because my mother was like it. She's the same: if there's supposed to be cushions on the chair, they've got to be on the chair and not on the floor.

I find I worry a lot about what other people think. You know, if somebody was to call unexpectedly . . . I can't sit there of a night with children's toys about. When they're in bed I have to clear everything up. My husband says I tidy up too often. But if I get the occasional night when he does stay in, I don't bother then. I do still clear away before I go to bed – empty ashtrays, wash the cups up. Sometimes he says, 'Leave it,' but I think I'd rather do it of a night-time.

When I'm ill I still come down and tidy up. I had flu last week but I still got up and tidied up everywhere and got the children ready for school. I didn't like to think somebody would knock at the door and come in and find me untidy. [Does your husband notice when it's tidy?] Well, he doesn't make much comment. I've got a terrible fad for changing the room round more or less for something to do, I suppose, because I sit in here so much. I had the settee in the middle of the room and I changed it around. He'll come in and I have to say, 'I've changed the room round, what do you think of it?' and he'll say, 'I like it,' or 'I don't like it.' Men don't really worry about furniture or rooms, do they?

I do work to a routine. I'd rather be late for work than not do what I usually do before I go to work. I don't know why I have a routine. I suppose that's why it's boring. You work to a routine so long it becomes a habit.

My mother's a very tidy housewife. I suppose I take after her in a lot of ways. I don't like my husband to come in and find the dinner not ready, and I don't like him to come in and find me ironing. He used to stipulate, as far as he was concerned he didn't want to see his wife washing and ironing, so I always have that done before he comes in. My mother's the same. I was never given the opportunity to help around the house when I was young. My mother would do things even when she was ill and then she'd turn around and say we did nothing for her.

I detest ironing, I can't even say why. I detest ironing shirts. The only thing I don't mind ironing is my little girl's things. I don't like ironing on the whole, but I have to do it – if I didn't do it, I'd get moaned at, there'd be no shirts: my husband wouldn't do it. I don't sit back and think who's going to do it, I'm not going to do it, because I know it's my job. I've *got* to do it.

I don't like washing paintwork – it's a very boring job. I don't mind hoovering. You might get a bit of a backache, but it's quite easy – except that I detest doing the stairs with the hoover. Polishing's alright – you just spray it on. I detest shopping – I never know what to get. I don't mind if I'm going out shopping for clothes or for something for the home, which isn't very often, but I don't like shopping for food, because I never know what to get each day. I don't like the price of the bill at the end of it. I hate Thursdays, the day I do most of my shopping, because the bill goes up every week.

I don't mind washing by hand, and I don't mind washing with the machine. I'm not overjoyed at the prospect, but I don't mind it. I don't like the cooking, but I like the eating. I can't abide washing dishes: I hate that. I eat, and I'm full up, and I've got to get up and start clearing the table, washing pots and pans. If I can get out of that, I will, and if my boys are in a very good mood, they'll offer to wash up for me.

I don't mind mending. If the children's elbows come out of their jumpers, I don't mind sitting there sewing. My boys are very heavy on clothes. They have to have uniform for school, clothes for playing in, and clothes for best. I used to knit everything for the children, but I don't now: I found that the clicking of the needles started to annoy me. I like buying clothes. If the children are dressed nice, *I* get the pleasure out of that. You get sort of pride from other people looking and thinking that your children are smart. I think the way you dress your child can have a psychological effect on them. My boys like modern clothes, and I do my best to keep them up in fashion, even if I go without myself. If they want a pair of bell-bottoms because they're in fashion, I like to buy them. I feel if they go round looking dirty and scruffy, people look down on me.

I was in hospital once and I wanted to see the children, and my husband took the boys out – only the boys – and he bought them a new suit each out of a children's boutique. I did like them but I told him it was unnecessary to go out and buy more because the clothes they had upstairs were smart enough.

[Do you find housework monotonous on the whole?]

Well, I suppose I do really, because it's the same thing every day. You can't sort of say, 'I'm not going to do it,' because you've got to do it. Take preparing a meal: it's got to be done, because if you didn't do it, the children wouldn't eat. I suppose you get so used to it, you do it automatically. When I'm doing housework, half the time I don't know what I'm thinking about. I'm sort of there, and I'm not there. Like when I'm doing the washing – I'm at the sink with my hands in water, and I drift off. I daydream when I'm doing anything really – I'm always going off into a trance, I don't hear people when they talk to me. I do it at work too: I stare into space, I'm working at the same time. I can't say there's something specific on my mind, because there isn't.

I always say I'd like a holiday. We've never had a holiday together since we've been married. I have took the children away for a week to Bognor in a caravan – just me and the children. But my husband hasn't come with us, he's always worked his holidays.

I'm a very lonely person. Apart from going to the pub on Sundays, and going to bingo, I don't go out. After he's gone out, I usually turn the television off; I don't like to watch it on my own. I'm not an addict, I prefer the silence to the noise. We never go anywhere together. I sometimes say I'd like to go to the pictures, but I've never got there yet in the last five years. I have a friend who comes down sometimes; she'll wait till she sees my husband's gone out – till she sees the car's gone. My friend's not married – she's my niece actually – if she goes out every night, I have to sit on my own. [Do you have friends at work?] No, not really. I keep to myself pretty much at work. There's only ten women work there, you see: we all have a laugh together. I don't usually see anybody in the afternoons. [Do you go out with the children in the daytime ever?]

If I get all my work done on a Saturday, I might go over and see my mother and father, but I haven't done that for a long time. It's two buses and a long walk. I don't go to other people's houses, they usually come to me. I don't like dogs, and both my sister-in-law and my friend along here have got dogs.

I'd like to get away sometimes, but you see my husband's a bit old-fashioned; he can go out, but I've got to stay in. I can go out with him, and I'm allowed to go to bingo once a week – with *his* sister – but if I suggested a dance or the pictures, I'm not allowed. He puts his foot down, he's rather possessive there. I think it's wrong, but my trouble is that from the time we've been married I've been a very weak person. I've let my husband rule my life, and now I'm trying to make changes, and it's too late, you see. We argue about my working, because I work in a warehouse where all men work, and he's always tel¹ing me to pack it in, but that is one thing where I have stood my own ground and said I won't pack it in.

I enjoy my job. I won't give my notice in because it's an easy-going firm, we've got no bosses over us, we're our own bosses, we work in a happy atmosphere, if you're off sick they do pay you and I like working there.

I left school at fifteen. I didn't stay on at school because I wasn't very brainy. I suppose I always had it in my mind to end up getting married and having children. My parents wanted me to be a short-hand typist. When I was at school I worked as a Saturday girl in Woolworths and I had to sign a contract to say that I'd work there fulltime, so I went there for a week to fulfil the contract when I left school. Then I went to Featherstone Brothers as a coil winder for about three months – it's an aircraft-maintenance factory – and then I went to the birthday-cards place, and I made birthday cards for about nine months. These jobs were all from fifteen to eighteen: I got married when I was eighteen. Next I did screw—plating in another factory for three months; then I went to a sweet factory and made peppermints – I ate more than I made! From there I went to Simpsons, where I stayed till I got married, and that was doing screw-plating too – wiring the screws to be dipped in metal. I started there on August the tenth, I got engaged on August the fourteenth, I got married on May the sixteenth, and I left in the June. I was having a baby.

[And when did you start the job you've got now?]

Oh, I have worked since then – practically all the time, on and off sort of thing. I didn't go to work when I had my first boy, because twelve months later I had another one, and when they were two and three I used to go office cleaning, in the mornings and evenings. My husband used to look after my children – I used to go early morning, half past four, and be home before he went to work. In the evening – I used to live in a flat then – the girl downstairs used to keep them down there with her. During the day I used to mind children: I had my sister's two, another two from up the road, my aunt's little girl who was five, and two from round the corner, so I had nine with my own two.

Then I went as a temporary in the evening – doing casual labour as a machine operator at Burley & Green's – that was after I had my little girl. She was six weeks old when I started that job. My mother used to have her and the two boys.

My sister always worked in an office – she was head of a department and I always wanted to be like her. When this job came up at Burley & Green's I bluffed my way in. The only time I'd seen those machines was when I'd swept round them office cleaning. A girl-friend of mine was working there of an evening, and she got me in. I liked working on machines actually, I like working with my hands. I used to be on the machine on my own in charge of invoices and paperwork and I used to think myself something more than what I actually was. I suppose I used to daydream then that I was a lot cleverer than what I was.

I packed up there because we got up to date with the work and they didn't want anybody. The little girl must have been about ten months then. And I went to another evening job. Then I moved out of my flat and I didn't work again till I moved here – oh, except I did one and a half weeks packing bits for motor cars. I never worked no more till I went to the school as a washer up, on the fourth of February last year. I had the summer holidays off with my children because I used to get half pay: they paid you a retainer. I got the job I've got now just as the holidays were ending.

[Are you going to stay at the job you've got now?]

I expect so. It's not bad money – £7 a week, and I need the money: that's why I go to work, not for the fun of it! I've always worked because I've needed the money, because he spends too much money on drink and therefore I've always had to work to make my own money up. I don't know how much he earns: he thinks that once a wife gets her housekeeping, that should be it. He gives me £13 one week, and £12 the next, because he has to pay the rent every other week. That money's for food, clothes, gas, electricity, payments on the television, and payments on the cooker. I get the family allowance, and I don't draw that, that's the children's, and I use that for their clothes. If he spends more than he thinks he's going to spend, I get stopped a pound. When any bills come in he always gives them to me. I get paid off my husband on a Thursday and in my job I get paid on a Thursday, and I put it all together, and then I spend the whole lot, near enough.

[Do you agree with mothers working generally?]

Yes. I think it does a mother good to get out. I would never leave my children with somebody they didn't know. You're going out to work *for* them; I mean if I didn't go to work I couldn't afford to dress my children.

I've changed jobs a lot because I get bored very quick. When I don't work I always get this restlessness – that I want to get out of the house. At home it's too easy to sit down and think. Going out to work is sort of escape from the home, I suppose. I find some days when the time comes for me to go home I don't like it. I'm more happier at work than I am at home. I don't know why. I think I regard my home as a prison; I did say that to Dr Robinson once. He said I was a very insecure person. But to me it *is* a prison because I'm not allowed freedom on my own bat. My husband can come and go as he pleases. Like Saturday, for example, he's going to watch Fulham play football, but if I came home and said I was going on an outing – like a works outing – I wouldn't be allowed to go. I say to him: 'You've got your freedom – it's only fair that I should go out,' and he says, 'It's all right for a man, but it's not all right for a woman.'

I always class my marriage as unhappy. My husband doesn't. He thinks this is it – this is marriage. I compare my marriage with my sister's – her and her husband have got more companionship than what we've got. My nieces come down and they talk about what they're doing, where they're going, and their jobs and I get very envious, because I never had any life of my own when I was younger. I always say I got married too young; I didn't see enough of life. I met my husband when I was sixteen, I got engaged when I was seventeen and I got married when I was eighteen.

I suppose I'm frightened of my husband to a certain extent. I've always been led to believe that a man is the boss of the home, and I feel I can't get that idea out of my mind. My marriage is like boss and employee: I take orders from my husband.

I often feel I'd like to put my coat on and walk out. I know I could always go back to my parents, but I think of my children, because this is their home, and my mother and father are getting old now, and therefore they wouldn't want three young children running about. I don't think it'd be much fun for my children. I don't walk out, of course. I suppose it's because I'm a weak willed person. In my mind I'd like to be different from what I am. I'd like to be a stronger person, able to put my foot down and lead my own life.
[Does your husband do anything in the house?]
He did, when we moved in here. I said I wanted the kitchen in tongued and grooved panelling in proper wood, and I bought the wood, and he did do that for me. But I've been waiting sixteen months for him to do this room. I want the picture rail down and – this is the wallpaper the council put on – I want it redecorated.

When I first came out of hospital after the operation I had, he was good then, but everything he does must be finished in time to still go out to the pub. He does say – about the washing up for instance – 'Leave that, and I'll do it,' but you see, I can't come in here and sit down knowing that it's all out there, so therefore I get up and do it and he goes back to sleep. He wouldn't go shopping. Sunday morning he might tidy up and run the hoover over the carpet, only sometimes I think he does it to save an argument. He doesn't usually buy for the children: they play football and they're always coming home needing new things for that, and he just shrugs his shoulders and says, 'That's your responsibility, not mine.' I get my housekeeping and that's that.
[Does he ever help with the children?]
Yes, he'll take them up to bed, if he's awake. He never took much interest in them as babies. He never changed a nappy, never! He would sometimes feed – more with the little girl, he idolizes her.

He wouldn't take a baby for a walk in a pram – he wouldn't be seen dead with a pram. He'd go into a small shop, but not a big one: he doesn't walk round the supermarket with me on Thursdays, he waits outside in the car. And that's another thing: I'm supposed to be learning to drive. I was having lessons, but I found I couldn't afford them. So he said I could go out in the car with him, but every time I want to do that we have to have an argument. I want to drive so I can go and do my shopping without having to drag it home, and so I can go and see my parents and take the children more places.

I think of myself as looking after my husband, like I look after my children, because he's always got a clean shirt, he's always got a meal to come home to, and he's always got me to come home to. I do sort of feel proud about that sometimes, but then I get annoyed at myself that I haven't got the courage *not* to be here.

I do get pleasure out of doing these little things for him, but I've got a very childish way about me, if I do something I've always got to show him. Like when I used to knit – I would rush and finish it to show him; I get pleasure in giving. He doesn't appreciate it always, but he sometimes gets up after a meal and says, 'That was nice, I enjoyed that.' He doesn't pay me compliments as a person. Sometimes when I go out I know I look nice – I've done my hair, I've got all my make-up on, and the clothes I wear out with my husband I don't wear to work or round the house. I wouldn't wear a coat out shopping that I'd wear with him, and I like to dress modern.

[Do you like looking after the children?]
I won't say I dislike it, but as I said before, my patience is gradually wearing thin. [Did you plan the children?] My first child I did. I had to get married, but my parents were against the marriage, so we planned that if we had to get married, they wouldn't stop it. When we got married I was four and a half months pregnant. I stopped work a couple of months later, because I don't carry babies very well. The second one wasn't planned. I'm afraid I was a bit green, I believed the old wives' tale that you couldn't fall if you were breast-feeding, and I did, and I didn't know I was having that boy till I was five months. I fed the first one till he was seven months. It was always drummed into me that a mother's milk is better for the baby, but I didn't feed my second one. I found I didn't have the time, and

I didn't want to do it in front of the other one, because he was only twelve months, and there was a lot of jealousy when I used to cuddle the baby to feed it. I stopped feeding that baby after three weeks.

I had miscarriages in between the second boy and the girl, and when I had her I couldn't feed her because she was only two pounds six born, she was premature, and she was fed intravenously by tube. I did plan her because I lost two babies, and also I lost a baby in 1969, a little girl I wanted, but she was stillborn on September the seventeenth. I can't have any more. I had an abortion last Easter and I was sterilized after. I'd been in hospital because I was in for eight weeks with my stillborn baby, I had placenta praevia;* the same thing happened again, I kept bleeding all the time. They said I wouldn't be able to carry the baby. I didn't mind having the termination but I think now – at the moment – it's having some reaction on me. It isn't that I wanted any more children – I didn't, moneywise, and also how far my patience had gone.

I'm going through a nervous depression at the moment. I suppose when your nerves are on edge the children feel it. I've noticed when I'm happy, they're happy; when I'm upset, they're upset, and my oldest boy's been a bit of a handful since he was a baby: he's a very highly strung child, one minute he's all loving and friends with everybody, and the next minute he's bashing up his brother and sister and he hates the whole world. My little girl's going through this stage where she whines a lot – she can't ask for something, she's got to scream for it. I can't stand noise. I thought I would go and talk to the doctor about it. He could help me, give me some pills.

I don't know whether it was because I used to see my friends wheeling prams, or what, but there was never any other question in my mind than getting married and having children. Even when I used to play with dolls as a child. Really, you're prepared for motherhood. I think now when I buy my little girl's toys . . . she's got a cot, and dolls, and she's got a pram, and you buy the ironing board and iron and a little washing machine – and it's all miniatures of what you have in real life later on. It's like being prepared for the future.

*A condition in which the afterbirth grows in the wrong place, over the entrance to the womb.

I don't think that's right. It was only the other day I thought it's like playing house all over again, but for real. And I think I'd rather buy her trains and motor cars – you know, something constructive for her to play with – instead of preparing her. I can't really explain how I feel about this. But I think right from birth you're like a robot, you're programmed: it's as if you're born, you get the toys – the prams and everything – and then later on you get the real things. It's all planned for you. It's not the same for boys – even when they're younger they're allowed much more freedom. With a girl it's the usual thing, you go into a shop, you can buy a more modern washing machine for them, or instead of a pram with one shade, it's a twin pram, or it's a new doll, but it's the same as when you're married, you can improve yourself by buying a new washing machine, or something else new. It's going on and on all the time. Sometimes when I'm sitting and thinking, and I think I'm preparing her for what I'm going through now, I don't want her to have the life I've had, even up till now; I'd rather her be more independent than me.

I think of myself as a housewife, but I don't think of myself as a cabbage. A lot of people think that they're housewives and they're cabbages. I don't like to think I'm only a housewife. A lot of people say if anybody says, 'What do you do?' 'Oh, I'm just a housewife.' I resent saying that: I don't say it. Either I say, 'I'm a shrink wrapper', or I say, 'I'm a wife and mother and I've got a part-time job.' These days people look down on housewives. There's more women fighting for equality and doing men's jobs, and a lot of women don't like staying in the home. There's more women work fulltime than part-time. I wouldn't like to work fulltime and run a home as well.

[Do you ever feel there's anything else you would rather be doing . . . ?]

Yes! Sitting on a beach in Majorca.

[What would you say are the best things about being a housewife?] You can please yourself pretty much when you do a thing. You haven't got to work to rule all the time. You're your own boss during the day. [And the worst things?] I suppose you get days when you feel you've got to get up and do the same old thing, you get bored stiff, you're stuck in the same routine. I think if you ask any housewife, if they're honest, they'll turn round and say that they feel like a drudge half the time. It's doing the same thing – boredom.

I always used to think my mother was a very miserable woman. Now I find myself getting very much like her, and that frightens me. The whole future frightens me. I think when the children are grown up, I'm going to be even more lonely.

[Do you think women get a better or worse deal in marriage than men?]

A worse deal. Well, I do anyway. I'm domineered – my life's ruled for me.

[Do you agree with men doing housework?]

Yes, I think they should do their share. They should help. [What would you think of a marriage in which the wife went out to work and the husband stayed at home?] Oh no, I wouldn't think nothing of that. I'd say he was a henpecked husband. No, I wouldn't agree with that. They should help, but not take over.

[Do you think there are any ways in which women are treated unfairly?]

I don't think of myself as everybody. I class myself as me. So if I say I'm being treated unfairly, I don't know about anybody else. I'm just me. [What do you think of the women's liberation movement?] I don't fancy burning my brassières. I say equality is all right to a certain extent. A woman can never be as equal as a man: although they're not inferior, they'll never be quite as equal. That's my opinion. If you're all for this liberation movement, now I couldn't imagine myself doing what my husband does. I couldn't do it. Lugging great sacks of rubbish about. If it's equality so far as women MPS, why not women dustmen? And I don't think women could do it. So I therefore say men are the stronger sex in some things, but not in all things.

Seven

Myths of Woman's Place
One: The Division of Labour by Sex

Industrial capitalism is the economic and social system in which the present alienation and oppression of women as housewives has arisen. But other forces also act to maintain the home-centredness of women's identity. A set of myths about woman's place in society provides the rationale for the ideology of gender roles in which femininity and domesticity are equated.

A myth is 'a purely fictitious narrative . . . embodying some popular idea concerning natural or historical phenomena'.[1] In the ideology of woman's place, two statements popularly believed to be true, but actually untrue, are these: 'Only women are, ever have been, or can be housewives,' and 'Only women as mothers are, ever have been, or can be the proper people to rear children.' The former can be called the 'myth of the division of labour by sex' and the latter the 'myth of motherhood'. Both myths are referred to directly and indirectly by housewives in the interviews quoted in the previous chapter, particularly when discussing the participation of men in domestic tasks, and also in considering the question of gender-role reversal in the family.

As anthropologists have discovered in the study of small-scale societies, the function of myth is not only or even chiefly symbolic or explanatory. The primary function of myth is to validate an existing social order. Myth enshrines conservative social values, raising tradition on a pedestal. It expresses and confirms, rather than explains or questions, the sources of cultural attitudes and values. The notions expressed in myth are always held as sacred – they are perceived and transmitted as sacred – and it is through its sacred aspect that myth justifies the claim that the conservation of the status quo is the all-important social task; it supports the view of the world held by people who say that 'it has always been and should always remain as they know it'.[2] Because myth anchors the present in the past it is a sociological charter for a future society which is an exact replica of the present one.

The myth of the division of labour by sex and the myth of motherhood are myths because as statements of fact they are untrue, and because, despite this lack of veracity, they are powerful forces acting to conserve the tradition of women's domestic identity. Myth stated as fact becomes fact: what is mythological appears real. Authenticity triumphs despite (or because of) the concealment of bias.

In this chapter and the following one, the two myths of the division of labour by sex and motherhood are examined, and their basis as myth is uncovered.

*

The myth of the division of labour by sex describes the relegation of women to a domestic role in the family group as natural, universal and necessary. It states that women are naturally housewives in all societies, and that women need to assume this role for society to survive. The myth does not always make these assertions categorically, but imprecise reiterations of necessity, universality and naturalness abound (just as they do in popular discussions on the subject of gender roles). Reference is usually made in the myth to scientific or academic work which is held to prove the point – in other words, to contain a detailed version of the myth and to present the pseudo-evidence for its credibility.

Three different sorts of 'expert' promulgate the myth of the division of labour by sex. There are the ethologists, whose self-conferred mission is to sketch in those parts of the myth which document the naturalness of woman's domestic role. Anthropologists, with data on the division of labour by sex in different societies, provide the evidence for its universality; and, finally, the sociological contribution is a stake in the necessity of the division of labour by sex which confines women to the home. To survive, it is said, society requires the restriction of women to the housewife–wife–mother roles. Of these three, the anthropological contribution is probably the most influential, and so will be given more attention than the other two.

1 Ethology

Ethology is concerned with the study of unlearned, species-specific behaviour. It emphasizes the *biological* substratum of human social behaviour: what is natural rather than merely social.

The ethologist claims that the division of labour by sex, with women as housewives and men as non-housewives, has 'direct biological roots'.[3] Such a claim enables the myth of the division of labour by sex to take on the quality of a 'myth of origin', and hence to gain in persuasive power. What the ethologist contributes is that part of the myth which 'explains' how it all started, which links the division of labour between female and male in industrial societies with the division of labour between female and male in animal societies both today and millennia ago.

Proponents and popularizers of the myth of origin related to the division of labour by sex include Desmond Morris (*The Naked Ape*), Lionel Tiger (*Men in Groups*), Lionel Tiger and Robin Fox (*The Imperial Animal*), and Robert Ardrey (*African Genesis*). This is the sort of assertion they make about the division of labour by sex:

The evidence is sufficiently extensive and heterogeneous in its theoretical, disciplinary and natural origin to lend confidence to the notion that the sexual division of labour is a cross-cultural constant . . . we are involved here with a phenomenon deeply rooted in the nature of human social life . . . It is a feature of social life at the heart of man's survival, the understanding of which must involve an approach to 'behavioural bedrock' – to the fundaments of the behavioural process.[4]

One of the few general rules about human cultures that anthropologists can safely affirm is that in all known societies a distinction is made between 'women's work' and 'men's work' . . . this goes back to the evolution of the hunting animal, where male and female were assigned radically different tasks . . . This basic pattern evolved in a hunting context that molded its content and direction.[5]

These verbose statements conceal an essentially false chain of reasoning. Tiger, Fox *et al.* look around at human society, make a (false) generalization about it, and then search around in evolution and animal societies for evidence to support it. Hence Tiger observes that the 'sexual division of labour is a cross-cultural constant'. Since the book in which he proclaims this is one about male bonding, he continues by saying 'the crux of my argument is that male bonding patterns reflect and arise out of man's history as a hunter'.[6] This boils down to the argument that the sexual division of labour is determined by the fact that once-upon-a-time (supposedly) men went hunting and women stayed at home. As Desmond Morris phrases this argument:

The females were too busy rearing the young to be able to play a major role in chasing and catching prey . . . the hunting ape . . . [had] to abandon the meandering, nomadic ways of its ancestors. A home base was necessary, a place to come back to with the spoils, where the females and young would be waiting and could share the food. This step . . . has had profound effects on many aspects of the behaviour of even the most sophisticated naked apes of today.[7]

A variety of subsidiary mythical assertions are used to support this argument. Facts such as differences in female–male growth-rates and reactions to rising environmental temperatures are dragged in, as well as the 'obvious' dangers to the reproductive process of a food-hunting female. It is also necessary to assert (to make the argument relevant to modern conditions) that 'working has replaced hunting, but has retained many of its basic characteristics. It involves a regular trip from the home base to the "hunting" grounds. It is a predominantly masculine pursuit . . . '[8] and so on. With a flagrant disregard for truth (housework is work, and involves daily excursions from the home base – shopping: 38 per cent of females work outside the home, and so on) a picture is built up in which the oppression of women to the home is validated by an image of Mrs Pregnant-or-Nursing Ape, waiting gratefully with a cooking pot in hand for the return of Mr Hunting Ape with his spoil. Mrs Ape then kept the home fires burning, just as Mrs Naked Ape does (or is encouraged to do) today.

The argument has two basic weaknesses. Firstly, it assumes that we know exactly how evolution occurred and that it was a more or less unilinear process. Neither of these statements is in fact true. The second obvious weakness inheres in the generalizations from animals to humans, and from humans back to animals. Very specific differences mark human beings off from their animal ancestors and counterparts, not least of which is the enormous dependence of the human species on learning processes: the human capacity to invent, perpetuate and change culture.

In outline the ethologists assert that 'man' began as a vegetarian tree-dwelling hairy ape. About 15 million years ago, with the climatic changes of the Pliocene, the environment changed and lush vegetation was replaced by scrub and grassland. The ape had to come down from the trees and adapt his capacities to a ground-based search for animal food. Hunting and housewifery were the adaptive capacities required by these changes, and therefore acquired by male and female respectively.

In her book *The Descent of Woman* Elaine Morgan calls this the 'Mighty Hunter' myth. She produces a wealth of evidence to show what is wrong with it on a factual level. There are three crucial points. The myth of the mighty hunter fails to explain why apes became weapon-users, and walkers-on-two-legs. The changeover from four legs to two is argued by the ethological school to have taken place on grounds of convenience: it produced faster speeds. Yet 'other things being equal, four legs are bound to run faster than two . . . Try to imagine any other quadruped discovering that – a cat? a dog? a horse? . . . ' As for discovering weapons, an animal 'does not suddenly adopt a totally new course of action, such as picking up a stick or a rock and throwing it. The idea would simply not occur to it, and even if it did, the animal would have no reason to suppose that it would work.'⁹

The animal species whose behaviour bears some relation to the aggressive, meat-eating, ground-dwelling ape of the myth are *not* those who, in evolutionary terms, could be called 'man's' closest relatives. The ethologist cites macaques and baboons, but these are monkeys, not apes. The ape species of chimpanzees and gorillas are much more closely related to *Homo-sapiens*. While baboons and macaques are largely ground-dwellers and are aggressive and bloodthirsty animals, chimpanzees and gorillas are mild-mannered vegetarians. Female–male differences in size and strength are greater among the former than among the latter. As a matter of fact, if the sexual division of labour between hunting males and babysitting females was as rigid as the myth claims among animals who were the ancestors of *Homo sapiens*, then the female–male difference in size and strength among humans today would be very much greater than it is. According to Björn Kúrten in *Not From the Apes*, even the descent of man from the apes is in question: 'It would be more correct to say that apes and monkeys descended from early ancestors of man.'¹⁰

The third crucial objection to the mighty-hunter myth hinges on its androcentricity. In title, phrasing, thesis, adduced evidence, and conclusion, this argument about the biological origins of the division of labour between man and woman is imbued with the male's self-interest. It is the 'Mighty Hunter' not the 'Mighty Housewife' myth: the activity which is valued is the masculine one. In describing his view of the division of labour, the ethologist inevitably places the masculine role first. The feminine role appears as an afterthought. This sequence has a concealed logic, since the whole argument about the traditional division of labour by sex being natural subverts the oppression of women to domesticity as a masculine convenience. For the prehominid male home is 'a place to come back to with the spoils, where the females and young will be waiting . . .'[11]: we are left to imagine what home might mean to the prehominid female. This description has immediate parallels with the place of men in the family today – compare it, for instance, with the description of a British coalmining community given in Chapter 4. The male, as Elaine Morgan puts it

sees himself quite unconsciously as the main line of evolution with a female satellite revolving around him as the moon revolves around the earth. This not only causes him to overlook valuable clues to our ancestry, but sometimes leads him into making statements that are arrant and demonstrable nonsense.

If the picture of the aggressive male striding out across the savannah for game is a fable,

the man who is reading the book (to say nothing of the man who is writing it) gets no end of a kick out of thinking that all that power and passion and brutal virility is seething within him, just below the skin . . . so he averts his eyes from the primate family tree, forgets that he descended from apes, and identifies with the baboon, even if it means making a monkey of himself.[12]

This androcentricity recurs in the anthropological and sociological contributions to the myth of the division of labour by sex. In the validation of the status quo through myth, androcentricity is called for, because the status quo is itself androcentric: the rights and responsibilities of women are less than the rights and responsibilities of men. The human individual who is represented in social structure and thinking is the male, not the female.

The mighty-hunter myth has many parallels with myths of origin found in small-scale societies. In *Magic, Science and Reli-*

gion the anthropologist Bronislaw Malinowski says that a myth of origin 'conveys much more to the native than is contained in the mere story . . . [the myth] is the context of social life, it is the gradual realisation by the native of how everything he is told to do has its precedent and pattern in bygone times'.[13] On this level, the function of the mighty-hunter myth is a straightforward one: the vindication of patriarchy.

As Malinowski observes, it is not possible to reconstruct history reliably from a myth of origin. As he also observes, a myth of origin tends to be worked hardest in times of social strain, when the state of affairs portrayed in the myth is called into question. When women's roles are changing, or when proposals are made that they should be changed, the interests of a male-supremacist social order call for a reiteration of the 'naturalness' of traditional gender roles. The popularity of the argument that the traditional pattern is natural therefore constitutes proof of its mythical character.

2 Anthropology

The ethologist argues backwards to nature from a situation in which the traditional division of labour by sex is supposedly a 'cross-cultural constant'. The anthropologist provides him with so-called 'evidence'.

George P. Murdock, one such anthropologist, has provided 'evidence' which has been very influential in the field of sociological/anthropological writing on this topic. In his *Social Structure* he describes the division of labour by sex as follows:

Man with his superior physical strength can better undertake the more strenuous tasks, such as lumbering, mining, quarrying, land clearance and housebuilding. Not handicapped, as is woman, by the physiological burdens of pregnancy and nursing, he can range farther afield to hunt, to fish, to herd, and to trade. Woman is at no disadvantage, however, in lighter tasks which can be performed in or near the home, e.g. the gathering of vegetable products, the fetching of water, the preparation of food, and the manufacture of clothing and utensils. All known human societies have developed specialisation and co-operation between the sexes roughly along this biologically determined line of cleavage . . .

The advantages inherent in a division of labour by sex presumably account for its universality . . . The man, perhaps returns from a day of hunting, chilled, unsuccessful, and with his clothing soiled and torn, to find warmth before a fire which he could not have maintained, to eat food gathered and cooked by the woman instead of going hungry, and to receive fresh garments for the morrow, prepared, mended, or laundered by her hands. Or perhaps the woman has found no vegetable food . . . the man in his ramblings after game can readily supply her wants.[14]

This claim to constancy rather than variability in the patterning of the division of labour by sex is mythical. Again, androcentricity is evident. The cosy ease with which Murdock's picture of woman's role in small-scale society may be assimilated to the (masculine) image of modern woman's domesticity should, for a start, create suspicion in the mind of the reader. 'Lighter tasks'; the 'gathering (digging) of vegetable products'; 'household chores'; 'superior' (male strength); 'handicapped' (a description of the female): these are all statements imbued with the values of Murdock's own Euro-American culture, a culture in which the male's work, but not the female's work, is prestigeful, a culture in which domestic work is devalued and has no status as work, and a culture in which housework, the care of a family, and other related domestic pursuits, are the only activities for the female to which universal approbation is granted.

Again, the order of female and male roles in this description betrays an identification with the masculine interest. The male role comes first. In discussing the advantages inherent in the division of labour by sex, Murdock cites first of all the advantage to the man ('The man perhaps returns from a day of hunting . . . ') and only secondarily the advantage to the woman. Why the man's garments should be laundered by the woman, rather than the woman's garments laundered by the man (both, of course, being soiled in the search for food) is left unspecified – as also are the feelings of the woman in this hypothetical but revealing situation. (The man is described as 'chilled' and 'hungry'.)

In this attempt to generalize about patterns of gender differentiation, the (male) anthropologist thus imputes to other societies the bias in favour of the male endemic in Western culture today. The myth reproduces, and hence validates, the gender-role norms of this male-oriented culture. In the women of non-industrialized societies, Murdock sees the woman of his own culture defined in relation to the male as weaker, more domesticated, less capable, more 'expressive' and less 'instrumental' in her family role.

The personal investment of the male anthropologist in the perpetuation of this myth is suggested by one female anthropologist, Annie Lebeuf:

> By a habit of thought deeply rooted in the Western mind women are relegated to the sphere of domestic tasks and private life, and men alone are considered equal to the task of shouldering the burden of public affairs. This anti-feminist attitude, which has prevented political equality between the sexes from being established in our country until quite recently (and even so, the equality is more de jure than de facto), should not allow us to prejudge the manner in which activities are shared between men and women in other cultures . . . [15]

A profoundly disturbing index of this bias is the discrepancy between Murdock's description of the division of labour by sex, and the original data on which these generalizations are based. Murdock's article 'Comparative Data on the Division of Labour by Sex', the basis of these generalizations, was published twelve years before his *Social Structure*, and contains material on the gender-differentiation of tasks collated by him and a group of his graduate students. From the original tabulation, a briefer version is reproduced below. It shows the number of cultures in which there is deviation from the rules claimed

The Allocation of Tasks by Gender in 224 Cultures[16]

Tasks	Number of cultures in which task is		
	Feminine	Shared	Masculine
Tasks claimed by Murdock (*Social Structure*) to be universally masculine:			
Lumbering	6	8	104
Mining and quarrying	1	2	35
Land clearance	13	44	73
Building of dwellings	36	73	100
Hunting	0	13	166
Fishing	4	56	98
Herding	5	12	38
Trade	7	56	51
Tasks claimed by Murdock (*Social Structure*) to be universally feminine:			
Gathering of vegetable products, etc.	137	50	20
Water-carrying	119	12	7
Cooking	158	38	5
Manufacture and repair of clothing	95	20	12
Some other tasks:			
Boatbuilding	1	8	91
Weapon-making	0	1	121
Basketry	82	19	25
Mat-making	61	12	16
Pottery	77	16	13
Burdenbearing	57	59	12
Agriculture: soil preparation	37	76	31
Agriculture: cultivation and tending of crops	44	89	10

NOTE: The total number of cultures in which each task is shown as feminine, shared or masculine does not necessarily add up to 224. In some cultures the task is either not performed, or else there is no information as to its gender.

by Murdock in his *Social Structure* for the gender-differentiation of particular tasks.

The table shows, for example, fourteen cultures in which lumbering is done either by women exclusively or by both sexes: thirteen cultures in which women are exclusively responsible for land clearance, thirty-six in which they alone are responsible for the building of dwellings. In fifty-six cultures, fishing is an activity assigned to both genders; in twenty-five men are responsible for basket-making, and in thirty-eight, cooking is a shared activity.

There are something like 4,000 other distinct human cultures whose division of labour by sex is not represented on this table. Murdock's sample of 224 societies is not, moreover, a random selection from the pool but a selection biased by the data-selection procedure he used – the Yale University Cross-Cultural Survey files.

The anthropological contention that 'woman–housewife and man–non–housewife' is a pattern reproduced in the social structure of all human communities is probably the most influential part of the whole division-of-labour-by-sex myth. For this reason, the arguments deserve some factual contradictions.

Like ethology, anthropology not only describes what (mythically) occurs, but answers the question as to why it occurs. Biology is held ultimately responsible. The female's more extensive and burdensome reproductive role and the male's 'superior' size and strength are the two biological bases, according to Murdock's account, of the traditional division of labour.

A close look at how childbearing and childrearing are managed in many small-scale societies produces the perception that pregnancy and lactation are burdensome occupations only in a culture that views them as such – which many do not. Activity during pregnancy and lactation is not ruled out by the 'facts' of biology, but variously prescribed or prohibited according to cultural custom. What nature (or biology) decrees is not gender-role differentiation, but reproductive specialization. Females conceive children, gestate and give birth to them, and – in pre-industrial cultures – enable them to survive by feeding them on human milk. Males impregnate females. But the fact that females bear children, while males only impregnate females, does not determine the division of labour between female and male in society at large. The web of cultural beliefs about masculine and feminine parenthood roles intervenes as a variable factor.

Among the Mbuti pygmies of the Congo forest, described in Chapter 2, gender differentiation is minimal. Childbirth is treated casually, and the mother's tie to her child imposes no restraints on her ordinary activity.

The mother is likely to be off on the hunt, or on the trail somewhere when birth takes place; there is no lessening of activity for her during pregnancy. Childbirth is said to be effected easily, with complications rarely happening. Any woman may act as midwife . . . Within two hours of delivery, if birth took place in the camp, the mother is apt to appear in the doorway of her hut, with a bundle wrapped in bark cloth held in her arms. Within the same period of time, if birth took place on the trail she will continue her journey.[17]

Both Mbuti parents have to obey certain food taboos until the child can crawl. Beyond this, the only other restriction on normal activity for either parent is the taboo on sexual intercourse between mother and father during the lactation period – a common (but not universal) means of 'family planning' in small-scale societies.

For the people of Alor, an Indonesian island, childbirth is integrated in a similar way with the normal daily activities of women. The subsistence economy is in women's hands: women are responsible for the cultivation and collection of all vegetable foods – the staple diet of the community. The most prized characteristic in a woman is her industriousness, her thorough commitment to the agricultural work which requires her absence from the home for a major part of each day. The reluctance of women to take on the responsibilities of child-bearing as well as their other duties is accepted as normal. 'We men are the ones who want children. Our wives don't. They just want to sleep with us.' Childbirth takes place in a corridor off the family living room. When the baby is born, the mother wraps it up and joins her relatives and friends. Birth is 'an easy and casual procedure'.* Ten to fourteen days after childbirth, a woman returns to regular field work, leaving her baby in the care of the father, an older sibling, or a grandmother.[18]

These two examples show that the freedom of the father is just as liable to be restricted following the birth of a child as is that of the mother. For the Mbuti, the two sets of taboos imposed by childbirth apply to father and mother equally. Among the Alor, it is the leisure of the father which is more likely to be curtailed by the advent of a child, the family being dependent on the woman's work for its food supply. The word for 'breastfeeding' in the Alor language is the same as for 'holding in the arms' and 'fondling' and is used of both females and males equally.

The impact of childbirth on the roles of parents is clearly a cultural construct. In both cases the variable which intervenes between the biological 'fact' of reproductive specialization and the cultural fact of gender-role differentiation is the complex of beliefs and values attached to the reproductive roles of female and male. Each culture may have its own validating myth.

The anthropological myth which validates our social pattern not only asserts that childbearing and childrearing are burdensome occupations but that they restrict women's activity so as to rule out any extra-domestic role. This is manifestly untrue. In most cultures all over the world, and in our own before industrialization, women have engaged in productive work,

---

* Mortality from childbirth is not necessarily higher in small-scale societies than in modern industrial society, and there is evidence that it may be lower. Hospitalized childbirth carries a risk of infection which 'primitive' childbirth does not. (See Ford, *A Comparative Study of Human Reproduction*, p. 58.)

which has required travel away from the home base and the expenditure of substantial physical energy. Where cultural beliefs sanction the participation of women in productive work, this activity has been made compatible with childcare. Sometimes childcare has been seen as the husband–father's responsibility, sometimes older children are relied on to care for younger ones, sometimes a whole kinship network is the childcare context, sometimes the women of the community evolve a system of communal childrearing. Often a combination of methods is used. The assertion that childrearing restricts women to the home is a duplication of that other myth, the myth of motherhood. It reproduces the values of one culture rather than describing the conditions of all human cultures.

The same is true of those characteristics of the division of labour by sex supposedly based on the male's superior size and strength. The myth merely repeats the belief of one culture about the biologically-based incapacity of the female to carry out heavy or demanding work. It distorts the contrary evidence which can be found in many other cultures.

The aborigines of Tasmania are one society in which the division of labour by sex deviates from this mythical pattern. These people assigned seal-hunting, fishing, and the catching of opossums to the women of the community. Opossum-catching was a particularly skilled and dangerous task. The pursued opossum retired to a hollow in a decayed branch at the top of a smooth-trunked gum tree: the woman had to climb the tree using only a rope and a sharp flint or hatchet, and then walk out along the projecting branch to extract the opossum from its retreat, flinging it to the ground below. The task was reported to be carried out with ease by a healthy woman, but 'one who had been out of health . . . could not get many steps off the ground, so that not only skill, but a considerable measure of strength appears necessary to ascend the gigantic gum trees.[19]'

For fishing, the Tasmanian women slung baskets round their waists and then dived down to prise crayfish off the underwater rocks with wooden chisels. They seemed 'quite at home in the water' and pursued their task with expertise, efficiency and perseverance. Their hunting of seals was described by a nineteenth-century observer in the following terms:

The women all walked into the water in couples, and swam to three rocks about fifty yards from the shore. There were about nine or ten seals upon each rock, lying apparently asleep. Two women went to each rock with their clubs in hand, crept closely up to a seal each, and lay down with their clubs alongside . . . After they had lain upon the rocks for nearly an hour, the sea occasionally washing over them . . . the women rose up on their seats, their clubs lifted up at arms' length, each struck a seal on the nose and killed him; in an instant they all jumped up as if by magic and killed one more each. After giving the seals several blows on the head and securing them, they commenced laughing aloud and began dancing. They each dragged a seal back into the water, and swam with it to the rocks . . . and then went back and brought another each, making twelve seals.[20]

Women as hunters and warriors are commonplace in some cultures. In the old African kingdom of Dahomey, Amazons were women enrolled as regular members of the king's army. In 1845 the Dahomean army consisted of 5,000 women and 7,000 men. A European observer in 1862 'attributed the origin of the corps to the masculine physique of the Dahomean women which enabled them to compete with men in enduring toil, hardship and privations'.[21] Most courageously of all to Western observers, these women took part in demanding training which necessitated at one point climbing a barrier of thorns fifteen feet high and six feet wide, on the other side of which was a ditch of burning wood.

This participation of women in armies is, of course, also found in modern times. In the Second World War, millions of women served in every branch of the regular armed services. That few saw actual combat is due, not to their physical unsuitability for it, but to the belief that war 'should be the one impregnable male bastion'.[22] Many countries, including China,

the U.S.S.R., Yugoslavia, Israel, Cuba and Vietnam, today
train women as combatants, and women guerilla fighters
appear with established regularity in news items.

Building and heavy agricultural work – the remaining
purportedly masculine activities – are other areas in which the
myth of the division of labour by sex distorts the truth. In one
study which surveys sixteen peoples at different stages of
economic development, four cultures where the building of
dwellings is in the hands of women are identifiable: the Semang
of the Malay, the bushmen of the Kalahari desert, the Kazak
of Central Asia, and the Masai of East Africa. For the latter
culture, the author of this work, Daryll Forde, offers an
account of the construction of an encampment:

The construction and maintenance of the kraal is the work of the
women. The oval huts are built close together in a circle round an
open space forty to a hundred yards in diameter. Encircling the
huts a stout fence of thorn bush is erected to keep out both wild
beasts and enemies . . . Each wife has her own hut, which she builds
and keeps in repair. The ground plan, which is rectangular with
rounded corners about four or five yards long and three or four
yards wide, is scratched on the ground. Long, pliant stakes are set
up a foot or so apart all round and strengthened by horizontal pieces
or ropes of withes a foot or so apart for about a yard from the
ground. Stouter uprights are set in the ground along the long axis
of the hut, and a roof pole is lashed to their tops about five feet from
the ground. The wall stakes are then bent over to meet the roof
pole, and when lashed to it form a low vault which is strengthened
with fairly close interlacing of thinner sticks . . . in the more permanent settlements the huts are walled and roofed with layers of long
grass a foot or more thick bound over the frame and finally covered
with a layer of fresh cow dung and mud which dries into a hard cake
and is renewed as required.[23]

As for agricultural work, the claim that the heavy tasks are
universally performed by men and only the relatively light and
undemanding ones by women appears to be a considerable
distortion of the true state of affairs. In Britian, heavy agricul-

tural work was performed by women until the last century, when technology began to reduce the need for heavy manual labour. Over much of the world, but particularly in Africa, the cultivation of the land has been a feminine role either predominantly or (often) exclusively. Forty years ago female farming with no male help (except with the felling of trees) characterized the whole of the Congo region, large parts of South-East and East Africa, and areas of West Africa too. The situation is much the same today, with women performing between 50 per cent and 80 per cent of the total agricultural work in a wide sample of communities all over Africa.

In her detailed study of *Woman's Role in Economic Development*, Esther Boserup discusses the question of the kind of work performed by men and women in agriculture:

Now it may be asked whether the work done by women tends perhaps to be much lighter than that done by men. The available information does not warrant a hard and fast answer to this question . . . Light tasks, such as the guarding of crops against animals and birds, appear to be done mainly by the very young or the very old of both sexes, and able-bodied women are not spared from hard work. One of the sample studies from a central African republic mentions that the women generally do the most exhausting and boring tasks, while the performance of the men is sometimes limited simply to being present in the fields to supervise the work of the women.[24]

The anthropologist Ethel M. Albert describes the role of women in Burundi, one African community:

[The women] have as their first duty cultivating the husband's fields. During the two or three weeks before the rainy season, a woman leaves the house each day a little after sunrise, pregnant or a baby on her back and another child trailing behind her, hoe in hand. She must prepare the soil and sow the seed . . . during the rainy season she must weed the peas, beans and millet. At harvest time, she is again very busy . . . She must harvest the crops and carry it [the harvest] from the fields to her yard in bundles of from 30 to 50 kilograms on her head; there she must dry and clean what she has harvested. Finally, she stores the food in large storage baskets and brews the sorghum beer . . . When the husband is home he will probably help his wife to clear a new plot of ground or to sow or harvest . . . [But] if he does not like to do woman's work, he stays at home while his wife goes to the fields or he visits a neighbour who has beer.[25]

This example – and there are many other similar ones – undermines the validity of the assumption that agriculture, women's role over much of the world throughout history, is an activity in which the help of men with their 'superior' physical strength is essential. In many societies, men are not considered superior in strength, in any case. In Burundi, both men and women 'agree on the stereotypic differences of physique and psychology between the two sexes. To begin with, it is believed that women are better suited by nature than men for manual labour. They work better and longer in the fields than men . . . Men and women both insist that women are made for work . . .'[26] As this anthropologist reported to an American conference on 'The Potential of Women', Burundi people could not understand how it was that the practice of allotting heavy work to the female was reversed in her (the anthropologist's) own culture – as she told them it was. 'My African neighbours,' she said,

had become accustomed to the idea that my country engaged in all manner of nonsensical practices. They were usually tactfully tolerant, but when I said that in my country, it was the men who did the heavy work . . . they did not conceal disapproval. This was a mistake, they maintained. Everybody knows that men are not suited *by nature* to heavy work . . . Men drink too much and do not eat enough to keep up their strength; they are more tense and travel about too much to develop the habits or the muscles needed for sustained work on the farms.

She stressed that these beliefs were based on the Africans' observations of their people's actual behaviour, and were held in 'an old fashioned patriarchal feudal kingdom in which nobody had ever heard of the equality of the sexes'.[27]

Countries with a tradition of female labour in heavy agriculture or burdenbearing often have a high proportion of female labour in mining, construction and transport sectors when undergoing economic development. In a number of Asian and Latin American countries, a quarter of the labour force in the mines is composed of women. Women are also used to transport weighty materials on building sites: in Ceylon 6 per cent, in Thailand 9 per cent, and in India 12 per cent, of the labour in the construction industry is female. The main job of these women is to pass bricks along a line to the bricklayer and to carry cement, lime and mortar on their heads. In Syrian towns, women work as masons and as general labourers in house construction. African contractors employ women in road construction, to draw water and carry sand and other materials. Chinese women do the unskilled work in the building trade, mostly digging foundations and moving earth. Vietnamese women work as load carriers and dock labourers.

Trade, says Murdock, is a typically masculine task, since men, not 'handicapped' by their reproductive roles, are able to range farther afield than women. As a percentage of all people employed in trade and commerce, women actually make up about half, or substantially more than half, in ten out of thirty-two African, Asian, and Latin American countries tabulated by Esther Boserup in her study. In six of these ten, three quarters or more of the women thus employed are classified as 'trading on their own account'.

Trading, like agriculture, is a physically demanding activity. For the African woman who trades, 'attendance at the markets, which are held on fixed days in the surrounding countryside, necessitates journeys – often long ones – on foot, with a load carried on the head, not to mention the baby astride its mother's back. It is not surprising,' she observes, 'that fat women are rarely to be seen in the African countryside.'[28]

Cultures differ greatly in their ideas about which sex should be involved in market trading. Ghana, which has an 80 per cent feminine trading community, may be contrasted with most

Arab countries, where the percentage of women trading is, by comparison, small (it varies from nil to 8 per cent). For the Arab woman, trading is not on the whole considered an appropriate occupation, while the African woman trader is a noted, respected and accepted figure.

A comment ventured by a British factory inspector (a female) in 1916 on women's work in the First World War draws attention to an aspect of the feminine role which escaped the attention of her contemporaries, as it apparently escapes the attention of anthropologists and others today:

It is permissible to wonder whether some of the surprise and admiration freely expressed in many quarters over new proofs of women's physical capacity and endurance is not in part attributable to lack of knowledge or appreciation of the very heavy and strenuous nature of much of normal pre-war work for women, domestic and industrial.[29]

It is incorrect to assume that women are peculiarly suited to domestic work and childcare *because* of their inferior physical capacity. Is domestic work light, physically undemanding and sedentary?

Water-fetching, a central domestic activity in most small-scale societies, demands not only the ability to carry heavy loads, but the daily walking of distances of a quarter of a mile and often more. The trip to the water supply must be made several times a day. The gathering of firewood for cooking and heating entails daily scavenging excursions of several miles. Preparation of food is commonly an exhausting affair, involving the grinding by hand of raw materials in readiness for the cooking pot. In one Guatemalan village

men rise at dawn . . . to begin the day's work in the fields . . . [But] women have already been up and about for some time, grinding tortillas for their husbands' morning meal, and for his midday meal in the fields . . . During a normal day the Chimalteco housewife must boil maize in lye to remove the shell for the family's meals, and she must grind the maize into a paste on her stone metate, a task that takes many hours of her day. Then she must carry water for the evening baths, sweep the house, bring firewood when necessary, tend the children . . . and wash . . . her clothes at the springs where many women spend two or three hours every day . . . On sunny days many women sit before their houses weaving the cloth for their family's clothes, a task requiring long hours and careful work.[30]

Childcare, a 'natural' task for women, would, in small-scale societies where children have to be carried for much of the time, be an impossible task were not women 'naturally' endowed with substantial resources of strength and energy. 'The mother carries her child [until it is three years old] astraddle on her thigh, and keeps it in place with a broad shoulder-strap of cotton or bark; as she also has to carry a large basket on her back, one child is clearly her maximum load.' Thus Claude Lévi-Strauss describes maternity among the South American Nambikwara tribe. The basket carried by the Nambikwara woman contains the entire possessions of the family; food, furniture, tools, etc., and is up to five feet high——'as tall, that is to say, as the women who bear it'.[31]

These women burdened with child and family possessions have also the role of searching for food. Armed with pointed sticks, they dig up roots and kill small animals. The role of providing food rather than merely preparing it, is, though omitted from anthropological generalizations about the division of labour by sex, a regular aspect of the 'primitive' woman's life. To the Aborigine family, for instance, the woman's economic role is essential. Meat is scarce, and without the women's constant search for vegetable foods, starvation would ensue. Like the Nambikwara women, they carry the entire household effects with them: blankets, clothes, tools, household equipment, amounting to 30 or 40 lb.

The daily life of modern housewives and mothers may be very different from this, but most would agree that their domestic duties are neither light nor sedentary. The image of housework and childcare as casual, undemanding labour is false.

The myth of the division of labour by sex hence misrepresents the truth: its generalization that men's and women's work in all human cultures has the same intrinsic patterning, due to their grounding in biological 'fact', is a reiteration of the values attached to the division of labour by sex in Western culture today. For every task that the anthropological myth claims as universally feminine or masculine, many contrasting examples can be cited. (This holds true of the 'feminine' domestic tasks as well as of the 'masculine' non-domestic ones.) It is simply not true that in every society there lurks the spectre of the woman–housewife: she is a figure specific to a particular kind of society. Not only is the division of labour by sex *not* universal, but there is no reason why it would be. Human cultures are diverse and endlessly variable. They owe their creation to human inventiveness rather than invincible biological forces.

3 Sociology

The sociological component of the division-of-labour-by-sex myth insists on the *necessity* of the traditional gender-role pattern – its necessity for the survival and maintenance of the existing social order. In this sense, the sociologist's contribution is less oblique than the other two. If the function of myth generally is to maintain the status quo, then the sociologist overtly declares this to be part of 'his' theoretical enterprise.*

The sociologist who contributes to the division-of-labour-by-sex myth tends to belong to what is known as the 'structural–functionalist' school. However, despite the fact that this approach is criticized within sociology itself, adherence to the belief that traditional gender roles are somehow necessary is widespread in sociological writing and implicit in the sociological approach to many areas of study including 'work' and 'the family'.

According to Talcott Parsons, the arch-theorist of the struc-

---

*'His' is appropriate here for two reasons. Firstly, most sociologists have been male, and secondly, sociology has to date been an androcentric enterprise.

tural–functionalist school: 'The importance of the family and its functions for society constitutes the primary set of reasons why there is a *social* as distinguished from purely reproductive differentiation of sex roles.'[32] In other words, the family's function in society *necessitates* a particular division of labour by sex. The family is a means of reconciling two opposed value-systems in modern society: the 'universalistic' and the 'particularistic'. In the modern occupational system inhere universalistic values: effective performance and achievement in a role are judged by 'objectively defined criteria'. On the other hand, in the kinship structure roles are determined by particularistic values based on biological relatedness. These values define statuses, rights, and obligations by ascribed rather than achieved differentiations between persons. While the particularistic value-system is the heritage of a kinship-oriented past, the universalistic value-system is, historically, an innovation. Its institutionalization in modern society means that adaptations on the part of the kinship structure are called for: labour has to be mobile. The need for mobile labour means that large kinship units are impractical, and the family is reduced in size. The essential function of the family in this analysis is to provide labour power for the economy. To act as a repository for kinship-oriented values, the family has to remain 'the' family, but to produce labour power it has to be as small as possible——hence the residual nuclear unit of two parents and 2·4 children.

All this appears logical, but is actually erroneous. Socialization systems other than the family fulfill the purpose of providing labour power for the occupational system, e.g. communal childrearing as practised in the Israeli kibbutzim. It is also erroneous to assert that the conflict between the two value-systems can *only* be dealt with in this way. Family values may be integrated with the values of the industrial enterprise: to a large extent this is what has happened in modern Japan.

But how do we get from the supposed necessity of the family to the 'necessary' domesticity of women – the 'social as opposed to purely biological differentiation of sex roles'? Parsons agrees that some explanation is necessary:

The problem with respect to the family is not *why* it [the differentiation of roles] appears there . . . but why the man takes the more instrumental role, the woman the more expressive . . . In our opinion the fundamental explanation of the allocation of roles between the biological sexes lies in the fact that the bearing and early nursing of children establish a strong presumptive primacy of the relation of mother to the small child and this in turn establishes a presumption that the man, who is exempted from these biological functions, should specialize in the alternative instrumental direction.[33]

Again, biology rears its ugly head. The sociological myth, like the ethological and anthropological ones, is underpinned by the assumption that biology necessarily determines the place of women in society – and thus, by derivation, the place of women in the family. Parsons 'presumes' that biology establishes primacy and that social sex-roles are founded on this. A few sentences later the presumption is translated into the dictates of necessity. He says that recent changes in the United States family have reinforced the traditional differentiation of sex roles: the isolation of the nuclear family from other kin 'focuses the responsibility of the mother role more sharply on the one adult woman . . . Furthermore the fact of the absence of the husband–father from the home premises so much of the time means that she has to take the primary responsibility for the children.'[34]

The myth is that *someone* has to take care of the children, and since fathers have to work, *mothers* must do the childrearing. 'Mother' here means not the biological mother role but the social childrearer role. The truth of the matter is the reverse of the myth: *because* women take care of children men are free to be away from the home, involved in their employment work.

If gestation and lactation do not actually determine women's childrearing role, then how remote a determinant they are of women's other family roles: home-care and husband-care.

Having dwelt at length on how the family has been and is being subject to size-reduction, Parsons fails to take up the point that much of women's time over the life cycle is now spent not in childcare but in home-care and husband-care. These latter activities require some justification other than a fictional grounding in biology, a justification which sociological theory provides in its argument about the distinction between 'instrumental' and 'expressive' family roles.

The terms 'instrumental' and 'expressive', describing masculine and feminine roles respectively, are crucial in the sociological myth. In the sociological analysis of family structure they neatly express the essential function of myth which is to *affirm* traditional gender-role values. Their meaning is easily clarified by a look at Morris Zelditch's paper on 'Role Differentiation in the Nuclear Family', an established sociological classic. In this paper, Zelditch purports to explain why instrumental and expressive roles in the family are differentiated. He maintains that 'the system must differentiate behaviours and attitudes in order to continue to exist as a system; and . . . some specialization . . . [must] occur in responsibility for the attitudes and behaviours involved'. What sort of differentiation is this? The 'instrumental' role-player is a 'task leader' and the 'expressive' role-player is a 'sociometric star'. The instrumental role-player is the husband–father, and his function is to manifest 'directive' behaviour, the 'inhibition of emotions' and 'the ability to accept hostile reactions from others'. The expressive role-player is the woman–housewife, and she specializes in 'the expression of emotions, supportive behaviour to others, the desire to please and be liked and a more generalized liking for other members'.[35] Her role is to act as the provider of emotional warmth and stability for the whole family, to maintain good, tension-free relationships between the family members; to keep the family together.

Why after all are *two* parents necessary? For one thing, to be a stable focus of integration, the integrative–expressive 'leader' can't be off on adaptive–instrumental errands all the time. For another, a stable secure attitude of members depends . . . on a *clear* structure being given to the situation, so that an *uncertain* responsibility for emotional warmth, for instance, raises significant problems for the stability of the system. And an uncertain managerial responsibility, an unclear definition of authority for decisions and for getting things done, is also clearly a threat to the stability of the system.[36]

When one considers what this means, its function as tradition-conserving myth becomes apparent. Again, the interest of men is primary. As with the anthropological discussion of the division of labour in small-scale societies, and the ethologists' description of the beginnings of human society, the sociologist puts the male role first: the instrumental role is referred to earlier than the expressive role, the man's absence from the home causes the woman to assume responsibility for duties within it, and not vice versa. The androcentric bias is built into the terms of the argument. 'Decision-making', for instance, means only those decision-making processes for which males have traditionally been responsible. Decisions about what meals to have, when to clean the house, and so on, are simply not counted. When Zelditch claims that the system must differentiate behaviours to guard against the dangers of 'uncertain responsibility' he is again arguing from the male viewpoint. Who is threatened by an uncertain responsibility for emotional warmth? Since the woman, according to Zelditch, is the one who provides it, she can hardly suffer from a situation in which she ceases to produce it or other people produce it instead. The same is true of 'decision-making'. The allocation of this responsibility to men in the interests of 'certainty' subjects women to the rule of patriarchy, which is broken when decision-making becomes a shared activity.

In practice the sociological argument means that the restriction of women to the family is a matter of convenience – not to women, but to men, to children, and to the institution of marriage and the family itself. It means that the family oppresses women, because the oppression of women is convenient, whilst their liberation would be inconvenient: a disruptive and destructive force. In particular their oppression in the house-wife role is belied by the assertion that the family role is an 'expressive' one, concerned with the abstract qualities of emotional warmth and supportive love. There is no mention of anything so prosaic, so instrumental as housework. The washing of dirty dishes and dirty clothes, the cooking of meals, the emptying of rubbish, the removal of dirt, the cleansing of excrement-stained cloth and bathroom equipment, are these really 'expressive' tasks – channels for the expression of emo-tional warmth and love? Do they actually provide an oppor-tunity for the expressive leader of the family (the woman–housewife) to care for the emotional interior of the family, to integrate the family as a group? Are they not instead directly antagonistic to the expression of caring emotions?

The sociological distinction between instrumental and ex-pressive roles first arose in the context of some experiments to do with small-group processes which were carried out at Harvard University in the years following the Second World War.[37] Small groups of six male undergraduates were placed in a room and asked to discuss a particular problem for a forty-minute period. It was found that two kinds of leader tended to emerge in this small-group situation, a 'best idea' man and a 'best liked' man. Out of this arose the idea, promulgated by Parsons and his colleagues, that in any small group a speciali-zation of roles will tend to occur, and that the family exhibits this same pattern because the family is merely a special case of a small group.

Rather than the family being a special case of a small group, the small group is a particular case of the family. In Chapter 4, it was argued that in a family-oriented society the patterns of gender roles within the family tend to radiate out from the family to illuminate other social structures. The family is our basic social unit: the pattern of gender roles exhibited by the family is the modal pattern of gender roles in our culture. The small-group experimenters at Harvard were merely witnessing the tendency for all structures in a gender-differentiated society to reflect the pattern of gender differentiation basic to it. The instrumental–expressive pattern in the all-male small group and the instrumental–expressive pattern in the female–male family group are signs of the same syndrome: the polarization of gender roles, behaviour and personality in society. The masculinity of males and the femininity of females is obvious in a two-sex situation, but in all-male or all-female groups a much greater range of gender behaviour is often observable among members of the same biological sex group. One symptom of this is the homosexual pair-bond which tends to reproduce the gender patterns of the heterosexual union; homosexuals themselves often complain about the difficulty they have in escaping from this pattern.

The error is to assume that what happens (in the small group, the family, or anywhere else) does so from necessity. The essence of the gender-role pattern which sociologists claim is essential to the survival of society in its present form is the economic exploitation of women as unpaid labourers, child-rearers, housewives, and servants of men's physical, emotional and occupational needs. This being the actual situation, the sociological construct is not only mere theory, but also validating myth for a social order founded on the domestic oppression of women. The social system must survive; the family must survive; the family entails a division of labour by sex, a differentiation of roles: women must be housewives.

Because the housewife role is a family role the myth of the division of labour by sex validates the institution of the family and makes its preservation mandatory. For the sociologist, and for the anthropologist and ethologist, the myth of the division of labour by sex is essentially the myth of the family. These stereotyped figures which people the myth are always pair-bonded, like the family, and the young are *their* young, as in the family. The family, like the division of labour by sex, is universal and natural. Yet since it is actually not universal or natural, these claims simply reiterate the premises on which our own family system is based. They spring from the intellectual's internalization of his* own cultural milieu: he hopes that what he believes in – the family and marriage – is more than a mere figment of his imagination. The family 'must' exist.

*Again, the androcentricity is a critical source of bias. See Barrington Moore, 'Thoughts on the Future of the Family'.

Eight

Myths of Woman's Place
Two: Motherhood

Of all the rationales offered for women's presence in the home, the myth of motherhood seems the most persuasive and the least questionable in its premises and conclusions, for even if the housewife role and the wife role are capable of change, the maternal role is not. Women's position in the family is founded in their maternity, now and for all time. Simple logic produces the conclusion that since women's maternal role is unalterable, their oppression as housewives might just as well continue. As with other myths, the function of the myth of motherhood is a validation of the status quo.

The myth of motherhood contains three popular assertions. The first is the most influential: that children need mothers. The second is the obverse of this: that mothers need their children. The third assertion is a generalization which holds that motherhood represents the greatest achievement of a woman's life: the sole true means of self-realization. Women, in other words, need to be mothers. 'Need' here is always vaguely specified, but usually means damage to mental or emotional health following on the denial of mothers to children, children to mothers, or motherhood to women.

The three assertions together form a closed circle: all women need to be mothers, all mothers need their children, all children need their mothers. Popular fiction, pseudo-psychology, and the pronouncements of so-called 'experts' faithfully reproduce them as facts rather than as unevidenced assumptions. Mother and child, child and mother are 'both almost intrinsic to each other;

they are really part of each other's being . . . Nature intended mother and child to be together . . . The mother is totally essential to the well-being of the child . . . '[1] and so on.

Like all myths, this one is powerful because it reiterates and affirms traditional forms of behaviour; it is, on one level, true. It is true that in Western society today children do need their mothers, mothers do need their children, and that there are desires induced in women which can only be satisfied through childbearing. To analyse the myth of motherhood is to understand how these 'facts' come to be true, and why, in terms of what is scientifically known about motherhood and childrearing, their generalization to all human cultures is invalid.

1 All Women Need to be Mothers

This component of the motherhood myth owes its credibility to two aspects of modern woman's situation: the early processes of feminine gender-role socialization, which stress maternity as all women's destiny; and psychoanalytic theory which provides the pseudo-scientific backing for this cultural emphasis on the importance of the parental role to women.

Psychoanalytic – Freudian – theory characterizes all women as the 'bearer of ova and maternal powers'.[2] It makes maternity a key theme on feminine psychosexual development. Theodore Lidz, a widely respected American psychiatrist, is representative of many modern psychiatrists in his promulgation of the view that woman's

biological purpose seems to require completion through conceiving, bearing and nurturing children . . . Her generative organs seem meaningless unless her womb has been filled, her breasts suckled . . . The woman's creativity as a mother becomes a central matter that provides meaning and balance to her life.[3]

This assertion comes from a chapter on parenthood in Lidz's book *The Person: His* [sic] *Development Through the Life*

Cycle. In another chapter, called 'The Neonate and the New Mother', Lidz discusses the expectant mother, again asserting the traditional Freudian view: 'if the mother has come to terms with being a woman, which includes some lingering regrets at not having been born a boy, she feels that her pregnancy is fulfilling her fate, completing her life as a woman, and she knows a creativity that compensates for past restrictions and limitations.'[4]

There are three basic elements of the Freudian position: the identification of the maternal role as an essential component of the feminine gender role; the classification of reproductive behaviour (motherhood) as merely one branch of psycho-sexual behaviour (femininity); the generalization of penis envy as universal in all 'normal' women, and thus the generalization of the desire and the need for motherhood as a normal feminine attribute. Motherhood is the practical resolution to penis envy. The desire for a (preferably male) child replaces the desire for the male organ. According to Freud, the female child

begins by making vain attempts to do the same as boys and later, with greater success, makes efforts to compensate for her defect – efforts which may lead, in the end, to a normal feminine attitude . . . If a little girl persists in her first wish——to grow into a boy – in extreme cases she will end as a manifest homosexual, and otherwise she will exhibit markedly masculine traits in the conduct of her later life, will choose a masculine vocation, and so on.[5]

It follows from these premises that the woman who chooses not to become a mother cannot be a 'feminine' woman: along with motherhood, she rejects womanhood. The choice is cast as a choice between alternative gender roles; to be feminine means to be, or to want to be, a mother: to reject motherhood means to be masculine. Lundberg's and Farnham's *Modern Woman: The Lost Sex*, an early example of the popularization of this Freudian perspective, shows clearly the identification of maternity with femininity and the equation of any other 'career' beyond the maternal one as 'masculine'. Published in

1947, this treatise blamed most contemporary ills on women's deviation from their proper gender role – maternity looming large in the list of feminine activities thus neglected in the course of women's progressive (pathological) masculinization. Childbearing and childrearing represent for women, assert Lundberg and Farnham, 'almost their whole inner feeling of personal well-being'.[6]

Far from being outdated, this view is a common component of the feminine image today. To have children but turn over their rearing to someone else – even their father – brings social disapproval: a mother who does this must be 'hard', 'unloving', and of course 'unfeminine'. A woman who does not have children is pitied. If her childlessness is willed, she is seen as deviant, abnormal: as one such woman explained her condition: 'I have never felt myself to be any less of a woman because of this [not wanting children] and nor has any man, as far as I am aware . . . But I [am] . . . accused of selfishness – and smugness, and even serious abnormality.'[7] Indeed, one of the motivations commonly attributed to women's liberationists is that they are frustrated through the lack of a maternal role.

These accusations of gender-role deviance are made in the same tone of absolute certainty which psychoanalytic theory uses to describe the true nature of women. The air of certainty provokes a diagnosis of arrogance. Along with everything else in the Freudian ragbag of concepts and precepts about womanhood, the roots of the psychoanalytic insistence that women need to be mothers lie in a patriarchal culture which denies personhood to women.

Psychoanalytic theory may foster an understanding of why women behave as they do in our culture, but its perspective is culture-bound. Not all cultures insist that women's main vocation is motherhood. Not all females everywhere are subject to the same processes of gender-role socialization as they are in the Western nuclear family. Many make parenthood a somewhat subsidiary vocation for both men and women. Womb envy is a much-neglected topic. If it were as reputable a passion as penis envy, we might gain a better understanding of how men behave as they do.

In other words, the function of psychoanalytic theory, so far as the myth of motherhood is concerned, is to keep women in their place – with their children – secure in the pseudo-knowledge that they are doing what it is in their natures to do, convinced that their desire for motherhood is self-constructed and self-fulfilling, rather than, as it actually is, a convenience to their culture, and an inconvenience to them.

In Western culture today, motherhood is the chief occupation for which females are reared. It is a major component of the feminine gender role as taught to a female child by her parents, and others with whom she comes into contact. Through this early learning the assertion 'all women need to be mothers' comes to be true. This explains why women in our culture (mothers, teachers, midwives, health visitors, nurses, paediatricians) appear to be 'good' with children and to have a 'natural instinct' for childcare.

One index of the early emphasis on maternity is the portrayal of women's roles in pre-school books. Maternity is *the* feminine ideal: in a 1972 study of American pre-school books most portrayed the adult woman as a mother or a wife: fairies and water maidens were the only other alternatives. No woman had a job, and motherhood was presented as a fulltime lifelong occupation. In two books, *What Boys Can Be* and *What Girls Can Be*, the goals were President of the United States and the mother of children respectively. British children's books portray feminine vocations as motherhood and housework. For Jane (of Peter and Jane), Janet (of Janet and John), Dora (of Dick and Dora), Carol (of Carol and John), Ruth (of Ruth and John), the major role of 'helping mother' with housework is interspersed with that other major activity, doll play.

The doll is the first symbol of maternity, recognized in our culture (but not in all others) as a feminine toy. Ninety-seven per cent of 9–11 year old boys and 100 per cent of 9–11 year old girls described the doll as an exclusively feminine toy in one study of sex-role identification. In the case of doll's furniture (bath, high chair) the agreement was 100 per cent in both sex groups. Pressures are exerted from parents, teachers and peers to make this identification of the doll as symbolizing maternity. 'Dolls are for girls, not for boys,' says one mother to her son. 'Everybody'll think you're sissy. You should play with cars and trucks.'[8] The parental attitude is not merely incidental. Studies have shown that the degree to which children identify objects – including dolls – as gender-differentiated is linked directly to the parents' attitudes.

The function of playing with toys in the gender-role socialization process is to establish a future pattern of response to the objects and activities for which the toys stand as symbols. Sheer familiarity with dolls provides the basis for 'anticipation and pleasure in relation to similar objects'[9] (babies). Childcare becomes the primary role perceived as suitable for women. A sample of eight- and eleven-year-old girls studied by Ruth Hartley assigned to women 'behaviours related to childcare, care of the interior of the house, and of clothes and food'. When asked what they themselves would *like* to do when grown up, these girls rejected all the behaviours they perceived as masculine, electing to be mothers and housewives. One of the few exceptions to this rule was that they said they would like to play with their male children, a responsibility which they assigned to fathers.

Two facets of this socialization process for women are directly related to the adult woman's attitudes to motherhood. In childhood women are led to want children not marriage. Marriage is accepted later as a legitimation of the desire to breed, as evidenced by these words of one unmarried mother:

If I want to live and have children, I've got to do it under the financial protection of a man; I have to marry him . . . and let him look after me, I can't do it by myself on my own. I have to sort of sell my personality to his, in exchange for him giving me the money to feed and clothe the children . . . [10]

This sharp realism, a no-nonsense attitude to marriage, was revealed in one study of adolescent girls' attitudes to work and marriage. Over a third of the 600 girls who wrote essays on the theme of their imagined future lives fantasized the death of their husbands before middle age. Once the men had provided them with children, and the children were past the age of dependence, the men were dispensable. In some cases the woman went back to work when her husband died, but a more common theme was for the widow to live with, or near, her children, repeating the mother–child intimacy of early married life. (Others replaced their husbands with a dog or with a life of social abandon: 'I was forty when my husband was killed in a plane crash. I was brokenhearted, but it could not be helped. Now I went to a lot more dances, I was hardly home at night.')[11]

A second aspect of women's socialization for motherhood is the lack of realism associated with doll play: it bears little relation to the real experience of childcare. Dolls are inanimate objects, offering no opportunity for the rehearsal of interactive episodes between mother and child. Their intrinsic hardness and coldness is a parody of the softness and warmth of the live human infant. Thus the sensory aspect of infant nurturance is denied. A failure to give the child 'enough reliable affectionate fondling to satisfy his [sic] sensuous needs'[12] is perhaps the major failing of the family today. The only sense dolls stimulate is the visual one, and here the image is again unrealistic: what we see is not the shape and appearance of the human body, but a manufactured resemblance to some stylized feminine (or less commonly masculine) form. The hair mimics some fashionable feminine style, the eyes are fringed with long, perfectly even lashes, the cheeks are rosebud pink, the lips have come straight out of a cosmetics advertisement in a women's magazine. Although some dolls are equipped to emit the word 'Mummy', some can 'walk', and some can be made to urinate, the genitals are conspicuously absent. More is indicated here than the general repression of female sexuality in our culture, for while a few imaginative manufacturers have recently added genitalized dolls to the repertoire, it is usually only the male dolls which have genitals. The form of the female doll remains the same: between 'her' legs there is a smooth unbroken surface. The message transmitted to the female child by this shape is a denial of *biological* femaleness, and thus of *biological* maternity. What she learns to value is not her inherent and quite un-changeable capacity to give birth to children, but the multitude of servicing activities she must perform for them: not the absolute value of her biological womanhood, but the relative value of her culturally learnt ability to 'take care' of children.

Doll play, which occupies more of a female's time in modern society than the care of her own children, induces a preoccupation with clothing, washing and grooming children. It denies – or rather is silent about – the biology of gestation and birth, the joy of body contact between mother and infant, the sen-suous pleasure of feeding a child with one's own body. The peculiarity of this situation is noted most often by anthropolo-gists because it is in strong contrast to the 'socialization for motherhood' experiences of the child in non-industrialized cultures. Here the younger sibling, not the doll, teaches mother-hood, and it is not the value of the servicing aspects of child-care which is internalized, but the unshakeable conviction of biological womanliness. 'In Bali,' writes Margaret Mead, 'little girls between two and three walk much of the time with purposely thrust out little bellies, and the older women tap them playfully as they pass: "pregnant?" they tease.' Thus, in a society where pregnancy is treated with openness and sim-plicity, the female child makes the connection between the simple inconspicuous folds of her genitals and the fact of birth: she learns the connection between her own undeveloped nipples, and the survival of infants. When she is weaned, she is told: 'You must stop being a baby, suckled by women, and start on the road to being a woman who yourself nurses babies.'[13]

Compared to the Balinese woman, representative of women in many small-scale societies, women in modern industrialized cultures are ill-prepared for biological maternity. They are led to think of themselves as mothers, and to want to *be* mothers, but the entire biological side of motherhood is suppressed. Breastfeeding is avoided as much as possible. Pregnancy is perceived and experienced as a pathological event: childbirth is an act which requires hospitalization. It is also a time of personal trauma: postnatal depression is common, and female admissions to mental hospitals are raised due to psychoses following childbirth. Only in a culture which itself idealizes motherhood can such personal reactions be comprehensible. Indeed, only in this kind of culture could there be a movement for 'natural' childbirth, and only from the habits of such a culture could there develop a 'world trend towards lactation failure'.[14]

The decline in the natural feeding of infants is a strange feature of a society which pays so much superficial attention to the dictates of medical science. All the knowledge we have indicates that, far from being a matter of similar outcomes, the bottlefeeding versus breastfeeding debate is a dilemma with only one safe solution for the baby: natural feeding. A British National Child Development Study, *From Birth to Seven*, discussed the advantages of breastfeeding over bottlefeeding in 1972:

Cases of gastroenteritis seen today occur almost entirely in bottle-fed babies. 'The breast-fed infant has always been safe from this serious infection' . . . the composition of cows' milk has certain important disadvantages compared with human milk. The electrolyte content of cows' milk, especially of sodium chloride and phosphates, is higher than in human milk; and cows' milk proteins may cause an antibody response if absorbed from the gut in the first few weeks of life. Risks of artificial feeding, including the incidence and danger of hypocalcaemic convulsions, and the possible role in 'cot death' of milk antibodies after absorption of cows' milk antigens from the gut have recently been stressed.[15]

As one researcher put it: 'Perhaps the time has come for doctors to realise that there are firm, objective reasons for encouraging mothers to breastfeed.'[16]

The reasons why breastfeeding is as unpopular as it is today (80 per cent of British babies receive little or no breast milk, and the percentage is similar in other industrialized cultures) have to do with 'modesty', 'embarrassment' and 'deep-seated revulsion'. The breast has become a sexual, not a nutritional object. Thus, for the 'respectable' woman it is an area to be hidden away. Breastfeeding entails prolonged stimulation of one of the most sensitive parts of the female body, which involves sensitive pleasure and causes the uterus to contract rhythmically. In a culture which represses female sexuality, this is something to be avoided. Women have learnt to reject their bodily sensations, either reproductive or sexual: this fact stands in curious contradiction to the glorification of the motherhood ideal in modern society.

It is not surprising, then, to find an ambivalent attitude to children. In the research study from which the interviews in this book are drawn, housewives were committed to 'liking' their children (they had internalized the myth of motherhood) but, on the other hand, children were resented. Another finding was the emotional investment in external aspects of childcare – keeping the child and its clothes clean. In part this derives from the need to integrate childcare with housework. Both become service activities. But in part it also springs from an inability to perceive the child as a person, whose emotional, psychological and intellectual needs take prior place over the 'need' to be well-dressed, well-washed and well-fed. 'She has some tendency to regard her children as though they were a combination of animated toy, stuffed animal and sparkling bauble,' say the authors of *Workingman's Wife*. 'A child is for her, in one of its major aspects, a passive object to be hugged close, or to deck out in appealing clothes . . . As an expression of her protective-ness . . . [she] devotes many hours a day to the physical care of her children.'[17]

Society in general idealizes only a particular kind of mother-hood: motherhood within marriage. Despite improvements in the legal situation of the unmarried mother, her actual situation is one of economic deprivation and discrimination. A 1970 British study of middle-class unmarried mothers (most studies have been based on working-class women) showed that despite the superior educational and other advantages of these women 'even they tend to experience a lot of difficulty in getting an adequate income, accommodation or day care for their children'. Discrimination by employers, landlords, etc., was a common experience: 'My baby is to be placed by the children's department. I live in one room. I have nobody to mind her . . . The foster mother would keep her no longer than eight weeks . . . There was no nursery available.'[18] If society valued the biological mother–child unit rather than the idealized image of the married-woman-and-child, then no improvements in the unmarried mother's situation would be needed.

To the image of mother and child a peculiar ambivalence attaches. People are fond of saying that there is no more honourable profession in modern society, yet it is one of the only two honourable professions which receive no financial recognition – the other one is housework. Clearly, society has a tremendous stake in insisting on a woman's natural fitness for the career of mother: the alternatives are all too expensive. A recent British court case took an appropriately dismal view of the value of maternal love:

Mr Justice Eveleigh, who had the task in the High Court of assessing in cash terms the loss to two young children of their mother in a car crash, said *he must disregard the loss of love and affection a mother gave* . . . The judge said it had been said that a mother's services were worth 50p an hour [italics added].[19]

However, a calculation on this basis produced such a massive sum that the judge was forced to find a different method of assessing a mother's value. He decided that the mother would have gone out to work and earned £8 a week. After adding a bit, 'for the fact that she had been a good mother and had been handy at decorating and gardening' he awarded the children, aged five and seven, £8,593 for their mother's death. At the same time he decided they were owed £1,007 for their father's loss of earnings over a two-year period subsequent to the same car crash.

One source of this ambivalent attitude to motherhood may be traced back to the conditions of childrearing in the family. Many of the protestations about the glory of motherhood are uttered by men, and it may be speculated that women speak with the same voice because they have assimilated the attitude of men. Men are brought up by women, their mothers, and then required to make the break from mother-dependence to father-identification. The mother pressures the male child to sever the bonds of mothering and he learns to reject feminine identification. In those first years the foundations of the male's legendary love–hate relationship with the female are laid down: the feeling 'This is not me, I must reject it' together with the feeling 'This is where I belong'. The 'good woman' is the mother, domesticated and non-sexual: the bad woman is the non-mother, desired because she *is* sexual. 'We must keep in mind,' said Konrad Lorenz, 'that mother-love is not more necessary to the survival of the species than the drive to copulation. Why, then, are those drives to copulation "brutish" and why is "maternal love" sublime?'[20]

Maternity, like housewifery, is a leveller among women. The expectation is set up that childbearing and childrearing are the areas in which the greatest life satisfactions can be found; consequently motherhood becomes a main life goal. 'They have always wanted children,' comment Rainwater, Coleman and Handel in their study of *Workingman's Wife*, 'and most of those who do not yet have children are regretful. They feel that having children is a fulfilment of themselves, and signals the realization of what they were always meant to be – mothers.'[21] The same intense concern for children explains the under-utilization of graduate women's skills. Social origins, report the authors of a recent British study of graduates, have a much less marked effect on attitudes to employment among women than among men, because the women all want to have children.

Six years after graduation nearly half of the women in the sample were engaged solely in 'domestic activities' – a withdrawal from employment accounted for chiefly by the fact of actual or expected motherhood. The authors of the study conclude that these graduates' choices of a maternal role

cannot be accounted for in terms of the marked unattractiveness of the alternatives which would presumably be the case for the vast majority of women who have no high-level skills whatsoever. Rather, in order to account for their choice, we have to look more at their assimilation of a broad set of attitudes towards motherhood and domesticity generally. In short, we have to examine the influence of an ideology about the 'place of woman' in home and society.[22]

Another crucial finding concerns the response of women to the experience of motherhood. The mystique which surrounds motherhood in our society means that before they become mothers, women have a highly romanticized picture of what motherhood is. Alice Rossi's study of women college graduates in America shows this clearly. On the basis of questionnaires sent to 1961 graduates, she made a distinction between 'homemaker' and 'pioneer' types. The homemakers were those women who stated that they had no other career goal beyond becoming housewives and mothers. However, when the homemakers experienced housewifery–motherhood in practice as opposed to theory, their expectations concerning the primacy of family roles in their lives took a marked drop. Before motherhood is experienced, they want more children than they do later, and while 16 per cent of single 'homemakers' approve of maternal employment in the pre-school period, 35 per cent of the married ones do. 'It is almost,' Rossi comments, 'as though . . . homemakers had romantic notions concerning marriage and family roles which the reality of marriage and motherhood tempers . . . Marriage and family roles are less fully satisfying to the homemakers than they expected them to be.'[23]

These aspects of motherhood in our society demonstrate the falsity of the contention that all women need to be mothers.

The behaviour of women as mothers is associated with the kind of upbringing they get, and with the cultural conditions under which they experience their maternity. It owes nothing to their possession of ovaries and wombs, any more than the behaviour of men as fathers proceeds directly from their possession of alternative genitals.

2 All Mothers Need Their Children

There is no such thing as the maternal instinct. There is no biologically based drive which propels women into childbearing or forces them to become childrearers once the children are there.

Nevertheless the 'maternal instinct' is a phenomenon of established popularity today. It is suggested that all women have this instinct, and asserted confidently that all mothers must have it. Irreparable damage to maternal mental health is claimed to follow from a situation in which a woman gives birth to a child and then hands over its rearing to someone else. Childcare by the biological mother is said to be necessary for the sake of the woman's 'own awakened motherliness' as well as for the newborn's needs.[24] (It is interesting that this contention relates to day-nursery care for babies, and other means of childcare used by economically underprivileged mothers, but has never been held to apply to the upper-class method of employing nannies or au pair girls to care for babies. It has been suggested that the au pair system may be particularly bad for children, since it subjects them to the care of people who may not understand their native language, are not particularly interested in children, and do not stay with the family for a long enough period of time.)

Complaints about thwarted maternal instincts are often made by the anti-abortion lobby. It is maintained that abortion is always followed by guilt feelings and sometimes by a complete mental–emotional disintegration. It is 'against nature'. 'There are few women,' asserts the report of the Royal College of

Obstetricians and Gynaecologists in Britain, 'no matter how desperate they may be to find themselves with an unwanted pregnancy, who do not have regrets at losing it. This fundamental reaction, *governed by maternal instinct* . . . [italics added].[25]

This is a distorted picture. For mothers-to-be who abort their babies because they do not want them, the psychiatric outlook is promising. If the maternal instinct is thwarted, the vast majority (353 out of 354 in one study) show no evidence of it. Women whose abortions are carried out for medical reasons, on the other hand, may suffer long-term regret; the babies they aborted were wanted ones. It was not 'nature' they acted against, but their simple desire to have, love and care for a child.

Conversely, social mothers manage very well without the aid of any biological maternal instinct. A contemporary British study charting the development of a group of 180 adopted children showed that by the age of 7 the adopted children were doing as well as and often better than non-adopted children. Moreover, their development was 'dramatically' better than that of illegitimate children who stayed with their biological mothers. According to the researchers responsible for this discovery, it undoes 'the myth of the blood tie'. 'A good mother is one who has the time, the means, and the will . . . not the blood,'[26] or, one could add, the 'instinct'.

The attraction of any mother–child pair is not biological, but affective; that is, nothing proceeds from the symbiosis of gestation and from the act of parturition which itself determines the mutual and lasting dependence of mother and child. Certain biologically determined mechanisms are present which under natural conditions reinforce the relationship between biological mother and child, but they do not demand it. The reflex which leads the newborn infant to turn its head when an object touches its cheek is one such mechanism. The point of the reflex is to enable the infant to search for and find its mother's breast. But under modern conditions, where the breast is increasingly replaced by the bottle, the bottle can be placed in the infant's mouth with accuracy by anyone. The infant's reflex does not then act as a stimulus for the physical contact of breastfeeding.

Smiling is another example of a biologically determined reflex that can cement the mother–child relationship. 'Since the infant will smile at the face of the mother and thereby reward itself and since the mother will in turn smile at the smile of the infant and thereby reward herself, concurrent smiling is mutually rewarding from the outset.'[27] 'Mother' here can, of course, mean 'social' not 'biological' mother.

The desire for motherhood is culturally induced, and the ability to mother is learnt. As two experts have put it '. . . the concept of a "maternal instinct" operating without prior learning or experience now lacks scientific endorsement.'[28] Hormonal changes in the mother do occur as a result of child-birth, but do not themselves transform the biological mother into a psychosocial one. It is not true that 'hormonally based drives irresistibly draw the mother to her child in the tropistic fashion of the moth drawn to the flame.'[29]

The importance of learning and the unavailability of instinct is implicitly recognized in some social practices surrounding motherhood. Women are not expected to deliver themselves – in contrast to women in small-scale societies who often are, having already learnt what childbirth is like by watching other women do it. Nor are they expected to know how to breastfeed: this most 'natural' part of motherhood is learnt also, and is not governed by some biological instinct. As one medical study concluded from observing the behaviour of new mothers, instinct has nothing to do with it, though mothers often believe that it has. 'The mothers secretly believe that they must lack innate maternal feeling and they are distressed by this apparent inadequacy.'[30] The essential capacity is not instinctual but imitative: because women in Western society do not see other women breastfeeding they lack the capacity to imitate successful breastfeeding themselves. This study observed 150 mothers and perceived that they often did not know how to position the baby at the breast, how to encourage the infant to take the nipple in its mouth, which the relevant areas of the nipple are, or how the shape of the mother's breast might interfere with the infant's breathing. Without the help of knowledgeable people successful breastfeeding could not be established.

Direct parallels occur in the animal world where it is learning, not instinct – as was once believed – which inspires successful reproductive behaviour. Laboratory-raised monkeys are inept at copulation. (Human beings also have to be taught the techniques of intercourse, and some involuntary childlessness even today is due to simple ignorance of the need for penile penetration.) Such monkeys, if they are female, do not know how to cope with birth – what to do with the baby, the placenta, the umbilical cord. Sometimes they are unable to distinguish between placenta and baby. They are inefficient breastfeeders. All the laboratory-raised rhesus monkeys in one study failed to nurse effectively and the babies had to be hand-reared. In the unnatural conditions of a zoo, their only salvation is the zookeeper, who saves chimpanzee babies from starvation by teaching their mothers how to suckle them. Under 'natural' conditions, monkeys and chimpanzees acquire reproductive knowledge from their elders and peers.

A crucial learning experience for both animals and humans is the experience of being mothered oneself. Being successfully mothered induces the desire and the capacity to repeat the experience. Primate research shows that unmothered monkeys do not respond to their infants: one such mother 'sat fixedly at one side of the cage staring into space, almost unaware of the infant . . . There was no sign of maternal response, and when the infant approached and attempted contact, the mother rebuffed it, often with vigour.'³¹ These mothers are as liable to crush their babies on the floor and kill them as to pick them up gently. Lack of mothering is important in the genesis of human child-beating behaviour or child neglect also. 'What provokes child beating? An incredible sense of aloneness, worthlessness, and strangely enough desire – desire for the child to take care of the unheeded needs of the attacker's own yesterdays.'[32] The small face in the pram is a reminder of what was missed and what can thus be granted only grudgingly to another: 'Lucky little pig. It's a good life being a baby. I'd like to be in there too.'[33] The infant can make up for this by 'loving' the mother. But crying, a universal characteristic of all babies, means rejection: 'When he cried it meant he didn't love me, so I hit him.'[34]

Caution must be exercised here. If the maternal instinct is a myth, then what is 'mothering'? 'Mothering' is not a mystical quality. The expression of love in a warm, caring relationship is its most essential ingredient. Other components, such as stimulation of visual, verbal and social capacities are also necessary. As Michael Rutter in his valuable *Maternal Deprivation Reassessed* put it, this definition of mothering 'implies that while warmth is a necessary part of mothering it is not specific to mothering. Rather it appears that warmth is a vital element in all kinds of family relationships.'[35] In particular, warmth is an equally important fact in father–child relationships: fathers are not exempt on biological grounds from an engagement in 'mothering' behaviour.

3 Children Need Their Mothers

This assertion is the most subversive part of the myth of motherhood. After all, in a child-oriented society, what could be more reprehensible than an apparent neglect of children's supposed needs?

The assertion makes three assumptions. The first is that children need their biological mothers. The second is that children need mothers rather than any other kind of caretaker. The third is that children need to be reared in the context of a one-to-one relationship. 'Need' here, as in the other assertions that make up the myth of motherhood, is imprecise, but a failure to have the need satisfied is usually held to result in some adverse and permanent development in the child's mental and emotional state.

The falsity of the first component in this assertion has been uncovered in the preceding section. The second statement that children need mothers as opposed to other kinds of caretaker is the critical one here.

Research psychologists may point out, as Michael Rutter does, that the essential ingredients in mothering are warmth and love and that these can be provided by any person who cares for a child, but popular opinion continues to believe in the face of all evidence that a mystical connection binds child to mother and to mother alone. A letter published in *The Times* demonstrates the adherence to this belief:

> It is with horror and a sinking heart that I read of the Government's intention to expand nursery education ... It is an established fact that children are closely attached to their mother ... from before birth to the age of about five or six ... For a child to develop fully and with its potential undamaged, it is essential that it should move through this period of intense attachment to its mother. Not even toys, brightly painted rooms or the companionship of other similarly deprived children can compensate for the withdrawal of this relationship ... [36]

As Rhona and Robert Rapoport observe in their book *Dual-Career Families*:

> A good deal of information and misinformation [about motherhood] from the writings of psychiatrists and paediatricians has come into popular usage through the mass media, and is applied indiscriminately to particular cases.[37]

But unhappily it is not only popular opinion which believes the myth: 'experts' continue to produce it as fact rather than fiction. A paediatrician writing in 1972 of behaviour problems in hospitalized children said:

> The child who behaves in this way [soiling, wetting, not letting his mother out of his sight] is reacting to the loss of a *normal maternal relationship* ...

Much more serious is the child who has been deprived of *mothering* from the start . . . Such a child is denied the opportunity of experiencing deep *maternal* affection; consequently his relationships with people, when he becomes an adult, are likely to be superficial . . .

Lack of *mothering* can occur without the physical loss of *mother*. If she is cold and lacking in affection . . . she will have a similar damaging effect on her child [italics added].[38]

An even more uncompromising statement was made by a research worker in child psychology, discussing a proposal that fathers should participate more fully than they do at present in childrearing:

The work-sharing idea has as its core the idea that the man and the woman are interchangeable. In looking after the child they are not . . . *a mass of uncontradicted research* shows that the baby needs a consistent single caretaker. Through that caretaker the baby experiences the world. *She* is his interpreter.

After the age of eight months, however,

infants are ready to make increasingly close contact with their fathers. But this does not mean that they need *mothering* less . . . [italics added].[39]

These monologues are not simply personal beliefs uttered as science. They represent internalizations of a myth thematically interwoven with all aspects of our culture.

Much of the present concern with mothering behaviour arose out of the study of institutionalized children. In a book published in 1943, Margaret Ribble's *The Rights of Infants*, the author imputed a wide variety of infant reactions to lack of, or inadequate, mothering: negativism, refusal to suck, hypertension, vomiting, wild screaming, stuporous sleep, diarrhoea, and marasmus (wasting away). Subsequent investigations by others, in particular René Spitz, described the deleterious effect of institutionalization and/or the infant's separation from mother. The principal syndromes they noted were weepiness, withdrawal, and lack of contact with the environment, refusal to act and stupor: syndromes they attributed to the loss of

maternal love. Later these observations were extended to
children in hospital. In a very moving film, *A Two-Year-Old
Goes to Hospital*, British child psychiatrists documented in 1953
the behaviour of a 'normal' child admitted to hospital for a
minor hernia repair operation. Laura, the child in the film, goes
through a cycle of withdrawal, protest and resumed control,
and then increasing withdrawal from the previously intimate
relationship with her mother.

A comparison arose between institutionalized and maternal
systems of childrearing, with the maternal system seen as not
only the *better* of the two, but the one that all children need.
The comparison is invidious. Many institutions have large
numbers of children to care for, and few staff, so that the
individual child gets much less attention, love, and stimulation
than a child in a one-to-one relationship – a child who is
'mothered'. A 1960 study comparing institutionalized and
home-reared infants found that home infants were shown
affection eighteen times more often than the other group.
Another study of a Canadian children's home carried out in
1967 made the following observations of what went on there,
a pattern probably replicated in countless other institutions:

> Each child is generally confined to one nursery and one outdoor
> experience each day in the garden . . . Every child is treated the same.
> At a certain age he [*sic*] is placed upon a pot and there is expected to
> stay until he has achieved success. When he becomes restless, as he
> naturally will, it is sometimes felt necessary to tie him to the pot,
> in order to keep him sitting there. Prolonged sitting on the pot is
> causing some prolapsed rectums . . . [in eating] every child is
> treated exactly the same. Little opportunity is given for each child to
> eat at his own pace, and no variety is offered as the children get
> older. Nor do the children have adequate opportunity to feed them-
> selves . . . the children still spend a great deal more time in bed than
> is good for them . . . There is a great lack of play equipment . . . [40]

A research programme designed to improve upon this
institution's methods of caring for children deduced that four
principles in particular were missing and necessary to children's

healthy development: (1) a concern for the uniqueness of each child; (2) opportunities for the child to establish a dependent and trusting relationship with one or more caretakers; (3) opportunities for the child to take initiative; (4) consistency in care and discipline.

Clearly these principles are more likely to be followed in families than in institutions, and *these* are the guidelines for mothering behaviour wherever it is located. The syndrome manifested by institutionalized children is not one of 'maternal deprivation'. These children are not deprived of their mothers: they have simply not been looked after consistently and lovingly by an adult or adults concerned with their intrinsic individuality as people.

A crucial distance separates children whose emotional development is stunted through faulty institutional care from those whose experiences in hospital prove emotionally traumatic. The syndrome here *is* one of maternal deprivation. The child's whole antecedent experience has produced a dependence on the relationship with the mother. The mother's prolonged absence from an environment which is strange and often painful to the child (the hospital) induces terror and anxiety. Again, the mother's presence or absence is not mystical in its effect. The real trauma is that the child feels betrayed by its mother: it is deprived through mother-separation, because its mother is the only person in the world it has learned to trust. Removal to hospital and the mother's subsequent absence are 'totally unsuspected from the emotional instinctive point of view of the child'.[41] As Konrad Lorenz goes on to observe: if the mother were a chimpanzee, she would start fighting the hospital staff tooth and claw, and this is what the human child rationally expects the mother to do.

The film *A Two-Year-Old Goes to Hospital* was made at the Tavistock Institute under the direction of John Bowlby, who, more than any other single person, has been responsible for promulgating the myth that children need their mothers. In *Forty-Four Juvenile Thieves*, published in 1946, he noted the frequency with which delinquents and affectionless psychopaths had a background of mother-separation and institutionalization. In *Child Care and the Growth of Love*, published in 1953 and based on a report to the World Health Organization, he declared that what is essential for mental health is that 'the infant and young child should experience a warm, intimate and continuous relationship with his mother . . . '[42] His views have been modified since, and his most recent work considers the mother–child relationship in the more general, less sex-specific context of 'attachment' behaviour. But his work has been very influential, and he bears at least some responsibility for the interpretations made of it. At the beginning of his career, Bowlby was concerned with child guidance, and during these years, as he puts it, 'I became convinced in my own heart that certain events of early childhood were of critical importance in determining personality development – particularly the child's relationship to his mother, and the mother's unconscious attitude to the child.' Subsequently, 'I was eager to make scientific these clinical observations on mother–child relationships . . . I must confess to a rather one-track, one-problem mind.'[43]

The urge to 'make scientific' a personal inner conviction is hardly a sound basis for arguing that children need their mothers' more or less fulltime attention throughout childhood. On this view have been based decades of policy decisions in many countries; mothers have been urged to stay at home and day nurseries have been closed down. It is still happening. At a conference reported in the *Guardian* in September 1972, it was said that 'very young children who are placed in crèches and day nurseries could have their mental development seriously impaired . . . An acute deprivation syndrome can quickly be set up when a baby does not receive *continual maternal care* [italics added].'[44] The report is headed 'Crèche Peril for Babies' and ends with the recommendation that women should be paid to stay at home and follow their 'maternal profession'.

Needless to say, the crucial sentence of this report is buried in the middle: it reveals that the research in question had been done in institutions where each baby received less than one hour's individual attention out of the twenty-four. There are bad institutions and good institutions, just as there are good mothers and bad mothers. In point of fact, few mothers are actually able to provide the sort of continual love and stimulation of a child's development which the myth of motherhood sets up as an ideal.

Most insidious of all in such reports is the use of the word 'maternal'. If the word 'paternal' were to be substituted for it (and there is no evidence that fathers could not, with experience, become good mothers) then the political implications of these findings would be very different. There would have to be a massive removal of men out of employment and back into the home. Hence the myth stands revealed for what it is: a political statement. As Mead observed almost twenty years ago: 'This . . . [the assertion that children need their mothers] is a new and subtle form of antifeminism in which men – under the guise of exalting the importance of maternity – are tying women more tightly to their children . . . '45

Not all reiterations of the myth of motherhood come from the mouths or pens of men but most of them do. To interpret the myth as a political weapon designed to keep women in their place is also to see it as a technique for the evasion of *paternal* responsibility.

Most research on childrearing has been concerned only with mothers, not fathers. A symptom of this is to be found in the four volumes (to date) of the Tavistock study group *Determinants of Infant Behaviour*. In the four indices of these volumes there are a total of 1,450 entries, only five of which refer to fathers. Three of these five concern paternal behaviour in monkeys. The fourth refers to a 'Mr K. who loves to rough-house with his children'. The fifth comments that there has never been any direct observation of father-infant interaction. A few studies do chart the importance of fathers in the child-rearing process and these are valuable evidence against the myth of motherhood: one of these studies, Robert Andry's *Delinquency and Parental Pathology*, is a survey of family relationships in two groups of delinquent and non-delinquent boys. Andry found that a major difference between the two groups was the inadequate love shown by the fathers of delinquent boys; so far as maternal affection was concerned, there was no difference between the two groups. These boys were suffering, in other words, from a deprivation of *paternal* love.

But because the myth of motherhood is also the validating myth for a denial of paternal responsibility, we do not read in the newspapers that fathers are being urged to devote more time to their children for the sake of the next generation's emotional health. Nor do we ever see it said that the working father is a problem: only working mothers are. Nobody has yet studied the impact of the father's employment-work role on his relationship with his children. In the dual-job family, it is the working mother who constitutes a problem because childcare is a mother's duty.

If the syndrome of the institutionalized child is one bogey constantly resurrected in the myth of motherhood, maternal employment is another one. Research findings actually show that the employment of mothers has no deleterious effects on any index of children's physical, social, intellectual or emotional development: there are no differences in psychosomatic scores, anxiety scores, school grades, or personality adjustment, according to maternal employment status.[46] Against the popular belief that juvenile delinquency stems from the fact of maternal employment must be set the finding that children of working mothers are actually *less* likely to become delinquent than children of mothers who stay at home.[47] Working mothers enjoy their children more, and are less irritable with them, than fulltime mothers.[48] Women who have employment outside the home are therefore not worse mothers because they work. There is no mystical gift bestowed on the child by its mother's presence in the home.

Employed mothers are only, after all, doing what women have done throughout history and in all cultures, which is to participate in the economically productive life of society. The essential variables so far as children are concerned are the quality of the care they receive and the mother's attitudes to her job, not the fact of employment on its own. A sociologist who has studied extensively the effects of maternal employment concludes:

Perhaps the most serious shortcoming in sociological perspective has been a failure to see clearly that someone other than the biological mother can play the role of supervisor of children in many cases as effectively, and in some more effectively, than the mother.[49]

But the myth of motherhood takes its toll. Employed mothers often feel guilty. They feel inadequate, and they worry about whether they are doing the best for their children. They have internalized the myth that there is something their children need that only they can give them.

Research findings have not conclusively laid to rest the belief that maternal employment is bad for children. The myth is still current in academic as well as popular circles. Barbara Seaman in her book *Free and Female* cites an amazing illustration of its persistence. In 1971 an American expert on the employment of mothers, Lois Hoffman, was asked to contribute an article on the subject to an encyclopaedia. She submitted an article which concluded that the evidence should be 'reassuring to working mothers'. The article was returned to her for approval, edited and interlaced with dire warnings about the potentially damaging effect on children of a mother's employment. Hoffman refused to allow the edited version to go forward, and no article ever appeared.

In the endless debate about the 'working mother' problem, the fact that the 'nonworking' mother is also a myth is, of course, conveniently forgotten. Mothers may be distracted by housework at times when their children need conversation, stimulating play, or physical affection. Financial proposals are made for encouraging mothers not to take employment, but nobody argues that the emotional needs of children require the assumption of at least some maternal household work by state agencies (or the greater participation of men in it).

This is also entirely logical within the terms of the myth. But it is contrary to the evidence, that 'like the other aspects of gender role . . . parental-role behaviour does not require and is not dependent on innate sex-specific mechanisms'.[50] Children 'need' fathers: this is a 'fact' which the adherence to motherhood obscures. In other cultures, and in animal societies too, males do often participate in childcare, and sometimes they carry the main responsibility for it. The Mbuti and Alorese cultures cited in Chapters 2 and 7 are examples of human societies which insist on paternal childcare. Among animals, the Hamadryas baboon and the wild Japanese monkey are notable for their pronounced paternal childcare behaviour.

Animal experiments in which virgin female rats and adult male rats caged with young rats for periods of time displayed 'mothering' behaviour suggest that a main reason why male mammals in general and male humans in particular do not behave maternally is because they have not been made (or allowed) to do so.

The emphasis placed in the myth of motherhood on the importance of the biological mother–child tie as exclusive and continuous is very strange when looked at in the context of other cultural practices. Under 'normal' conditions in most small-scale societies the mother is too busy with her own productive work (and with her other children) to concentrate her energies on a one-to-one relationship with a particular child. In these societies, there are various forms of communal childcare, including communal breastfeeding, where all lactating mothers share their supply of milk among all unweaned children in the group. 'Wet nursing' is a Western variant on this theme. 'Induced' lactation is a further variant, in which a woman who has not yet had children, or who has not had any for some years, establishes her milk supply to nourish a needy child. Lactation is induced principally by putting the child to the breast, but also by extra intake of fluids. Animals use the same technique. In monkeys, for instance, where the mother's death renders an infant milkless, another 'mother' will adopt it and produce milk to feed it.

The remaining contention that underpins the myth of motherhood is that successful childrearing can only take place in the context of a one-to-one relationship.

Research into the attachment behaviour of young children suggests that multiple attachments, not single attachments, are the rule at the beginning. In one group of sixty infants under one year old, there were very few cases in which the mother was the only person to whom the infants showed attachment.

From the very beginning of this particular phase of development, it appears to be the rule rather than the exception that several individuals are selected as the objects of the infant's attachment responses . . . One of our most striking examples is provided by the infant who showed far more intense attachment behaviour towards the ten-year-old girl living next door than towards the members of his own family – despite the much greater availability of his parents, and despite the fact that the neighbour's daughter never fed him and rarely cuddled him . . . To concentrate only on the child–mother relationship would therefore be misleading and artificial.[51]

Initially the infant is capable of 'indiscriminate' attachment – that is, attachment to any of the individuals who come into contact with it. At around seven months a phase of 'discriminate' attachment begins, in which a certain amount of narrowing down takes place. The disjunction between the two phases is gradual. It is suggested that the change in the quality of attachment behaviour 'depends entirely on the learning opportunities held out to the infant in his particular social environment'.[52] Where these learning opportunities favour the predominance of the mother, as they will always do in a 'normal' family, the mother is likely to be at the top of the infant's attachment hierarchy, but the child's capacity for relationships is not inherently monotropic: where the childrearing context provides opportunities for multiple attachments, these will usually be developed with great success.

'Maternal deprivation' is hence a syndrome which can only occur in a culture oriented around an exclusive mother–child bond. In different cultural settings, the close and exclusive attachment of mother and child never develops. The child cannot be deprived through a lack of 'mother' love.

In Samoa, typical of many small-scale societies, people live in households of between fifteen and twenty people. The close relationship of mother and child is not found. Children are cared for and learn from many adults – aunts, cousins, sisters, grandmothers, fathers, uncles, brothers – and they learn that all can be depended on to provide. 'From the first months of its life, when the child is handed . . . from one woman's hands to another's, the lesson is learned of not caring for one person greatly, not setting high hopes on any one relationship.'[53] Under these conditions, children are also freed from the potential trauma of losing their mothers – through accidental separation or maternal death. There are always others who will care for them.

In the Israeli kibbutzim there has been a deliberate attempt to bring about a similar situation. Children in the kibbutz do not live with and are not reared principally by their mothers. They live instead in children's houses and are cared for by people especially trained in childcare and education. The infant generally goes to live in the infants' house within a few days of its birth and remains there for six months, during which time its mother visits to breastfeed. After six months, it is weaned and is taken to visit its parents in their room for a definite period each day; this period becomes longer as the infant grows. The contact with the mother is continuous in the sense that it is repeated – but it is brief each time: the mother breastfeeds and plays with the child but is not responsible for routine care, for nappy changing, bathing, dressing, and the feeding of artificial milk or solid food. Moreover she does not have a permanent substitute in the children's house. One person and one helper are responsible for each small group of infants, with a change of personnel at about eight months, again at 18–24 months, and thereafter at (roughly) ages four and seven. Quite often in the daytime the substitute collective mother is not available to the children on demand, and she rarely is so in the night, when a variety of different 'night watches' take over. The two continuities in the child's life are the kibbutz as a collectivity, and other infants. When she moves from one house to another, the infant's three or four small age-mates move too, and she is within sight and touch of her peer group most of the time. When other children might be watching their mothers doing housework the kibbutz child plays with other children.

Kibbutz children do not show signs of 'maternal deprivation', nor are they retarded in development. They are happy children with a sense of security and confidence about the world. They have emotional control and greater overall maturity than their non-kibbutz-reared counterparts.[54] But their security comes from the kibbutz and from their collective socialization within age-grades, not from the family in general or the mother in particular.

One result of childrearing which emphasizes peer interaction, as the kibbutz system does, or multiple non-intense attachments as in Samoa, is that children become emotionally dependent on each other rather than on adults. A different kind of personality is produced, a personality that lacks 'emotional depth'. Adults reared in this way have not, as children, experienced the subtle adjustments, sensitivities and intimacies that occur in a one-to-one relationship maintained over time. Deep mutuality is not something of which they have learned to be capable. Quite simply, they cannot form intense relationships because they are not intense people. As Bruno Bettelheim observes in his study *Children of the Dream*, 'intense' has the same root as 'tense'. Whatever is intense is also tense. Though kibbutz-reared adults lack depth, they are also free from the personality scarring that can result from the extreme closeness and precarious interdependence of the one-to-one relationship. 'In the kibbutz, with its multiple mothering, the infant has neither the utter security that may come from feeling himself at the core of his mother's existence, nor will he know the bondage it can bring.'[55]

In terms of the relationship between childcare practices and adult personality, a system of dependence on the mother–child bond produces one result, a system of collective socialization or 'multiple mothering' another. The two systems are appropriate for different kinds of society. This does not mean that the advantages and disadvantages of the two systems cannot be compared. If they are, it seems obvious that the one which carries the most disadvantages is the system founded on the exclusive social–emotional attachment of biological mother and child.

In our defence of biology and its mystique we are blind to the dangers of power. Women as the guardians of children possess great power. They are the moulders of their children's personalities and the arbiters of their development. But women as mothers are also powerful in an unrecognized way. The modern family system subjects the child to 'massive inputs' of the mother's personality. They are immensely vulnerable to the mother's day-to-day moods, feelings and behaviour. 'Every maternal quirk, every maternal hang-up will be experienced by the child as heavily amplified noise from which there is no respite.'[56] According to the study *Mothers of Six Cultures*, Western mothers show more 'emotional instability' than other mothers in their relationships with children. The instability is due in part to the amount of time they spend alone with their children (more than mothers in other cultures) and in part to their own doubts about the correctness of their behaviour as mothers.

The mother's role is to be bound closely to her child, but not too closely; to be possessive, but not too possessive. The balance is difficult to achieve, but in today's isolated conditions of motherhood it is essential, and the mother knows it is essential. The demand that she be a 'good' mother is an ideal:

it is a practical recognition of the child's intense vulnerability.
The mother must be good because nobody can cure her mis-
takes. They are embedded in the life of the child for ever.

The social image of children's vulnerability is real: children
are vulnerable. Confined in the one-to-one relationship with
the mother they are, first of all, vulnerable to the quality of the
feelings she has for them. The child may meet insufficient love,
hatred or rejection. Research by Professor C. Henry Kempe,
who coined the phrase 'battered baby', shows that about one in
five mothers has difficulty with the love-aspect of the mother–
child relationship. Violence against children is one possible
outcome: so is 'failure to thrive'. 'The mother, emotionally
unable to care for her child, just sets it aside . . .'[57]

Contrary to the popular image of the 'baby batterer' such
mothers are usually partners in stable marriages and only a
minority are suffering from psychotic or major personality dis-
orders.[58] 'Baby battering' is distinct from child neglect: a
neglected child is abandoned by its parents, but a battered child
is the object of intense emotional investment. Characteristic of
the 'battering' syndrome is the parent's perception that the
child has failed to live up to parental expectations. The parent
takes control and tries to force the child to conform to an ideal.
Battered children are almost always well-fed, well-clothed and
clean; the physical appearance of the child matters, and is
preserved whatever the damage wrought by the abusing parent
in other areas.[59]

More women than men batter children because women are
the childrearing parents. A mother's investment in her child's
physical appearance is an extension of the concern she has for
the appearance of her home: a concern induced in her through
her upbringing for domesticity. Housewife and mother roles
merge to the detriment of the people involved: mothers suffer
from the physical and mental conflict imposed by their dual
role, children from the need to compete with housework for
their mothers' attention. The extra hours of domestic work
put in by fulltime housewife–mothers (compared with their

employed sisters) are not spent in stimulating childcare. Repetitive housework occupies these extra hours.

This point was made forcefully by Charlotte Perkins Gilman, an early apostle of the women's movement in the United States. In a book called *The Home: Its Work and Influence* published in 1903, she said:

> Follow the hours in the day of the housewife: count the minutes spent in the care and service of the child, as compared with those given to the planning of meals, the purchase of supplies, the labour either of personally cleaning things or of seeing that other persons do it: the 'duties' to society of the woman exempt from the actual house-labour.
>
> 'But,' we protest, 'all this is for the child – the meals, the well-kept house, the clothes – the whole thing!'
>
> Yes? And in what way do the meals we so elaborately order and prepare, the daintily furnished home, the much trimmed clothing, contribute to the body-growth, mind-growth and soul-growth of the child?[60]

Her percipient analysis of the situation led her to make what was then a highly revolutionary demand: that housework be socialized – taken out of the home – and childcare become a community function.

All these problems with motherhood in our society are probably more common than we suppose. Few of them can be solved or masked by the support of the kin group: there is rarely a grandmother, uncle or older sibling to step in and take the mother's place. The 'normal' mother in a 'normal' family is on her own.

Thus another condition hidden by the myth of motherhood is the mother's intense vulnerability to the personality of her child. This, like fatherhood, is an unresearched area. Studies of battered babies suggest that the child itself may carry some responsibility: 'Nurses and social workers have confessed understandingly why a parent might batter "that child".'[61] Some of these children get battered in sequential foster home placements. One scientist has documented the different behaviour of a foster mother towards two infants placed with her at the same time. George was a highly responsive and active baby. The foster mother gave him a great deal of attention. Jack was a passive baby with a low responsiveness to all kinds of stimuli. The foster mother referred to him as 'the other one' and 'poor little thing'. She had as little to do with him as possible.[62]

What is dangerous in the 'normal' mother–child situation is that the child can demand and get the *total* attention of the mother. Annoying behaviour produced repeatedly by the child affects mother alone. Items such as 'continuous questioning accompanied by total uninterest in answer', 'continous leaping upon sitting or lying parent', 'types of aggressive and mono- tonous singing' and 'demands for food which is then discarded' are present in the behavioural repertoire of all 'normal' children. Their effect on the captive mother can be disastrous, for in this situation they do not have to be excessive to appear unreasonable. A more gradual reaction than the urge to batter is an erosion of self-confidence, a growing feeling of worthless- ness:

As the child becomes increasingly skilful in preventing his [*sic*] mother from attending to anything external to himself, her talents for these things deteriorate accordingly, and add to her feelings of inadequacy. Since it seems to her that she can satisfy the needs neither of her child nor of her household, she may become seriously depressed.[63]

Part of the danger inherent in the mother–child relationship is contingent on the situation of women. In the hands of the mother, society places the all-important task of rearing healthy new citizens, but the mother who carries this immense trust, the mother whose role is thus revered, is also the woman whose status in society is inferior. Despite her role as childrearer, she is not the first sex, but the second. This situation is fraught with danger. As J. S. Mill described it: 'Where liberty cannot be hoped for, and power can, power becomes the grand object of human desire.'[64] Or, as one mother, a hundred years later, expressed the same danger: 'It is in the very nature of a mother's position in our society, to avenge her own frustrations on a small, helpless child; whether this takes the form of tyranny, or of a smothering affection that asks the child to be a substitute for all she has missed.'[65]

To suggest that all mothers seek surrogate power in their relationship with their children would be oversimplification. It would read as an attribution of blame, which would also be wrong. A woman's desire to experience power and control within the family is mixed with the desire to obtain joy in childrearing and cannot be separated from it. It is the position of women in society as a whole, their dependent position in the family, the cultural expectation that the maternal role should be the most important one for all women, that makes the exaggerated wish to possess one's child an entirely reasonable reaction. Deprived and oppressed, women see in motherhood their only source of pleasure, reward and fulfilment: 'It came to me as a simple and absolute premonition ... I knew without doubt then what it was I wanted . . . It was not some thing, but some body that would be mine, peculiarly and particularly mine, and not in any way anyone else's at all.'[66]

The logical development of this response is 'maternal over-protection': a syndrome in which the mother's possessiveness is so complete that the child is never allowed to become independent. She 'holds her child tightly with one hand and makes the gesture of pushing away the rest of the world with the other. Her energies are directed to preserving her infant as infant for all time.'[67] Maternal overprotection may often not be recognized because it is not easily separable from 'normal' maternal love.

Thorough examination of the contention that all women need to be mothers, that mothers need their children, and that children need their mothers, uncovers no evidence for their truth, save that supplied by cultural mechanisms. Women brought up for motherhood need motherhood; children who experience 'mothering' but very little else cannot do without mothering; motherhood is not necessarily paramount to women, nor the mother to the child.

Along with the myth of the division of labour by sex, the myth of motherhood is a major source of women's oppression. Both myths act to confirm women's domesticity: their lasting psychological identification with the domestic world.

Nine

Breaking the Circle

'No nation can be free,' wrote Lenin, 'when half the population is enslaved in the kitchen.'[1] The meaning of this statement is both actual and metaphorical: the kitchen is the symbol of women's domesticity, and the lifelong activities and identities of women outside the kitchen are determined and defined by their domesticity.

Three political statements point the way to the liberation of housewives:

The housewife role must be abolished.

The family must be abolished.

Gender roles must be abolished.

1 The Housewife Role

The call for abolition of the housewife role follows directly from the kind of work role it is, and would stand whatever the sex of the worker. Housework is work directly opposed to the possibility of human self-actualization. The same job requirements are imposed on all kinds of women with all kinds of skills and abilities, but the basic activities of housework require little aptitude of any kind, save for a dutiful application to the goal of carrying them out. In an account of the occupations followed by mentally subnormal people, Leta S. Hollingsworth wrote in 1922:

> There seems to be no occupation which supports feebleminded men as well as housework and prostitution support feebleminded women ... The girl who cannot compete mentally need not become

an object of concern ... because she may drop into the non-competi-
tive vocational life of the household, where she naturally performs
many routine tasks, requiring but rudimentary intelligence, such
as peeling vegetables, washing dishes.

(An added advantage is that, 'if physically unobjectionable as
may be the case, she may marry, thus fastening herself to
economic support in a customary fashion'.)[2]

Work can only be self-actualizing when it provides motivation for the worker. Studies of industrial workers' attitudes
have led to a general distinction between two kinds of job
characteristics: those which provide motivation and those that
do not. 'Motivators' include 'a challenging job which allows
a feeling of achievement, responsibility, growth, advancement,
enjoyment of work itself, and earned recognition'. In the
second group of 'non-motivators' are 'such matters as pay,
supplemental benefits, company policy and administration,
behavioural supervision, working conditions'[3] and other
factors peripheral to the actual job.

Housework lacks any motivating factor. Essentially what
this means is that the housewife cannot get any information
about herself from the work she does. 'When the person feels
he [*sic*] is performing well in the work itself, it is "satisfying"
in a very deep sense of the word; it confirms the self. The
struggle to attain this through work is what is "motivating".'[4]
In housework there is no possibility of growth or advancement:
feelings of achievement are transitory, enjoyment of work itself
is a rare experience, and no opportunity for earned recognition
is offered. The responsibility of the housewife's job *is* motivating: from it stems the need to define work in terms specific to
the self as individual; but because of the housewife's psychological and actual isolation the result is often not satisfying at
all.

Earned recognition follows self-actualization as a second
quality housework cannot supply. It is 'a manifestation of
justice, an act of approval which confirms successful achievement and individual worth'.[5] Husbands do not serve as reliable

sources of approval for the housewife as worker, but in any case the recognition has to be earned, which means that the reward – verbal or otherwise – must be exactly commensurate with the energy expended and the results achieved. 'Unearned recognition in the form of friendliness, reassurance, small talk and personal interest,' says one six-year study of an instruments company in Texas, 'is not a substitute for earned recognition, but it is essential as a *maintenance* factor, *particularly in the absence of opportunity to earn recognition through job performance*' [italics added.][6] In other words, the husband's sympathetic and appreciative comments will *keep* the housewife at her work while they will not have the capacity to reward her in a more fundamental way.

The basic satisfaction that produces feelings of self-actualization cannot be gained from 'the conditions that surround the doing of a job . . . *it is only from the performance of a task that the individual can get the rewards that will reinforce his aspirations*' [italics added].[7]

This means that the inherent deprivations of housework as work cannot be banished by the mere improvement of housework conditions: better and nicer houses, more machines, more coffee mornings, or housewives' clubs. Solutions along these lines are often prescribed as medicine for the housewife's dilemma. Essentially they are prescriptions for adjustment to a pathogenic situation. Certainly it is the case that dissatisfied workers are highly sensitive to their environment and may often complain about it: housewives follow the practice of other workers, and in their demands for a new house or a new washing machine encapsulate the protest of fundamental discontent. Any improvement in the housewife's working conditions is purely a means of keeping women in their place.

Attempts to raise the status of the housewife's work have been notable for their failure. The technique of calling housewives 'home-makers' has had no real effect: with it we may compare the undertaker's transmutation into a mortician, a defensive and mocked attempt at self-professionalization. The work is the same and has the same stereotype whatever it is called. Housework has recently acquired a new status which underlines its basically 'menial' nature: it has become, in Britain, a form of punishment meted out to the criminal offender. In January 1973, the first offender to be punished in this way, Peter Giles, began his sentence by cleaning an old age pensioner's flat. 'It may come as a surprise to the magistrate who dealt with Mr Giles, and many uninitiated men everywhere,' wrote one protesting female journalist, 'that thousands of women in this country are interned for varying periods of time, week in and week out, performing the new ultimate deterrent known as "housework". Many are finding it increasingly difficult to remember what offence they committed in the first place.'[8]

Because housework is not intrinsically self-actualizing, many women try to make it so. The argument that housewifery is creative home-making stems from this motivation: the strive to elaborate the fundamental processes of housework into something bigger, better, more difficult and more rewarding. This is partly a claim for the use of skill and a right to status: making bread is more difficult than buying it from a shop, sewing clothes more taxing than acquiring them ready-made, and so on. It is also an attempt to express individuality. Every housewife knows that most women are housewives, and that every one of them does housework, but she has the defiant feeling that she is not like them: she is different. In the specification of standards and routines as rules for doing housework she expresses herself. This is a rational response to a 'levelling' situation. Nobody likes to be exactly the same as everyone else: a minimum of differentiation is psychologically necessary.

But neither self-actualization nor individuality can successfully be found in housework on more than a momentary basis. Both are lost as standards and routines multiply and the pleasurable knowledge of self-reward becomes the frenetic pursuit of goals outside oneself, the product of one's own imagination objectified as mocking agents of oppression.

Today only one avenue offers possibilities for an improvement in the status of domestic work, and that is the struggle of employed female domestic workers to improve *their* status and conditions. The recent campaign of the night cleaners in Britain for unionization, increased pay, sick pay, adequate staffing of buildings, and so forth, has made a strong claim for the essential dignity of the custodial domestic worker:

You say I'm a human being and I've got dignity, I work because I have to eat and live . . . But I sell my work at *my* price because I'm a human being not a slave . . . if you believe that, believe in the dignity of your own work, then you organise yourselves to make sure the employer appreciates the dignity of your work, that you're as good as he is, and you'll do his cleaning for proper payment. You won't do his cleaning because your role in life is to clean the houses of the rich, or to clean the office blocks of the powerful. It's a job like any other job.[9]

But it is easier to feel a dignity in shared work than in isolated work. Conscious of her dignity as worker, the housewife must remain isolated, privatized, and self-defining in her approach to housework.

Perhaps housewives should be paid for their work? The political contention that the housewife role must be abolished needs to counter this objection. Proposals in favour of 'a housewife's wage' are made today by both liberationists and anti-liberationists. The liberationist advocates wages for housework because she sees it as a crucial recognition of women's traditional unpaid labour in the home, and a step in the improvement of women's social status.* Anti-liberationists argue for the same development on different premises. Their premise is one of 'hygiene': that women's place is, and should be, in the home, and everything should be done to make it as pleasant as possible. This is the crux of the argument: if housewives are

---

*In the politics of the women's liberation movement the demand for paid housework has been coming to the fore recently. At the November 1972 conference it was a main issue. In the Italian movement, the demand receives particularly strong support.

paid, the status quo will be maintained. A system of state payment for the woman–housewife's labour in the home will
recognize and perpetuate the validity of the equation 'woman
= housewife'. Through the family-oriented structure of modern
society moreover, the system will also recognize and perpetuate
the privatization and social isolation of the housewife's work:
one woman per family, one housewife per home. The treatment
of housework as wage labour will ensure that the self-definition
of housework – one of its most dissatisfying aspects – will
endure. A new form of oppression for women will be added
to the old ones: the housewife, already exploited as people-
producer and object-consumer by the capitalist state, will be
exploited as its wage-labourer too. As wage labourer she will
not easily generate the political power other groups of workers
can exercise: for her conditions of work are inimical to the
organization of housewives in trade unions with collective
bargaining power and the ultimate deterrent of strike action.
In practice, a housewife's wage would be a state 'grant' rather
than a wage. Its character would be that of a benevolent hand-
out, rather than a payment earned of *right* for work done. The
result would be the integration of housework with other paid
work roles which are stereotyped as feminine, and therefore
suffer from an inferiorization of status, conditions and rewards.

Many proposals for a housewife's wage are actually proposals
for paid childrearing. This is a different matter altogether. Since
the state invests so much money in the education of children
(beyond the magic age of school entry) and in child health and
development generally, it is reasonable to suggest that some
financial recognition should be given to the childcare role of
the parent in the home.

'Family allowances', cash payments to mothers of two or
more children, have been payable in Britain since 1946. Their
cash value is small, but their social value to the mother is substantial. The system was originally intended to be, in part, a
payment to the housewife for her work. Eleanor Rathbone,
feminist, economist, author, and Member of Parliament, was

the system's founder. In her moving work *The Disinherited Family*, published in 1924, she argued a defence of motherhood and housework as 'work'.

It may be questioned whether it has ever occurred to any but a negligible fraction of Medical Officers of Health, inspectors, councillors, committee men and subscribers concerned in child welfare schemes, that if motherhood is a craft . . . it differs from every other craft known to man in that there is no money remuneration for the mother's task, no guarantee of her maintenance while she performs it and (most important yet most ignored of all) no consequential relationship recognised by society between the quantity and quality of her product and the quantity and quality of the tools and materials which she has at her disposal. Children are the mother's product, food, clothing and other necessaries her materials and tools . . .

This highly pertinent analysis continues with an evaluation of that other role, housewife:

In a hundred ways our social customs, our domestic architecture, our ideas of decoration and dress, show signs of the undervaluation of domestic work, especially that of housewives . . . There is, I suppose, no occupation in the world which has an influence on the efficiency and happiness of the members of nearly all other occupations so continuous and so permeating as that of the working housewife . . . On nearly every day of his life, from cradle to grave, the future or present wage-earner is affected in his health, his spirits, his temper, his ambitions, his outlook on society and judgement of its arrangements, by the conditions of his home . . . Potentially the work of that woman is as highly skilled as that of half a dozen ordinary craftsmen. Actually that work is performed in most households by the feminine equivalent of an industrious but untrained workman, who has picked up his trade by rule of thumb and is equipped with an insufficient number of atrociously bad tools.[10]

Rathbone, like other feminists of this era, had a thorough grasp of the role industrialization had played in the creation of women's situation. The family's loss of function and the woman's subjected status within it were signs of the family's economic disinheritance. A 'family allowance' was in her eyes a means of social restitution – of giving back to the family what society owed it. The basic economics of the system were worked out by Eleanor Rathbone and a group of her friends who met regularly for this purpose from 1918 onwards in a Soho club. But by 1940 (six years before the introduction of the scheme) the idea of payment to the housewife for her domestic labour had been dropped. The limited funds available were one reason: another was political unacceptability.

Rathbone saw family allowances as a means of paying women for their labour in childcare: like modern-day liberationists, her concern was to dignify women's unpaid work in the home. But the payment of a cash benefit to the mother is no less sex-discriminatory than the payment of a wage to housewives: both maintain women's traditional identification with domestic roles. *If*, therefore, there is to be any state payment for childrearing, along the lines of a 'family allowance' system, the interests of women will only be served if the 'parent' rather than the 'mother' is entitled to it.

A second common objection to any criticism of the housewife role, including its proposed abolition, is that women like being housewives. '*Some* women like it,' goes the logic, 'and those who don't can do something else.' This contention ignores the shaping of women's identity by their social situation. It is not merely what a woman wants that is at issue, but what she is induced to want, and what she is prevented – by social attitudes – from believing she can have, or be. Moulded in this fashion by restrictive stereotypes, the majority of women do not have any serious option but to conform. Thus they affirm their status: 'We are happy, we like being housewives.' Or, 'What's wrong with being a wife? I *like* looking after my husband.' Or, 'I love my children.' They have to reject the liberationist attitude and liberationists themselves have to be seen as deviant: 'Have you ever noticed,' asked a woman writing to *Shrew*, the newspaper of the London Women's Liberation Workshop, in 1972, that the majority of women's-lib supporters do not appear to be married? It would therefore seem that these workers for women's rights are really only after equal pay, or to dominate the male through jealousy. As for me, I love being a woman, a housewife, a mother, and above all a real wife to my husband . . . I suggest all who want equality go immediately to Red China or Russia and take a long look at what being equal means. Perhaps then they will see sense, return to good old England, and buy a new bra.[11]

Many of the fiercest diatribes against liberation come from women themselves. A tendency to atavism is shared by both genders.

A woman's declaration of happiness with housewifery is a necessary identification, but as a true statement it must be suspected. Women's generally subordinate position in society means that there are inbuilt obstacles to the housewife's real-ization of her oppression.

Society's denial of housework as work is one such obstacle. When society does not recognize housework as work, how can the housewife legitimately claim to be suffering from work-dissatisfaction? The sociologist provides a macrocosmic expla-nation of this process according to which wants and needs are confined to a limited context:

If lower participants [women] were habitually to compare their positions with the financial rewards, status, autonomy and intrinsic job-interest of higher management [men] it is difficult to see how industrial society [marriage] in its present form could maintain its legitimacy. It might be supposed therefore that power groups [men] would take an active interest in encouraging people [women] to adopt the most modest reference groups which they could be per-suaded to accept, since this would contribute to order and stability for the status quo [brackets added].[12]

Another pressure is to conceal dissatisfaction: not to express it directly, but to channel it into more subtle forms of protest. The social stereotype of women as emotional, hysterical and unstable makes this easy. Elina Haavio-Mannila, a Finnish sociologist, asked women about their satisfaction with family, work, leisure and life generally. She also asked them about the presence and incidence of anxiety symptoms (nervousness, headache, insomnia, nightmares, etc.). On the whole the women in the survey were more satisfied than the men, but they experienced more anxiety symptoms. This discrepancy was particularly evident in the lower social-class group: the satisfaction of these women was apparently high, but they felt more anxiety than the middle- and upper-class woman, and more than any of the men. The greatest number of anxiety symptoms were reported by fulltime housewives, again with the lower-class women worse off than their counterparts higher in the social strata. Haavio-Mannila concludes:

The frequent expression of satisfaction connected with a large amount of anxiety among lower-stratum women can be considered as a product of the generally underprivileged status given to women. Women were content with their lot even though objectively they were underdogs. The stress inherent in women's underdog position gets its expression in anxiety, not in open dissatisfaction with work, family, leisure and life. Men in a similar position are more openly dissatisfied and have less anxiety.[13]

It is a common research finding that women express more satisfaction than men do with monotonous, unskilled, badly paid and low-status types of work. Of course the usual (masculine) interpretation of this is that women 'are not dissatisfied with such work. Work does not have the central importance and meaning in their lives that it does for men, since their most important roles are those of wives and mothers.'[14] Significantly the so-called ability of women to accept dissatisfying jobs is interpreted as very valuable to men: it stops *them* being alienated: 'Women, who tend to be more satisfied than men with the prevailing unskilled routine jobs, "cushion" the occupational floor in machine industries, raising the ceiling slightly for the men who might otherwise be frustrated in low positions.' (The cure for the male worker's alienation is thus simple: get women out of the home into dead-end jobs, and men, seeing they are better off, will feel more satisfied.) Robert Blauner's *Alienation and Freedom* (from which the above quotations are taken) is a splendid documentation of the social expectation that women ought to be satisfied with dreary work (though in fact it claims to be an objective analysis of the relationship between alienation and different work structures).

Other findings of anxiety symptoms, and alcohol and drug dependence among women may be similarly linked with the social pressures on women to manifest their housework-dissatisfaction in covert ways. The International Yearbook of Neurology, Psychiatry and Neurosurgery recognizes what it terms simply 'housewife's disease'. A United States study of psychological-stress symptoms finds the highest symptom rates among fulltime housewives (compared with employed housewives and employed men). The fulltime housewives had high symptom rates for fainting, hand trembling, inertia, nervous breakdowns, heart palpitations, and dizziness. Retired men showed similar rates, suggesting that restriction to the home, with its concomitant social isolation, is a critical factor. Agoraphobia is a disability which afflicts housewives particularly, when their psychological suffering at being restricted to the home becomes physical as well. Records of drug consumption, particularly of psychotropic drugs (sedatives, tranquillizers, anti-depressants, appetite reducers, etc.), show that in the ten years between 1957 and 1967 consumption of these drugs increased by 80 per cent, and that three quarters of these drug-users are women.[15] There is no breakdown of the figures by domestic-role status – housewife or non-housewife – but since 85 per cent of all women are housewives, some connection (especially in view of the other evidence) seems likely.

In America, lobotomy – a type of brain surgery – has as one of its targets women: 'neurotic individuals who are still able to work and live at home'. As a means of enforced social adjustment, it is also currently being used for prison inmates and for hyperactive institutionalized children – both of these categories bearing echoes of the figure of the housewife, frenetic and houseproud, imprisoned in the solitude of her own home.

An affirmation of contentment with the housewife role is actually a form of antifeminism, whatever the gender of the person who displays it. Declared contentment with a subordinate role – which the housewife role undoubtedly is – is a rationalization of inferior status. For a man to say, 'But my wife is happy as a housewife,' is for him to put upon her an obligatory loyalty to her inferiorization. It means, 'I *want* her to be happy as a housewife,' and is in no way different from the statement, 'But my slave/servant is happy as he/she is.' Unlike other minority groups, women have a peculiar kind of relationship with their oppressors: men who wish to marry must marry women, and vice versa for women, who experience greater pressures towards marriage than do men. A number of contradictions follow from this. The first is that 'a dominant group member may be willing to marry a member of a group which, in general, he would not wish admitted to his club'.[16] Women are all right in their place (as housewives). Another contradiction is that although marriage places a woman in a subordinate role (wife–housewife) it is also a means of elevating her status. Like the domestic servant of eighteenth-century England, the housewife takes on the social status of her master (husband). Hence the emotional investment in continued subordination.

Proposals for breaking the equation 'woman = housewife' should not therefore be discredited on grounds of women's apparent contentment with the status quo. This is not a valid counter-argument, nor is the argument that everything would be all right if the housewife's working conditions were improved and she were paid for her work. It becomes clear that a second political statement follows from the first: the abolition of the housewife role calls for the abolition of the family.

2 The Family

Women's domesticity is a circle of learnt deprivation and induced subjugation: a circle decisively centred on family life.

'The appropriate symbol for housework (and for housework *alone*) is not the interminable conveyor belt, but a compulsive circle like a pet mouse in its cage spinning round on its wheel, unable to get off.'[17] Caught up in perpetual motion, women are too bemused by it to see how their suspension in this domestic world is brought about, or how they might break the ceaseless movement of the circle and step out and beyond it.

Women are instructed in their oppression as housewives by other women. The learning of domesticity by daughters from mothers is a lasting lesson, driven home through the psychological identification of mother and daughter. Unlike the father-son relationship, the structure of the modern family ensures that the mother–daughter relationship is essentially continuous and in some sense always symbiotic: before birth the baby is part of the mother, but after birth the female baby remains part of the mother, through identity of anatomy, through empathy and identification on the part of the mother. When the behaviour of mothers with young babies is studied, there is a clear differentiation according to the sex of the child. Mothers of sons approach the baby with a respect for the baby's otherness from the maternal self, his autonomy and independence. They stimulate the child to action, accepting the need to create a response in this 'other person'. But with daughters, the pattern of behaviour is different. The mother knows what the baby is: she is female. Any attempt to relate to the baby as another, a separate, person would be spurious. For the need to stimulate is substituted the desire to imitate, a confirmation of shared femaleness, the belief in a common identity.[18]

Another source of the message's strength is the integration of learning for domesticity with learning for femininity and the learning of 'good child' behaviour generally. In a multitude of trivial daily interactions, the female's identity is built up, an identity in which the components of femininity are integrated with the conception of self as person and self as child, so that the three images, female, child, person, are not in any way separable. To sit with one's legs crossed, to help one's mother make the beds, to wear pretty clothes, to be polite to adults, to behave well at mealtimes, to learn the virtues of honesty and kindness – the items of rewarded behaviour that compose a girl's socialization are not transmitted to her as categorized qualities of different roles. There is only one role expected of her and her identity comes from the social expectations that create this role.

In this process, even details of the housewife's occupational behaviour are transmitted to the child, and thus not only an identification with the role itself, but an internalization of ways of doing housework, may be traced back to the mother–daughter relationship. One study of children in an experimental-choice situation has critical relevance to the processes involved. Forty-eight children aged 3 to 5 were divided into two groups, and each group was allocated a model, one of whom showed 'nurturant' behaviour towards the children, the other of whom did not. Then both model and subjects were asked by the experimenter to perform a simple task – guessing which of two boxes contained a picture sticker. The model, previously instructed by the experimenter, entered the room first and deliberately produced items of behaviour that had nothing to do with the stated goal – finding the sticker. In one trial, for instance, the model walked towards the boxes, saying 'March, march, march.' She then aggressively knocked a small rubber doll off the lid of the box, said, 'Open the box,' removed the sticker and pasted it on the wall. In each case the child entered the room after the model and was observed to see whether or not she reproduced the model's behaviour.

The results of this experiment showed that 'children display a good deal of social learning of an incidental imitative sort, and that nurturance is one condition facilitating such imitative learning'. Some models took an extremely circuitous route to the box, a route which doubled the distance to be travelled and was clearly incompatible with the subjects' eagerness to get to the containers. Nevertheless, report the researchers, 'many subjects dutifully followed the example set by the model'. In other words, children will learn to imitate certain behaviours *'which are totally irrelevant to the successful performance of the orienting task'* [italics added].[19]

In its application to the occupational identification of the female child with housework, this study suggests that daughters will imitate aspects of the mother's behaviour which are dysfunctional from the viewpoint of simply getting the work done, and will internalize these items of behaviour, applying them to their own approach to housework. The finding that nurturance favours the development of 'incidental' learning patterns means the close relationship of mother and daughter is a context which encourages the process to occur.

The family, from the viewpoint of women as housewives, is precisely as dangerous as the experimental situation in which children can, through love, be induced to replicate behaviour which has no logic or meaning. Because mother is the ever-present and ideally ever-loving person, all her idiosyncracies and psychological deformities are the model for future action.

The family's gift to women is a direct apprenticeship in the housewife role. For this reason, the abolition of the housewife role requires the abolition of the family, and the substitution of more open and variable relationships: not man–provider, woman–housewife and dependent children, but people living together in a chosen and freely perpetuated intimacy, in a space that allows each to breathe and find her or his own separate destiny.

If the family goes, so, of course, does marriage. In the family (or anywhere else for that matter) all verbal language is impositional: 'housewife' means woman, not man, 'mother' (child-rearer) means female parent, not male parent. Superficial changes in the relationships between female and male over recent years have not altered women's traditional oppression to domesticity. Information given by housewives in the study cited earlier about the kind of help their husbands offer with housework and childcare, and about the patterning of marital roles generally, gives an impression of substantial segregation between the lives of husband and wife. The increased 'egalitarianism' of modern marriage (in so far as egalitarianism exists) has not directly affected the institutionalized segregation of marital roles. A greater equality may characterize the relationship between husband and wife in some areas – legal rights, for instance – but mother and father roles, husband and wife roles, remain distinct, and – most conspicuous of all – the allocation to women of the housewife role endures. Apparent changes, such as the increasing likelihood of a wife's employment, may not be changes at all, and we should not be taken in by surface appearances, nor by that pseudo-egalitarian phrase the 'dual-career' (or 'dual-job') marriage. Research shows that if a wife takes employment, her role does not automatically take on the power and authority conventionally associated with the husband's role in marriage. Any gain in equality, or any confirmation of the status quo, is achieved 'only in interaction with the pre-existing ideologies and personalities of the actors.'[20] The capacity of the housewife's employment to affect fundamentally and permanently the structure of marital roles is undermined by the ideology of non-interchangeability, of role-segregation, subscribed to by the married couple – the ideology of gender differentiation which is basic to marriage as an institution.

An ideological rejection of marriage and family life is not enough. Marriage may lose its legality, yet retain its flavour of oppression for the female partner. The family may be banished only in name, the structure of personal relationships perpetuating the axis of gender differentiation that the family, in essence, means. This invidious tendency may be seen clearly at work in modern commune movements, where a traditional division of labour between female and male is maintained, and of course in the U.S.S.R., where revolution called for both the abolition of the housewife role and the abolition of the family, but neither was achieved: 'When you ask a husband to help, the answer is always the same: "Do you want me to do a woman's work? Why, the neighbours would laugh at me".'[21]

So it is not enough, or it is redundant, depending on how you phrase it, to say that the abolition of the housewife role means the abolition of the family too.

3 Gender

We need an ideological revolution, a revolution in the ideology of gender roles current in our culture, a revolution in concepts of gender identity. We need to abolish gender roles themselves. This is the third political statement, and it proceeds directly from the logic of the other two. Abolish the housewife role, therefore abolish the family, but this is not enough, so the abolition of gender is called for.

Of many possible objections to this statement, a trivial but common one is that society is already witnessing the elimination of gender differences. This is doubtful. A tendency for men to grow their hair and for women to wear trousers does not mean that both are abdicating their gender stereotypes. It means only that men are growing their hair and women are wearing trousers. (A closer look reveals that, even on this level, a great deal of gender differentiation still takes place. The day when men freely walk around with mascaraed eyes and lipsticked mouths, and when women's hair is obviously greasy and neglected, might portend some actual, rather than mythical, gender liberation.) Only when men *en masse* are refusing to worry about the size and strength of their erections, about their careers and their earning power and their cars, when they cease to think of women as bitchy creatures to be put upon, as aesthetic and sexual objects for the decoration of the environment and the masculine ego, when they cease to bond with other men at football matches and in pubs while women wash dishes and are denied any media interest in *their* world, will something actually be happening to gender roles. Women, for their part, must substitute, for a superficial commitment to sex equality and trouser-wearing, not an emulation of the male's life style, but a true desire to liberate their own personalities

from the constraints of gender, before any meaningful change
can properly be discerned in their behaviour.

Many other objections to the contention that gender roles
should be abolished boil down to one anxiety: sex. The root of
this anxiety is a confusion between gender and sex. Gender is
a cultural role which has nothing directly to do with sexuality –
the drive to physical–genital contact and/or copulation. Points
of overlap are only that the aggressiveness and passivity of the
masculine and feminine gender roles respectively have been
carried over into the area of their sexuality, and that the female's
sexuality has traditionally been repressed in a male-oriented
culture to conform to the subjugated stereotype of the feminine woman. But physical attraction between men and women,
the urge to copulate, the drive to reproduce, is not going to
mysteriously disappear if women stop being housewives, if
men stop opening doors for women, if men rear children. In so
far as sexual attraction is based (at the moment) on these
trivial signs of gender identity, some re-conditioning will have
to take place. But all we need to change are our reflexes.

To change these, and other reflexes, a raising of consciousness
is needed. We need to see how we are moulded by the roles we
are given, and how to rearrange our identities when the social
edifice of role and role-expectation is made to crumble away.
In all areas of life the call should be 'people not gender'.
People should be committed to unravelling and reshaping the
old bonds of family relationships into new bonds of less intense
love and hate, to a desire to see children reared without the
trauma of dependence on mother-at-home and father-at-work,
to a dedication to the restructuring of employment work to
accommodate these more flexible life-styles.

Abolish the housewife role, abolish the family, abolish gender
roles – mighty statements, but do they defy translation into
practice? What can we do?

Breaking the circle entails the liberation of women to personhood in an institutional, legal, economic and political sense.
All those reforms not yet achieved which bring the sexes

closer together in terms of their social rights and responsibilities are prerequisites for the abolition of gender-differentiation, but their achievement will not mystically guarantee anybody's liberation. People must change themselves.

Women can take three immediate steps towards their liberation from enforced domesticity. First, they can reject uncompromisingly any attempt to stereotype them as housewives. 'Housewife' is a political label after all, a shorthand symbol for the convenience to a male-oriented society of women's continued captivity in a world of domestic affairs – a one-word reference to those myths of woman's place which chart their presence in the home as a natural and universal necessity. Because it is a political label, its rejection is also political. The critical battles here are to be fought on the level of bureaucratic processes as well as within personal relationships. Why write 'occupation: housewife' on a form when 'occupation: unpaid domestic worker', 'occupation: childrearer', 'occupation: person' or 'occupation: doctor/factory worker/waitress' (or whatever it is/was) can be written instead?

For many women, rejection of the housewife label will carry its most crucial significance in the female–male relationship, married or otherwise. *He* may agree with the sentiment in theory, but say in practice, 'I don't mind sharing the housework, but I don't do it very well. We should each do the things we're best at.' (Or, 'I don't mind sharing the work, but you'll have to show me how to do it.' Or, 'We have different standards and why should I have to work to your standards. That's unfair.') Apparent rationality conceals a concern to perpetuate the identification of women with domesticity: 'I don't like the dull, stupid, boring jobs so you should do them.'[22] The dialogue is amazingly intense and persistent: it is therefore political, not trivial. The measure of the woman–housewife's oppression is the strength of the man–non-housewife's resistance to 'real' (not merely theoretical) change.

A second step women can take they can *only* take because as childrearers they are the potential instigators of change. They can teach their daughters how *not* to be housewives (and their sons how to *do* housework). The important lesson to be learnt here is merely how to get the necessary minimum of housework done in the shortest possible time. For daughters, there must also be a constant affirmation of the female's capacities outside the home. More than just a 'Yes, you can be a builder, motor cyclist, pilot if you want to' is required: a sense of *excitement* must be communicated about the areas of self-realization which lie beyond the kitchen door.

And, finally, women must change themselves *now*. Women must fight the standards set up by their conditioning: standards which insist that anything less than domestic perfection is a crime against their own natures. Since they have no inherent natures, that crime is of their own imagining. It is on their conditioning that destruction needs to be inflicted, for these standards and ways of doing housework go back into the unconscious. They must be made conscious before the battle can be won.

References

Full bibliographic details will be found in the List of Sources, pp. 251–66.

Chapter One. What is a Housewife?

1. Hunt, *A Survey of Women's Employment*, vol. I, p. 5.
2. *Oxford English Dictionary*.
3. *Guardian*, 20 August 1970.
4. Adapted from Wells, *Social Institutions*, p. 168.
5. *Evening Standard*, 24 August 1970.
6. General Register Office, *Sample Census 1966*, summary tables, p. xv.
7. Quoted in *The Times*, 7 November 1972.
8. *Guardian*, 2 November 1970.
9. ibid., 10 March 1970.
10. Quoted in *Shrew*, July 1971, p. 2.
11. Oakley, *The Sociology of Housework*.
12. See List of Sources, pp. 259–60.
13. This is the estimate of Professor Henry Kempe, the American paediatrician who invented the phrase 'the battered baby', cited in *Guardian*, 26 June 1970.
14. Banton, *Roles*, p. 21.
15. Quoted in White, *Women's Magazines*, p. 276.
16. Berger and Luckmann, *The Social Construction of Reality*, pp. 66–7.

Chapter Two. Women's Roles in Pre-Industrial Society

1. Rapoport and Rapoport, 'Work and Family in Contemporary Society', p. 385.
2. This description of Mbuti life comes from Turnbull, *Wayward Servants*.
3. Mary Douglas describes the Lele of Kasai in Forde, *African Worlds*.
4. See Boserup, *Woman's Role in Economic Development*.
5. See for example Kaberry, *Women of the Grassfields*.
6. Clark, *Working Life of Women*, p. 5.

7. ibid., p. 7.
8. Smelser, *Social Change and the Industrial Revolution*, pp. 54-5.
9. Quoted in Clark, *Working Life of Women*, p. 94.
10. Clark, *Working Life of Women*, pp. 197-8.
11. Quoted in Clark, *Working Life of Women*, p. 198.
12. See Hill, *Women in English Life*, vol. I, p. 47.
13. Welch, *Pewterers*; quoted in Clark, *Working Life of Women*, p. 191.
14. ibid., p. 35.
15. Quoted in Clark, *Working Life of Women*, p. 194.
16. Laslett in *The World We Have Lost* computes a figure of between 1 in 10 and 6 in 10 of all first baptisms recorded within 9 months of marriage. In 1970 about 1 in 10 of all legitimate births were pre-maritally conceived (General Register Office, *Statistical Review 1970*, p. 141 and p. 195).
17. Pinchbeck and Hewitt, *Children in English Society*, p. 13.
18. Laslett, *The World We Have Lost*, p. 90.
19. Clark, *Working Life of Women*, p. 39.
20. ibid., p. 145.
21. Quoted in Hewitt, *Wives and Mothers*, pp. 2-3.
22. George, *London Life in the Eighteenth Century*, pp. 427-9.
23. Barley, *The English Farmhouse and Cottage*, pp. 42-3.
24. Pinchbeck and Hewitt, *Children in English Society*, p. 4.
25. Cited in Pinchbeck and Hewitt, *Children in English Society*, p. 7. It is doubtful whether mothers were as detached as some fathers in their attitudes towards the death of children.
26. Pinchbeck and Hewitt, *Children in English Society*, p. 8.
27. Laslett, *The World We Have Lost*, p. 3.
28. Cited in Clark, *Working Life of Women*, p. 157.
29. ibid., p. 5.
30. MacFarlane, *The Family Life of Ralph Josselin*.
31. Clark, *Working Life of Women*, p. 152.
32. This fascinating book by an anonymous author is discussed by Stenton, *The English Woman in History*, (pp. 61 *et seq.*; pp. 148-9).
33. Quoted in Hamilton, *History of the Homeland*, pp. 316-17.

Chapter Three. Women and Industrialization

1. Parsons, 'The Social Structure of the Family', p. 193.
2. Peckham Rye Group, *A Woman's Work is Never Done*, p. 5.
3. Beales, *The Industrial Revolution*, p. 30.
4. Harris, *The Family*, pp. 100-102.
5. Quoted in Pinchbeck, *Women Workers*, p. 150.

6. ibid., p. 148.
7. ibid., p. 122.
8. Hammond and Hammond, *The Town Labourer*, p. 156.
9. Pinchbeck, *Women Workers*, p. 156.
10. Quoted in Hamilton, *History of the Homeland*, pp. 323–4.
11. Quoted in Pinchbeck, *Women Workers*, p. 109.
12. Quoted in Hewitt, *Wives and Mothers*, p. 191.
13. Quoted in Pinchbeck, *Women Workers*, pp. 235–6.
14. ibid., p. 237.
15. Bell, *Storming the Citadel*, p. 24.
16. Neff, *Victorian Working Women*, p. 187.
17. Pinchbeck, *Women Workers*, p. 244, p. 249.
18. Hamilton, *History of the Homeland*, p. 315.
19. Quoted in Hill, *Women in English Life*, vol. II, p. 200.
20. Quoted in Pinchbeck, *Women Workers*, p. 262.
21. Engels, *Condition of the Working Class*, p. 148.
22. ibid., pp. 160–61.
23. Phillips and Tomkinson, *English Women in Life and Letters*, p. 398.
24. Tonna, *The Wrongs of Women*, pp. 119–20.
25. Engels, *Condition of the Working Class*, p. 144 and p. 146.
26. This is the conclusion of modern studies on the relationship between maternal employment and reproductive casualty. See Illsley, *The Sociological Study of Reproduction*, pp. 108–10.
27. Hewitt, *Wives and Mothers*, p. 140.
28. Hamilton, *History of the Homeland*, p. 321.
29. Hill, *Women in English Life*, vol. II, p. 338.
30. Reeves, *Round About a Pound a Week*, pp. 151–5.
31. Crow, *The Victorian Woman*, p. 49.
32. ibid., pp. 49–50, p. 134.
33. ibid., p. 317.
34. Pinchbeck and Hewitt, *Children in English Society*, p. 297.
35. Hamilton, *History of the Homeland*, p. 339.
36. Nottingham, 'Towards an Analysis of the Effects of Two World Wars on the Role and Status of Women', p. 667.
37. Cole and Postgate, *The Common People*, p. 532.
38. Strachey, 'Changes in Employment', p. 128.
39. Cole and Postgate, *The Common People*, p. 533.
40. White, *Women's Magazines*, p. 280.

Chapter Four. The Situation of Women Today

1. Parsons, 'The American Family', p. 16.
2. Westermarck cited in Fletcher, *The Family and Marriage*, p. 22.

3. Dennis, *Coal is Our Life*, p. 174, pp. 179–82.

4. ibid., p. 207.

5. ibid., pp. 221–3.

6. ibid., p. 228.

7. ibid., pp. 229–30.

8. See Slater, *The Pursuit of Loneliness*, chapter 3, on attitudes to children.

9. Kessen, *The Child*, p. 7.

10. Mead, 'The Contemporary American Family', pp. 5–6.

11. Blood and Wolfe, *Husbands and Wives*, p. 20.

12. Winnicott, *The Child, the Family and the Outside World*, pp. 114–15.

13. George and Wilding, *Motherless Families*, pp. 40–41, p. 45.

14. ibid., p. 81.

15. ibid., pp. 86–7.

16. Dicks, *Marital Tensions*, p. 154 and p. 33.

17. *The Times*, 11 May 1972.

18. Department of Health and Social Security, *Cohabitation*, p. 1.

19. *Guardian*, 7 March 1972.

20. Reported in *The Times*, 2 May 1972.

21. Benet, *Secretary*, p. 69, p. 74.

22. Etzkowitz, 'The Male Sister', p. 432.

23. Timbury and Timbury, 'Glasgow Medical Students', p. 217.

24. Kelsall, *Graduates*, p. 142 and p. 144.

25. ibid., p. 146.

26. Rossi, 'Barriers to the Career Choice of Engineering, Medicine or Science', p. 53.

27. Parsons, 'Age and Sex in the Social Structure', p. 609.

28. United Nations General Assembly Resolution adopted 10 December 1948.

29. Williams, *American Society*, p. 495.

30. Komarovsky, 'Cultural Contradictions and Sex Roles', p. 187 and p. 185.

31. ibid., p. 184.

32. Epstein, *Woman's Place*, p. 19.

33. Steinemann, 'A Study of the Concept of the Feminine Role', p. 284.

34. See Oakley, *Sex, Gender and Society*.

35. Steinemann, 'A Study of the Concept of the Feminine Role', p. 288.

36. Woodward, *The Strange Career of Jim Crow*, p. 11.

37. Holter, *Sex Roles and Social Structure*, p. 17.

38. Newcomer, *A Century of Higher Education*, p. 210.

39. *The Englishwoman*, November 1919, p. 16.

40. Newcomer, *A Century of Higher Education*, p. 210.

41. Leach, *Culture and Nature*, p. 3.

42. Liljestrom, 'The Swedish Model', p. 208 and p. 207.
43. Whiting, *Six Cultures*, p. 1003.
44. Robbins Report, *Higher Education*, p. 211.
45. Fawcett Society, *Women in a Changing World*, p. 15.
46. Epstein, *Woman's Place*, pp. 22–3.
47. Quoted in Kock, 'Two Cheers for Equality', p. 211.

Chapter Five. Housewives and Their Work Today

1. See Oakley, *The Sociology of Housework*. The sample was randomly selected from the records of two general practices (one in a working-class, one in a middle-class area) in London. Only married women aged between twenty and thirty and with at least one child under five at the time of interview were included.
2. See Hartley, 'A Developmental View of Female Sex Role Identification'.
3. An example is 'Ashton' described in Chapter 4.
4. These figures are taken from John H. Goldthorpe *et al.*, *The Affluent Worker: Industrial Attitudes and Behaviour*, (University Press, Cambridge, 1968), p. 18.
5. The validity of generalizing on the basis of forty interviews is discussed in Oakley, *The Sociology of Housework*.

Chapter Seven. Myths of Woman's Place: 1 The Division of Labour by Sex

1. *Oxford English Dictionary*.
2. Mair, *An Introduction to Social Anthropology*, p.229.
3. Tiger, *Men in Groups*, p. 88.
4. ibid., p. 95.
5. Tiger and Fox, *The Imperial Animal*, pp. 142–3, p. 148.
6. Tiger, *Men in Groups*, p. 95.
7. Morris, *The Naked Ape*, p. 21.
8. ibid., pp. 164–5.
9. Morgan, *The Descent of Woman*, p. 13 and p. 15.
10. Kúrten, *Not From the Apes*, p. 1.
11. Morris, *The Naked Ape*, p. 21.
12. Morgan, *The Descent of Woman*, p. 9 and p. 206.
13. Malinowski, *Magic, Science and Religion*, pp. 115–16.
14. Murdock, *Social Structure*, pp. 7–8.
15. Lebeuf, 'The Role of Women', p. 23.
16. Adapted from George P. Murdock, 'Comparative Data on the Division of Labour by Sex', p. 552.

17. Turnbull, *Wayward Servants*, p. 129.
18. Dubois, *People of Alor*, p. 109, p. 30.
19. Roth, *The Aborigines of Tasmania*, p. 100.
20. ibid., pp. 102–3.
21. Cited in Seligman, *Races of Africa*, p. 74.
22. Laffin, *Women in Battle*, p. 11.
23. Forde, *Habitat, Economy and Society*, pp. 293–4.
24. Boserup, *Woman's Role in Economic Development*, p. 17, pp. 20–22.
25. Albert, 'Women in Burundi', p. 200.
26. ibid., p. 192.
27. Albert, 'The Roles of Women', pp. 109–10.
28. Paulme, *Women of Tropical Africa*, pp. 7–8.
29. Quoted in Davidoff, *The Employment of Married Women*, p. 44.
30. Wagley, 'Economics of a Guatemalan Village', pp. 25–6.
31. Lévi-Strauss, *World on the Wane*, p. 273, pp. 267–8.
32. Parsons, 'The American Family', p. 22.
33. ibid., p. 23.
34. ibid.
35. Zelditch, 'Role Differentiation in the Nuclear Family', p. 312, p. 309.
36. ibid., p. 312.
37. See Bales and Slater, 'Role Differentiation in Small Decision-Making Groups'.

Chapter Eight. Myths of Woman's Place: 2 Motherhood

1. Tiger and Fox, *The Imperial Animal*, p. 56, p. 64.
2. Erikson, 'Inner and Outer Space', p. 18.
3. Lidz, *The Person*, p. 443.
4. ibid., p. 93.
5. Freud, *An Outline of Psychoanalysis*, p. 50.
6. Lundberg and Farnham, *Modern Woman*, p. 122.
7. *The Times*, 28 September 1970.
8. Rabban, 'Sex-Role Identification', p. 131.
9. Hartley, 'A Developmental View of Female Sex-Role Identification', p. 355.
10. Parker, *In No Man's Land*, p. 57.
11. Joseph, 'Attitudes to Work and Marriage', p. 183.
12. Lomas, 'The Study of Family Relationships', p. 15.
13. Mead, *Male and Female*, p. 97, p. 150.
14. Mead and Newton, 'Cultural Patterning of Perinatal Behaviour' p. 184.
15. Davie, *From Birth to Seven*, p. 72.

16. Quoted ibid.
17. Rainwater *et al.*, *Workingman's Wife*, p. 89.
18. Holman, 'Unsupported Mothers', pp. 776–7.
19. *The Times*, 19 February 1971.
20. Quoted in Tanner and Inhelder, *Discussions on Child Development*, vol. I, p. 227.
21. Rainwater *et al.*, *Workingman's Wife*, p. 88.
22. Kelsall, *Graduates*, pp. 147–8.
23. Rossi, 'Barriers to the Career Choice of Engineering, Medicine or Science', p. 81.
24. Erikson, 'Inner and Outer Space', p. 18.
25. *British Medical Journal*, 2 April 1966, p. 852.
26. *Guardian*, 28 June 1972.
27. Tomkins, 'The Biopsychosociality of the Family', p. 214.
28. Hampson and Hampson, 'The Ontogenesis of Sexual Behaviour in Man', p. 1421.
29. Tomkins, 'The Biopsychosociality of the Family', p. 127.
30. *Lancet*, 12 March 1955, p. 575.
31. Harlow and Harlow, 'The Effect of Rearing Conditions on Behaviour', p. 171.
32. Gil, *Violence Against Children*, p. 32.
33. A mother reported in the *Guardian*, 26 April 1972.
34. A mother reported in *The Times*, 24 June 1970.
35. Rutter, *Maternal Deprivation Reassessed*, pp. 16–17.
36. *The Times*, 8 December 1972.
37. Rapoport and Rapoport, *Dual-Career Families*, p. 288.
38. *The Times*, 17 May 1972.
39. ibid., 12 February 1971.
40. Flint, *The Child and the Institution*, p. 15.
41. Quoted in Tanner and Inhelder, *Discussions on Child Development*, vol. II, p. 225.
42. Bowlby, *Child Care and the Growth of Love*, p. 11.
43. Quoted in Tanner and Inhelder, *Discussions on Child Development*, vol. I, pp. 26–7.
44. *Guardian*, 7 September 1972.
45. Mead, 'Some Theoretical Considerations on the Problem of Mother–Child Separation', p. 447.
46. Burchinal, 'Personality Characteristics of Children', p. 120.
47. West, *Present Conduct and Future Delinquency*, p. 66.
48. Sharp and Nye, 'Maternal Mental Health', p. 324; Feld, 'Feelings of Adjustment', p. 357.
49. Nye, 'Adjustment of the Mother', p. 392.

50. Hampson and Hampson, 'The Ontogenesis of Sexual Behaviour in Man', p. 1469.

51. Schaffer, 'Some Issues for Research', p. 187.

52. ibid., p. 197.

53. Mead, *Coming of Age in Samoa*, p. 160.

54. See Bettelheim, *The Children of the Dream*, chapters 5 and 6.

55. ibid., p. 271.

56. Slater, *The Pursuit of Loneliness*, p. 69.

57. *The Times*, 24 June 1970.

58. *Guardian*, 26 April 1972.

59. Steele and Pollock, 'A Psychiatric Study of Parents Who Abuse Infants', p. 11.

60. This quotation comes from a passage of Gilman's book included in the anthology edited by Salper, *Female Liberation*, (p. 113).

61. Gil, *Violence Against Children*, p. 30.

62. Johnson and Medinnus, *Child Psychology*, pp. 302–3.

63. Andrewski, 'The Baby as Dictator', p. 907.

64. Mill, *On Liberty*, quoted in Sampson, *The Psychology of Power*, p. 100.

65. Gail, 'The Housewife', p. 153.

66. Parker, *In No Man's Land*, p. 141.

67. Levy, *Maternal Overprotection*, p. 38.

Chapter Nine. Breaking the Circle

1. Quoted in an early feminist work. I have been unable to find the exact source of this quotation in Lenin's writings.

2. Hollingsworth, 'Differential Actions Upon the Sexes', pp. 194–6.

3. Myers, 'Who Are Your Motivated Workers?', p. 73.

4. Lodahl, 'Patterns of Job Attitudes', p. 512.

5. Myers, 'Who Are Your Motivated Workers?', pp. 82–3.

6. ibid., p. 83.

7. Lodahl, 'Patterns of Job Attitudes', p. 486.

8. *Evening Standard*, 22 January 1973.

9. *Shrew*, December 1971, p. 11.

10. Rathbone, *The Disinherited Family*, p. 65.

11. *Shrew*, June 1972, p. 8.

12. Fox, *A Sociology of Work*, p. 78.

13. Haavio-Mannila, 'Satisfaction with Family, Work, Leisure and Life', p. 597.

14. Blauner, *Alienation and Freedom*, p. 176.

15. Balint, *Treatment or Diagnosis*, p. 176.

16. Hacker, 'Women as a Minority Group', p. 64.

17. Peckham Rye Group, *A Woman's Work is Never Done*, p. 5.

18. Moss, 'Sex, Age and State as Determinants of Mother-Infant Interaction', p. 300.

19. Bandura and Huston, 'Identification as a Process of Incidental Learning', p. 384.

20. Hoffman, 'Parental Power Relations and the Division of Household Tasks', p. 230.

21. Geiger, *The Family in Soviet Russia*, p. 184.

22. Mainardi, 'The Politics of Housework', pp. 448–9.

List of Sources

This list is not intended to be a comprehensive bibliography. It represents the sources consulted in the writing of this book. However, I have put an asterisk by those which are most interesting for the general reader who wishes to read further on the topic of women.

Anthropology

ALBERT, ETHEL M.: 'The Roles of Women: A Question of Values' in Seymour M. Farber and Roger H. L. Wilson (eds.), *The Potential of Women*, McGraw-Hill, New York, 1963.

'Women of Burundi: A Study of Social Values' in Paulme, 1963.

ARDENER, EDWIN: 'Belief and the Problem of Women' in J. S. La Fontaine (ed.), *The Interpretation of Ritual*, Tavistock Publications, London, 1972; Barnes & Noble, New York, 1972.

ARDREY, ROBERT: *African Genesis*, Fontana Books, London, 1961; Atheneum, New York, 1961.

*BOSERUP, ESTER: *Woman's Role in Economic Development*, Allen & Unwin, London, 1970; St. Martin's Press, New York, 1970.

DOUGLAS, MARY: 'The Lele of Kasai' in Daryll Forde (ed.), *African Worlds*, University Press, Oxford, 1954; Oxford University Press, New York, 1954 (paperback).

DUBOIS, CORA: *People of Alor*, University of Minnesota Press, Minneapolis, 1944.

*FORD, C. S.: *A Comparative Study of Human Reproduction*, Yale University Press, New Haven, 1945.

FORD, C. S. and BEACH, F. A.: *Patterns of Sexual Behaviour*, Methuen, London, 1965; Harper & Row, New York, 1951.

FORDE, DARYLL: *Habitat, Economy and Society*, Methuen, London, 1957; E. P. Dutton, New York, 1950.

HERSKOVITZ, MELVILLE J.: *Dahomey: An Ancient West African Kingdom*, Northwestern University Press, Evanston, 1967.

KABERRY, PHYLLIS: *Women of the Grassfields,* H.M.S.O., London, 1952; 2nd ed., Humanities Press, New York, 1968.

KÜRTEN, BJÖRN: *Not From the Apes,* Gollancz, London, 1972; Pantheon Books, New York, 1971.

LAFFIN, JOHN: *Women in Battle,* Abelard-Schuman, London, 1967; Abelard-Schuman, New York, 1968.

LEACH, E. R.: 'Culture and Nature or *La Femme Sauvage*', The Stevenson Lecture, November 1968, Bedford College, University of London.

LEBEUF, ANNIE D.: 'The Role of Women in the Political Organisation of African Societies' in Paulme, 1963.

LÉVI-STRAUSS, C.: *World on the Wane,* Hutchinson, London, 1961.

MAIR, LUCY: *An Introduction to Social Anthropology,* Clarendon Press, Oxford, 1965; Oxford University Press, New York, 1965.

MALINOWSKI, BRONISLAW: *Magic, Science and Religion,* Doubleday, New York, 1954.

MEAD, MARGARET: *Coming of Age in Samoa,* Penguin Books, Harmondsworth, 1943; William Morrow, New York, 1928.
Male and Female, Penguin Books, Harmondsworth, 1962; William Morrow, New York, 1949.

*MORGAN, ELAINE: *The Descent of Woman,* Souvenir Press, London, 1972; Stein & Day, New York, 1972.

MORRIS, DESMOND: *The Naked Ape,* Corgi, London, 1968; McGraw-Hill, New York, 1968.

MURDOCK, GEORGE P.: 'Comparative Data on the Division of Labour by Sex', *Social Forces,* 1937, pp. 551–3.
Social Structure, Free Press, New York, 1965.

*PAULME, DENISE (ed.): *Women of Tropical Africa,* Routledge & Kegan Paul, London, 1963; University of California Press, Berkeley, 1963.

ROTH, H. LING: *The Aborigines of Tasmania,* F. King & Son, Halifax, 1899; 3rd ed., Humanities Press, New York, 1969, reprint of 1899 ed.

SELIGMAN, G.: *Races of Africa,* Thornton Butterworth Ltd., London, 1930; Holt, New York, 1931.

TIGER, LIONEL: *Men in Groups,* Random House, New York, 1969.

TIGER, LIONEL and FOX, ROBIN: *The Imperial Animal,* Secker & Warburg, London, 1972; Holt, Rinehart & Winston, New York, 1971.

TURNBULL, COLIN: *Wayward Servants,* Eyre & Spottiswoode, London, 1965; Doubleday, New York, 1965.

WAGLEY, C.: 'Economics of a Guatemalan Village', *Supplement to the American Anthropologist,* 1941.

WHITING, BEATRICE (ed.): *Six Cultures: Studies of Childrearing,* John Wiley, New York, 1963.

Education

Department of Education and Science: *Statistics of Education 1970,* Volume 1, 'Schools' (1971); Volume 4, 'Teachers' (1972) and Volume 6, 'Universities' (1973).

GINZBERG, ELI, *et al.*: *Life Styles of Educated Women,* Columbia University Press, New York, 1966.

HAVEMANN, ERNEST and WEST, PATRICIA SALTER: *They Went to College,* Harcourt Brace, New York, 1952.

KAMM, JOSEPHINE: *Hope Deferred: Girls' Education in English History,* Methuen, London, 1965.

KELSALL, R. K., POOLE, ANNE and KUHN, ANNETTE: *Graduates: The Sociology of an Elite,* Methuen, London, 1972; Barnes & Noble, New York, 1972.

*KOMAROVSKY, MIRRA: *Women in the Modern World: Their Education and Dilemmas,* Little, Brown & Co., Boston, 1953.

NEWCOMER, MABEL: *A Century of Higher Education for American Women,* Harper, New York, 1959.

Robbins Committee Report: *Higher Education,* H.M.S.O., London, 1963.

TIMBURY, MORAG C. and TIMBURY G. C.: 'Glasgow Women Medical Students: Some Facts and Figures', *British Medical Journal,* 24 July 1971.

Employment

BELLE, E. MOBERLY: *Storming the Citadel: The Rise of the Woman Doctor,* Constable, London, 1953.

*BENET, MARY KATHLEEN: *Secretary: An Enquiry into the Female Ghetto,* Sidgwick & Jackson, London, 1972; *The Secretarial Ghetto,* McGraw-Hill, New York, 1973.

BLAUNER, ROBERT: *Alienation and Freedom: The Factory Worker and his Industry,* Phoenix Books, 1967; University of Chicago Press, Chicago, 1964.

DAVIDOFF, LEONORE: *The Employment of Married Women in England 1850–1950,* Unpublished M.A. thesis, University of London, 1956.

*EPSTEIN, CYNTHIA FUCHS: *Woman's Place: Options and Limits in Professional Careers,* University of California Press, Berkeley, 1970.

ETZKOWITZ, HENRY: 'The Male Sister: Sexual Separation of Labour in Society', *Journal of Marriage and the Family,* 1971, pp. 431–4.

Fawcett Society: *Women in a Changing World,* Report of a conference held at the Livery Hall, Guildhall, London, April 1967.

FOGARTY, MICHAEL P., RAPOPORT, RHONA and RAPOPORT, ROBERT N.: *Sex, Career and Family,* Allen & Unwin, London, 1971; Sage Publications, Beverly Hills, Calif., 1971.

Women and Top Jobs, Allen & Unwin, London, 1971; Fernhill House, New York, 1971.

FOX, ALAN: *A Sociology of Work in Industry,* Collier-Macmillan, London, 1971; Macmillan, New York, 1971.

General Register Office: *Census 1961 England and Wales,* Socio-Economic Tables, H.M.S.O., London.

Sample Census 1966 England and Wales, Summary Tables and Economic Activity Tables, H.M.S.O., London.

GROSS, EDWARD: '*Plus ça Change* . . . The Sexual Structure of Occupations Over Time', *Social Problems,* 1968.

HAAVIO-MANNILA, ELINA: 'Satisfaction with Family, Work, Leisure and Life Among Men and Women', *Human Relations,* 1971, pp. 585–601.

HANNA, MAX: 'The Typecast Third', *New Society,* 1 February 1973.

HUNT, AUDREY: *A Survey of Women's Employment,* Government Social Survey, H.M.S.O., London, 1968.

KINGSTON, N. and WOLFE, P. D.: *Graduates in Industry,* British Institute of Management, 1972.

*KLEIN, VIOLA: *Britain's Married Women Workers,* Routledge & Kegan Paul, London, 1965; Fernhill House, New York, 1965.

Labour Party: *Discrimination Against Women* (Opposition Green Paper), Transport House, London, 1972.

LLOYD, LEONORA: *Women Workers in Britain,* Socialist Women Publications, 1972.

LODAHL, THOMAS M.: 'Patterns of Job Attitudes in Two Assembly Technologies', *Administrative Science Quarterly,* 1964, pp. 482–519.

MYERS, M. SCOTT: 'Who Are Your Motivated Workers?', *Harvard Business Review,* 1964, pp. 73–88.

National Manpower Council: *Womanpower,* Columbia University Press, New York, 1957.

*PATAI, RAPHAEL (ed.): *Women in the Modern World,* Free Press, New York, 1967.

POLOMA, MARGARET M. and GARLAND, T. NEAL: 'The Married Professional Woman: A Study in the Tolerance of Domestication', *Journal of Marriage and the Family,* 1971, pp. 531–9.

ROSSI, ALICE S.: 'Barriers to the Career Choice of Engineering, Medicine or Science Among American Women', in Jacquelyn A. Mattfield and Carol G. Van Aken (eds.), *Women and the Scientific Professions,* M.I.T. Press, Cambridge, Mass., 1965.

SULLEROT, EVELYNE: *Historie et sociologie du travail féminin,* Gonthier, Paris, 1968.

TITMUSS, RICHARD M.: Foreword to Pearl Jephcott, *Married Women Working,* Allen & Unwin, London, 1962; Humanities Press, New York, 1963.

WILD, RAY and HILL, A. B.: *Women in the Factory,* Institute of Personnel Management, 1970.

WOMEN'S BUREAU, DEPARTMENT OF LABOR, CANADA: *Women in the Labor Force in Nine Countries of Europe,* 1962.

The Family

ABEGGLEN, J. C.: *The Japanese Factory,* Free Press, Glencoe, 1958.

BALES, ROBERT F. and SLATER, PHILIP E.: 'Role Differentiation in Small Decision-Making Groups', in Parsons and Bales, 1956.

BLOOD, ROBERT O. and WOLFE, DONALD M.: *Husbands and Wives,* Free Press, New York, 1960.

BOTT, ELIZABETH: *Family and Social Network,* Tavistock Publications, London, 1957 (revised edition, 1971); 2nd ed., Free Press, New York, 1972.

COOPER, DAVID: *The Death of the Family,* Allen Lane, London, 1971; Pantheon Books, New York, 1970.

DENNIS, NORMAN, FERNANDO, HENRIQUES and SLAUGHTER, CLIFFORD: *Coal Is Our Life,* Eyre & Spottiswoode, London, 1956; 2nd ed., Barnes & Noble, New York, 1969.

DICKS, HENRY V.: *Marital Tensions,* Routledge & Kegan Paul, London, 1967; Basic Books, New York, 1967.

*DREITZEL, HANS PETER (ed.): *Family, Marriage and the Struggle of the Sexes,* Macmillan, New York, 1972 (see especially the section on 'Communal Living and the Obsolescence of the Nuclear Family'):

EDWARDS, JOHN N. (ed.): *The Family and Change,* Knopf, New York, 1969.

EHRLICH, CAROL: 'The Male Sociologist's Burden: The Place of Women in Marriage and Family Texts', *Journal of Marriage and the Family,* 1971, pp. 421–30.

FLETCHER, RONALD: *The Family and Marriage,* Penguin Books, Harmondsworth, 1962.

GEIGER, H. KENT: *The Family in Soviet Russia,* Harvard University Press, Cambridge, Mass., 1968.

GEORGE, VICTOR and WILDING, PAUL: *Motherless Families,* Routledge & Kegan Paul, London and Boston, 1972.

GIL, DAVID G.: *Violence Against Children: Physical Child Abuse in the United States,* Harvard University Press, Cambridge, Mass., 1970.

HARRIS, C. C.: *The Family*, Allen & Unwin, London, 1969; Praeger, New York, 1970.

HOFFMAN, LOIS W.: 'Parental Power Relations and the Division of Household Tasks', in F. Ivan Nye and Lois W. Hoffman (eds.), *The Employed Mother in America*, Rand McNally, Chicago, 1963.

KESSEN, WILLIAM: *The Child*, John Wiley, New York, 1965.

KLEIN, JOSEPHINE: *Samples From English Cultures*, Routledge & Kegan Paul, London, 1965; Humanities Press, New York, 1965; vol. I (especially chap. 4 'Aspects of Traditional Working Class Life').

*KOMAROVSKY, MIRRA: *Blue-Collar Marriage*, Vintage Books, New York, 1967.

LAWS, JUDITH LONG: 'A Feminist Review of the Marital Adjustment Literature: The Rape of the Locke', *Journal of Marriage and the Family*, 1971, pp. 483–516.

MEAD, MARGARET: 'The Contemporary American Family as an Anthropologist Sees It', in Judson T. Landis and Mary G. Landis (eds.), *Readings in Marriage and the Family*, Prentice-Hall, New Jersey, 1953.

MEAD, MARGARET and WOLFENSTEIN, MARTHA (eds.): *Childhood in Contemporary Cultures*, University of Chicago Press, Chicago, 1955.

MOORE, BARRINGTON JR.: 'Thoughts on the Future of the Family', in Edwards, 1969.

OAKLEY, ANN: 'Are Husbands Good Housewives?', *New Society*, 17 February 1972.

'The Family, Marriage and its Relationship to Illness', in David Tuckett (ed.), *The Sociology of Medicine*, Tavistock Publications, London (forthcoming).

PARSONS, TALCOTT: 'Age and Sex in the Social Structure of the United States', *American Sociological Review*, 1942, pp. 604–16.

'The Social Structure of the Family', in Ruth N. Ashen (ed.), *The Family: Its Function and Destiny*, Harper, New York, 1949.

'The American Family: Its Relations to Personality and the Social Structure', in Parsons and Bales, 1956.

PARSONS, TALCOTT and BALES, ROBERT F.: *Family: Socialization and Interaction Process*, Routledge & Kegan Paul, London, 1956; Free Press, New York, 1955.

RAINWATER, LEE, COLEMAN, RICHARD P. and HANDEL, GERALD: *Workingman's Wife*, Oceana Publications, New York, 1959.

*RAPOPORT, RHONA and RAPOPORT, ROBERT: *Dual-Career Families*, Penguin Books, Harmondsworth, 1971.

'Work and Family in Contemporary Society', in Edwards, 1969.

*SLATER, PHILIP E.: *The Pursuit of Loneliness: American Culture at the Breaking Point*, Beacon Press, Boston, 1970.

STEELE, BRANDT F. and POLLOCK, CARL B.: 'A Psychiatric Study of Parents Who Abuse Infants and Small Children', in Ray E. Helfer and C. Henry Kampe (eds.), *The Battered Child*, University of Chicago Press, Chicago, 1968.

TUNSTALL, JEREMY: *The Fishermen*, MacGibbon & Kee, London, 1962.

VARGA, ROBERT: 'Dilemmas of a Househusband', *Saturday Review of Literature*, 2 January 1965.

WINNICOTT, D. W.: *The Child, the Family and the Outside World*, Penguin Books, Harmondsworth, 1964.

ZELDITCH, MORRIS: 'Role Differentiation in the Nuclear Family', in Parsons and Bales, 1956.

Feminism

BRITTAIN, VERA: *Lady Into Woman*, Andrew Dakers, London, 1953.

*JANEWAY, ELIZABETH: *Man's World: Woman's Place*, Michael Joseph, London, 1971; William Morrow, New York, 1971.

KOCK, ADRIENNE: 'Two Cheers for Equality', in Seymour M. Farber and Roger H. L. Wilson (eds.), *The Potential of Women*, McGraw-Hill, New York, 1963.

*MILLETT, KATE: *Sexual Politics*, Rupert Hart-Davis, London, 1972; Doubleday, New York, 1970.

*MITCHELL, JULIET: *Woman's Estate*, Penguin Books, Harmondsworth, 1971; Pantheon Books, New York, 1972.

*RATHBONE, ELEANOR F.: *The Disinherited Family: A Plea for the Endowment of the Family*, Edward Arnold, London, 1924.

*ROSSI, ALICE S.: 'Equality Between the Sexes: An Immodest Proposal', in R. J. Lifton (ed.), *The Woman in America*, Houghton Mifflin, Boston, 1965.

SALPER, ROBERTA (ed.): *Female Liberation*, Knopf, New York, 1972.

SCHREINER, OLIVE: *Woman and Labour*, T. Fisher Unwin, London, 1911; 5th ed., Johnson Reprint Corp. (subs. of Academic Press), New York, 1971, reprint of 1911 ed.

General Sociology

BANTON, MICHAEL: *Roles*, Tavistock Publications, London, 1965; Basic Books, New York, 1965.

BERGER, PETER L. and LUCKMANN, THOMAS: *The Social Construction of Reality*, Allen Lane, London, 1966; Doubleday, New York, 1966.

GENERAL REGISTER OFFICE: *Statistical Review of England and Wales 1970,* Part II, Population Tables, H.M.S.O., London, 1972.

RYDER, JUDITH and SILVER, HAROLD: *Modern English Society,* Methuen, London, 1970; Barnes & Noble, New York, 1970.

WELLS, ALAN: *Social Institutions,* Heinemann, London, 1970; Basic Books, New York, 1971.

WILLIAMS, ROBIN M.: *American Society: A Sociological Interpretation,* Knopf, New York, 1970.

History

*ARIES, PHILIPPE: *Centuries of Childhood,* Jonathan Cape, London, 1962; Knopf, New York, 1962.

ASHTON, T. S.: *The Industrial Revolution,* University Press, Oxford, 1948; Oxford University Press, New York, 1957.

*BAKER, ELIZABETH FAULKNER: *Technology and Women's Work,* Columbia University Press, New York, 1964.

BANDEL, BETTY: 'The English Chroniclers' Attitude Toward Women', *Journal of the History of Ideas,* 1955, pp. 113–18.

BEALES, H. L.: *The Industrial Revolution 1750–1850,* Frank Cass, London, 1958; 2nd ed., Augustus M. Kelley, New York, 1958, reprint of 1928 ed.

BEARD, MARY R.: *Woman as Force in History: A Study in Traditions and Realities,* Macmillan, New York, 1946.

CHECKLAND, S. G.: *The Rise of Industrial Society in England 1815–1885,* Longmans, London, 1964; St. Martin's Press, New York, 1965.

*CLARK, ALICE: *The Working Life of Women in the Seventeenth Century,* G. Routledge & Sons, London, 1919 (reissued by Frank Cass, 1968); Augustus M. Kelley, New York, 1967, reissue of 1911 ed.

COLE, G. D. H. and POSTGATE, RAYMOND: *The Common People 1746–1946,* Methuen, London, 1961; Barnes & Noble, New York, 1961.

COULTON, G. C.: *Medieval Panorama: The English Scene from Conquest to Reformation,* University Press, Cambridge, 1938; Macmillan, New York, 1938.

*CROW, DUNCAN: *The Victorian Woman,* Allen & Unwin, London, 1971; Stein & Day, New York, 1972.

ENGELS, FREDERICK: *The Condition of the Working Class in England in 1844,* Allen & Unwin, London, 1952.

GEORGE, DOROTHY: *London Life in the Eighteenth Century,* Kegan Paul, Trench, Trubner & Co., London, 1925; Knopf, New York, 1925.

HAMILTON, HENRY: *History of the Homeland,* Allen & Unwin, London, 1965; Humanities Press, New York, 1947.

HAMMOND, J. L. and HAMMOND, BARBARA: *The Town Labourer 1760–1832,* Longmans, Green & Co., London, 1919; Augustus M. Kelley, New York, 1973, reprint of 1917 ed.
Lord Shaftesbury, Penguin Books, Harmondsworth, 1939; Shoe String Press, Hamden, Conn., 1969, reprint of 1936 ed.

*HEWITT, MARGARET: *Wives and Mothers in Victorian Industry,* Rockcliff, London, 1958.

HILL, GEORGIANA: *Women in English Life from Medieval to Modern Times,* Richard Bentley & Sons, London, 1896.

HUTCHINS, B. L.: *Women in Modern Industry,* G. Bell & Sons, London, 1915; Macmillan, New York, 1915.

KLEIN, VIOLA: 'The Emancipation of Women: Its Motives and Achievements', in H. Grisewood (ed.), *Ideas and Beliefs of the Victorians,* Sylvan Press, London, 1949; E. P. Dutton, New York, n.d.

KUCZYNSKI, JÜRGEN: *A Short History of Labour Conditions in Great Britain 1750 to the Present Day,* Frederick Müller, London, 1942; Barnes & Noble, 1972, reprint of 1944 ed.

LASLETT, PETER: *The World We Have Lost,* Methuen, London, 1965; Charles Scribner's Sons, New York, 1966.

MACFARLANE, ALAN: *The Family Life of Ralph Josselin; A Seventeenth-Century Clergyman,* University Press, Cambridge, 1970.

MCGREGOR, O. R.: 'The Social Position of Women in England 1850–1914: A Bibliography', *British Journal of Sociology,* 1955, pp. 48–60.

*NEFF, WANDA FRAIKEN: *Victorian Working Women,* Allen & Unwin, London, 1929 (reissued by Frank Cass, 1966); Columbia University Press, 1929; reissued by AMS Press, New York, n.d.

NOTTINGHAM, ELIZABETH K.: 'Towards an Analysis of the Effects of Two World Wars on the Role and Status of Middle-Class Women in the English-Speaking World', *American Journal of Sociology,* 1947, pp. 666–75.

PHILLIPS, M. and TOMPKINSON, W. S.: *English Women in Life and Letters,* University Press, Oxford, 1926; reprinted by Benjamin Blom, New York, 1972.

*PINCHBECK, IVY: *Women Workers and the Industrial Revolution 1750–1850,* Routledge & Kegan Paul, London, 1930 (reissued by Frank Cass, 1969); reissued by Augustus M. Kelley, New York, 1971.

*PINCHBECK, IVY and HEWITT, MARGARET: *Children in English Society,* vol. I, 'From Tudor Times to the Eighteenth Century', Routledge & Kegan Paul, London, 1969; University of Toronto Press, Toronto, 1970.

POWELL, CHILTON LATHAM: *English Domestic Relations 1487–1653,* Columbia University Press, New York, 1917; reprinted by Russell & Russell, New York, 1972.

POWER, EILEEN: 'The Position of Women', in G. C. Crump and E. F. Jacob (eds.), *The Legacy of the Middle Ages,* Clarendon Press, Oxford, 1926; Oxford University Press, New York, 1926.

ROGERS, J. E. THOROLD: *Six Centuries of Work and Wages,* W. Swan Sonnenschein & Co., London, 1884; G. P. Putnam's Sons, New York, 1884, vol. 1.

SMELSER, NEIL: *Social Change and the Industrial Revolution,* Routledge & Kegan Paul, London, 1959; University of Chicago Press, Chicago, 1959.

*SMUTS, ROBERT W.: *Women and Work in America,* Columbia University Press, New York, 1959.

*STENTON, DORIS MARY: *The English Woman in History,* Allen & Unwin, London, 1957; Fernhill House, New York, 1957.

STERN, BERNHARD J.: 'The Family and Cultural Change', *American Sociological Review,* 1939, pp. 200–207.

STRACHEY, RAY: 'Changes in Employment', in Ray Strachey (ed.), *Our Freedom and Its Results,* Hogarth Press, London, 1936.

TITMUSS, RICHARD M.: *Problems of Social Policy,* H.M.S.O., London, 1950; reprinted by Greenwood Press, Westport, Conn., 1971.

TONNA, CHARLOTTE: *The Wrongs of Women,* John Taylor & Co., New York, 1844.

TROTTER, ELEANOR: *Seventeenth-Century Life in a Country Parish,* University Press, Cambridge, 1919.

WHITE, CYNTHIA L.: *Women's Magazines 1693–1968,* Michael Joseph, London, 1970; Humanities Press, New York, 1970.

WHITELOCK, DOROTHY: *The Beginnings of English Society,* Penguin Books, Harmondsworth, 1952.

WOMEN'S COOOPERATIVE GUILD: *Maternity: Letters from Working Women,* G. Bell & Sons, London, 1915.

WRIGHT, LOUIS B.: *Middle-Class Culture in Elizabethan England,* Cornell University Press, Ithaca, 1958 (especially chap. 7, 'Instruction in Domestic Relations').

Housework

1. HOUSEWORK HOURS

The following studies give information on housework hours, and figures from them have been used in the table on p. 7.

Rural Studies

(U.S. 1929) UNITED STATES BUREAU OF HOME ECONOMICS SURVEY: cited in Maud Wilson, 'Use of Time by Oregon Farm Homemakers', *Oregon Experiment Station Bulletin*, 256, November, 1929.

(U.S. 1929) ibid.

(U.S. 1956) MAY COWLES and RUTH DIETZ: 'Time Spent in Home-making by a Selected Group of Wisconsin Farm Homemakers', *Journal of Home Economics,* January, 1956.

(France 1959) ALAIN GIRARD: 'Le Budget temps de la femme mariée dans la campagne', *Population,* 1959, pp. 253–84.

Urban Studies

(U.S. 1929) UNITED STATES BUREAU OF HOME ECONOMICS SURVEY: reference as above.

(U.S. 1945) BRYN MAWR: 'Women During the War and After', cited in Myrdal, Alva and Klein, Viola, *Women's Two Roles,* Routledge & Kegan Paul, London, 1956; revised ed., Humanities Press, New York, 1970.

(France 1948) JEAN STOETZEL: 'Une Etude de budget temps de la femme mariée dans les agglomerations urbaines', *Population,* 1948, pp. 47–62.

(Britain 1950) C. A. MOSER: 'Social Research: The Diary Method', *Social Service,* 1950, pp. 80–84.

(Britain 1951) MASS OBSERVATION BULLETIN: 'The Housewife's Day', no. 42 May/June.

(France 1958) ALAIN GIRARD: 'Le Budget temps de la femme mariée dans les agglomerations urbaines', *Population,* 1958, pp. 591–618.

(Britain 1971) ANN OAKLEY: *The Sociology of Housework.*

2. GENERAL

BACKETT, E. MAURICE: *Domestic Accidents,* Public Health Papers 26, World Health Organization, Geneva, 1965.

BRADLEY, ROSE M.: *The English Housewife in the Seventeenth and Eighteenth Centuries,* Edward Arnold, London, 1912.

BURTON, ELAINE: *Domestic Work: Britain's Largest Industry,* Frederick Müller, London, 1944.

DAVIS, DOROTHY: *A History of Shopping,* Routledge & Kegan Paul, London, 1966; *Fairs, Shops, and Supermarkets,* University of Toronto Press, Toronto, 1966.

DRUMMOND, J. C. and WILBRAHAM, ANNE: *The Englishman's Food: A History of Five Centuries of English Diet,* Jonathan Cape, London, 1939; Albert Saifer, Orange, N.J., 1972.

ELLIOT, DOROTHY M.: 'The Status of Domestic Work in the United Kingdom', *International Labour Review*, 1951, pp. 125–48.

*FRIEDAN, BETTY: *The Feminine Mystique*, Gollancz, London, 1963; W. W. Norton, New York, 1963 (especially chap. 3, 'House-wifery Expands to Fill the Time Available').

*GAIL, SUZANNE: 'The Housewife': in Ronald Fraser (ed.), *Work: Twenty Personal Accounts*, Penguin Books, Harmondsworth, 1968.

GAVRON, HANNAH: *The Captive Wife*, Penguin Books, Harmondsworth, 1966; Humanities Press, New York, 1966.

HECHT, J. JEAN: *The Domestic Servant Class in Eighteenth-Century England*, Routledge & Kegan Paul, London, 1956; Fernhill House, New York, 1956.

LOPATA, HELEN Z.: *Occupation: Housewife*, Oxford University Press, New York, 1971.

*MAINARDI, PAT: 'The Politics of Housework', in Robin Morgan (ed.), *Sisterhood Is Powerful*, Vintage Books, New York, 1970.

MARSHALL, DOROTHY: *The English Domestic Servant in History*, Historical Association Pamphlet, 1949.

*OAKLEY, ANN: *The Sociology of Housework*, Martin Robertson, London, in press.

PECKHAM RYE WOMEN'S LIBERATION GROUP: *A Woman's Work Is Never Done*, Agitprop, 1970.

REEVES, MRS PEMBER: *Round About a Pound a Week*, G. Bell & Sons, London, 1913; Augustus M. Kelley, New York, 1972, reprint of 1913 ed.

*RICE, MARGERY SPRING: *Working-Class Wives*, Penguin Books, Harmondsworth, 1939.

3. DOMESTIC ARCHITECTURE

BARLEY, M. W.: *The English Farmhouse and Cottage*, Routledge & Kegan Paul, London, 1961; Hillary House, New York, 1962.

BAYNE-POWELL, ROSAMOND: *Housekeeping in the Eighteenth Century*, John Murray, 1956.

BRAUN, HUGH: *Old English Houses*, Faber & Faber, London, 1962; Lawrence Verry, Mystic, Conn., 1962.

CHAPMAN, DENNIS: *The Home and Social Status*, Routledge & Kegan Paul, London, 1955; Grove Press, New York, 1955.

HENDERSON, ANDREW: *The Family House in England*, Phoenix House, London, 1964; Lawrence Verry, Mystic, Conn., 1964.

Motherhood

ANDREWSKI, IRIS: 'The Baby as Dictator', *New Society*, 15 December 1966.

BANDURA, ALBERT and HUSTON, ALETHA C.: 'Identification as a Process of Incidental Learning', in Thomas D. Spencer and Norman Kass (eds.), *Perspectives in Child Psychology*, McGraw-Hill, London and New York, 1970.

BURCHINAL, LEE: 'Personality Characteristics of Children', in Nye and Hoffman, 1963.

DAVIE, RONALD, BUTLER, NEVILLE and GOLDSTEIN, HARVEY: *From Birth to Seven: A Report of the National Child Development Study*, Longman, London, 1972; Humanities Press, New York, 1972.

FELD, SHEILA: 'Feelings of Adjustment', in Nye and Hoffman, 1963.

HOLMAN, ROBERT: 'Unsupported Mothers', *New Society*, 29 October 1970.

ILLSLEY, RAYMOND: 'The Sociological Study of Reproduction and Its Outcome' in Richardson and Guttmacher, 1967.

LEVY, DAVID: *Maternal Overprotection*, Columbia University Press, New York, 1943.

LOUGHTON, MARY: 'The Young Mothers', *New Society*, 11 September 1969.

MEAD, MARGARET: 'Some Theoretical Considerations on the Problem of Mother–Child Separation', *American Journal of Orthopsychiatry*, 1954, pp. 471–81.

MEAD, MARGARET and NEWTON, NILES: 'Cultural Patterning of Perinatal Behaviour', in Richardson and Guttmacher, 1967.

MINTURN, L. and LAMBERT W. W.: *Mothers of Six Cultures: Antecedents of Childrearing*, John Wiley, New York, 1964.

MOSS, H. A.: 'Sex, Age and State as Determinants of Mother–Infant Interaction', in K. Danziger (ed.), *Readings in Child Socialization*, Pergamon Press, Oxford, 1970; Pergamon Press, Elmsford, N.Y., 1970.

NYE, F. IVAN: 'Adjustment of the Mother: Summary and a Frame of Reference', in Nye and Hoffman, 1963.

NYE, F. IVAN and HOFFMAN, LOIS W. (eds.): *The Employed Mother in America*, Rand McNalley, Chicago, 1963.

OAKLEY, ANN: 'The Myth of Motherhood', *New Society*, 26 February 1970.

PARKER, TONY: *In No Man's Land*, Panther Books, London, 1972; Harper & Row, New York, 1972.

*RICHARDSON, STEPHEN A. and GUTTMACHER, ALAN F. (eds.): *Child-bearing: Its Social and Psychological Aspects,* Williams & Wilkins, Baltimore, 1967.

*RUTTER, MICHAEL: *Maternal Deprivation Reassessed,* Penguin Books, Harmondsworth and Baltimore, 1972.

SEGLOW, JEAN, PRINGLE, MIA KELLMER and WEDGE, PETER: *Growing Up Adopted,* National Foundation for Educational Research, 1972; Fernhill House, New York, 1972.

SHARP, LAWRENCE J. and NYE, F. IVAN: 'Maternal Mental Health', in Nye and Hoffman, 1963.

TOMKINS, SILVAN S.: 'The Biopsychosociality of the Family', in Ansley J. Coale, Lloyd A. Fallers, Marion J. Levy, David M. Schneider, Silvan S. Tomkins (eds.), *Aspects of the Analysis of Family Structure,* Princeton University Press, Princeton, 1965.

YUDKIN, SIMON and HOLME, ANTHEA: *Working Mothers and Their Children,* Sphere Books, 1969.

A GROUP OF STUDIES ON INDUCED LACTATION

GREENWAY, P. J.: 'Artificially Induced Lactation in Humans', *East African Medical Journal,* 1939, p. 346.

MEAD, MARGARET and NEWTON, NILES: 'Cultural Patterning of Perinatal Behaviour' (p. 143) in Richardson and Guttmacher, 1967.

PLOSS, H. and BARTELS, M.: *Das Weib,* 8th edition, Leipzig, 1905.

RAPHAEL, DANA: *The Tender Gift: Breastfeeding,* Prentice-Hall, 1973 (chap. 9, 'Breastfeeding of the Adopted Child').

WIESCHOFF, H. A.: 'Artificial Stimulation of Lactation in Primitive Cultures', *Bulletin of the History of Medicine,* 1940, pp. 1403–15.

SOME ANIMAL STUDIES INTERESTING ON THE MATERNAL ROLE

HARLOW, HARRY F.: 'Sexual Behavior in the Rhesus Monkey', in Frank A. Beach (ed.), *Sex and Behavior,* John Wiley, New York, 1965.

HARLOW, HARRY F. and HARLOW, MARGARET K.: 'Social Deprivation in Monkeys', *Scientific American,* 207, 1962.

'The Effect of Rearing Conditions on Behavior' in John Money (ed.), *Sex Research: New Developments,* Holt, Rinehart & Winston, New York, 1965.

HARLOW, HARRY F., HARLOW, MARGARET K., and HANSEN, E. W.: 'The Maternal Affectional System in Monkeys', in Harriet L. Rheingold (ed.), *Maternal Behavior in Mammals,* John Wiley, New York, 1963.

ITANI, JUNCHIRO: 'Paternal Care in the Wild Japanese Monkey', *Journal of Primatology,* 1959, pp. 61–87.

KUMMER, HANS: *Social Organisation of Hamadryas Baboons: A Field Study,* University of Chicago Press, Chicago, 1968.

MCQUEEN-WILLIAMS, M.: 'Maternal Behavior in Male Rats', *Science,* no. 82, 1935.

WIESNER, B. P. and SHEARD, N. M.: *Maternal Behaviour in the Rat,* Oliver & Boyd, London, 1935.

Psychology

*AINSWORTH, MARY D., et al.: *Deprivation of Maternal Care: A Reassessment of its Effects* (published with John Bowlby, *Maternal Care and Mental Health*), Schocken Books, New York, 1966.

ANDRY, ROBERT G.: *Delinquency and Parental Pathology,* Methuen, London, 1960; 2nd ed., Charles C. Thomas, Springfield, Ill., 1972.

BALINT, MICHAEL, *et al.*: *Treatment or Diagnosis: A Study of Repeat Prescriptions in General Practice,* Tavistock Publications, London, 1970; J. B. Lippincott, Philadelphia, 1970.

BOWLBY, JOHN: *Forty-Four Juvenile Thieves: Their Characters and Home Life,* Baillière, Tindall & Cox, London, 1946.

    Child Care and the Growth of Love, Penguin Books, Harmondsworth and Baltimore, 1953.

    Attachment and Loss: I Attachment, Hogarth Press, London, 1969; Basic Books, New York, 1969.

ERIKSON, ERIK: 'Inner and Outer Space: Reflections on Womanhood', in R. J. Lifton (ed.), *The Woman in America,* Houghton Mifflin, Boston, 1965.

FLINT, BETTY M.: *The Child and the Institution,* University of London Press, London, 1967; University of Toronto Press, Toronto, 1966.

FOSS, B. M. (ed.): *Determinants of Infant Behaviour,* 4 vols., Methuen, London, 1961, 1963, 1965, 1969; Barnes & Noble, New York, same dates.

FREUD, SIGMUND: *An Outline of Psychoanalysis,* trans. James Strachey, Hogarth Press, London, 1969; W. W. Norton, New York, 1970.

HOLLINGSWORTH, LETA S.: 'Differential Actions upon the Sexes of Forces Which Tend to Segregate the Feebleminded', in James J. Jenkins and Donald G. Patterson (eds.), *Studies in Individual Differences,* Methuen, London, 1961; Appleton-Century-Crofts, New York, 1961. (The Hollingsworth article was originally published in 1922.)

JOHNSON, RONALD C. and MEDINNUS, GENE R.: *Child Psychology,* John Wiley, New York, 1965.

LIDZ, THEODORE: *The Person: His Development Throughout the Life Cycle,* Basic Books, New York, 1968.

*LOMAS, PETER: 'The Study of Family Relationships in Contemporary Society', in Peter Lomas (ed.), *The Predicament of the Family*, Hogarth Press, London, 1967; International Universities Press, New York, 1967.

LUNDBERG, FERDINAND and FARNHAM, MARYNIA F.: *Modern Woman: The Lost Sex*, Harper and Bros, New York, 1947.

RIBBLE, MARGARET: *The Rights of Infants*, Columbia University Press, New York, 1943.

*SAMPSON, R. V.: *The Psychology of Power*, Pantheon, New York, 1966.

SCHAFFER, H. R.: 'Some Issues for Research in the Study of Attachment Behaviour', in B. M. Foss, vol. II, 1963.

TANNER, J. M. and INHELDER, BARBEL (eds.): *Discussions on Child Development*, 4 vols., Tavistock Publications, London, 1956, 1956, 1958, 1960; International Universities Press, New York, 1971.

UNITED STATES DEPARTMENT OF HEALTH, EDUCATION AND WELFARE: National Center for Health Statistics, series II, number 37, August 1970, *Selected Symptoms of Psychological Stress*.

WEST, D. J.: *Present Conduct and Future Delinquency*, Heinemann, London, 1969; International Universities Press, New York, 1969.

Social Welfare

DEPARTMENT OF HEALTH AND SOCIAL SECURITY: *Cohabitation: The Administration of the Relevant Provisions of the Ministry of Social Security Act 1966*, Report by the Supplementary Benefits Commission to the Secretary of State for Social Services, H.M.S.O., London, 1972.

HOSKINS, DALMAR and BIXBY, LENORE E.: *Women and Social Security: Law and Policy in Five Countries*, United States Department of Health, Education and Welfare, 1973.

LAND, HILARY: 'Women, Work and Social Security', *Social and Economic Administration*, 1971, pp. 183–91.

SCHWEINITZ, KARL DE: *England's Road to Social Security*, A. S. Barnes and Co., New York, 1961.

WYNN, MARGARET: *Family Policy*, Michael Joseph, London, 1970.

Sociology of Women, Gender Roles and Minority Groups

*BERNARD, JESSIE: *Women and the Public Interest*, Aldine-Atherton, Chicago, 1971.

BETTELHEIM, BRUNO: *The Children of the Dream*, Paladin, London, 1971; Macmillan, New York, 1969.

*DAHLSTROM, EDMUND (ed.): *The Changing Roles of Men and Women,* Duckworth, London, 1967; revised ed., Beacon Press, Boston, 1971.

FERRISS, ABBOTT L.: *Indicators of Trends in the Status of American Women,* Russell Sage Foundation, New York, 1971.

FIELD, MARK G.: 'Workers (and Mothers): Soviet Women Today', in Donald R. Brown (ed.), *The Role and Status of Women in the Soviet Union,* Teachers College Press, Columbia University, New York, 1968.

*HACKER, HELEN: 'Women as a Minority Group', *Social Forces,* 1951, pp. 60–69.

HAMPSON, JOHN L. and HAMPSON, JOAN: 'The Ontogenesis of Sexual Behaviour in Man', in William C. Young (ed.), *Sex and Internal Secretions,* Baillière, Tindall & Cox, London, 1961; 3rd ed., 2 vols., Williams & Wilkins, Baltimore, 1961.

HARTLEY, RUTH E.: 'Some Implications of Current Changes in Sex-Role Patterns', *Merrill-Palmer Quarterly,* 1960, pp. 153–64.

'A Developmental View of Female Sex-Role Identification', in B. J. Biddle and E. J. Thomas (eds.), *Role Theory,* John Wiley, New York, 1966.

HARTLEY, RUTH E. and KLEIN, ARMIN: 'Sex-Role Concepts Among Elementary-School-Age Girls', *Journal of Marriage and the Family,* 1959, pp. 59–64.

*HOLSTER, HARRIET: *Sex Roles and Social Structure,* Universitetsforlaget, Oslo, 1970.

JOFFE, CAROLE: 'Sex-Role Socialisation and the Nursery School: As the Twig Is Bent', *Journal of Marriage and the Family,* 1971, pp. 467–75.

JOSEPH, JOYCE: 'A Research Note on Attitudes to Work and Marriage of Six Hundred Adolescent Girls', *British Journal of Sociology,* 1961, pp. 176–83.

KOMAROVSKY, MIRRA: 'Cultural Contradictions and Sex Roles', *American Journal of Sociology,* 1946, pp. 182–9.

LILJESTRÖM, RITA: 'The Swedish Model', in Seward and Williamson, 1970.

MYRDAL, GUNNAR: 'A Parallel to the Negro Problem', *An American Dilemma,* Harper & Row, New York, 1962, Appendix 5.

OAKLEY, ANN: 'Sisters Unite', *New Society,* 11 March 1971.

Sex, Gender and Society, Maurice Temple Smith, London, 1972; Harper & Row, New York, 1973.

RABBAN, MEYER: 'Sex-Role Identification in Young Children in Two Diverse Social Groups', *Genetic Psychology Monographs* 42, 1950.

RABIN, A. I.: 'The Sexes: Ideology and Reality in the Israeli Kibbutz', in Seward and Williamson, 1970.

SEAMAN, BARBARA: *Free and Female*, Coward, McCann and Geoghegan, New York, 1972.

SEWARD, GEORGENE and WILLIAMSON, ROBERT (eds.): *Sex Roles in Changing Society*, Random House, New York, 1970.

SPIRO, MELFORD E.: *Kibbutz: Venture in Utopia*, Schocken Books, New York, 1963.

STEINEMANN, ANNE: 'A Study of the Concept of the Feminine Role in Fifty-One Middle-Class Families', *Genetic Psychology Monographs* 67, 1963.

*SULLEROT, EVELYNE: *Woman, Society and Change*, Weidenfeld & Nicolson, London, 1971; McGraw-Hill, New York, 1971.

WEITZMAN, LEONORE J., *et al.*: 'Sex Role Socialisation in Picture Books for Pre-School Children', *American Journal of Sociology*, 1972, pp. 1125–50.

WOODWARD, C. VANN: *The Strange Career of Jim Crow*, 2nd edition, Galaxy Books, New York, 1966; revised ed., Oxford University Press, New York, 1966.

Index

abortion, 199–200
adopted children, 200
Africa, 172, 173
agriculture: declining opportunities in, 40, 41, 55; in pre-industrial Britain, 14–15, 173; in small-scale societies, 172, 173ff
Albert, Ethel M., 'Women of Burundi', quoted, 174–5
Alor, Indonesia, 169, 212
ambivalence, 60, 80–90 passim, 91
Andrewski, Iris, 'The Baby as Dictator', quoted, 219
Andry, Robert, Delinquency and Parental Pathology, 209–10
anthropology, male-oriented, 163–165, 170
apprentices, apprenticeship, 18, 19, 25, 26, 42; for housewifery, 95–6, 236
Ardrey, Robert, African Genesis, 158
Arkwright, Sir Richard, 35
Asia, Central, 172

baby battering, 217, 218. See also child-beating
Bali, 193
Barley, M. W., The English Farmhouse and Cottage, quoted, 24
Beales, H. L., The Industrial Revolution, quoted, 33
Bedford College, 85
Beecher, Catherine, The American Woman's Home, 52

Beeton, Mrs Isabella, Book of Household Management, 52
Belgium, 74
Benet, Mary Kathleen, Secretary: An Enquiry into the Female Ghetto, quoted, 73–4
Bernard, Jessie, Women and the Public Interest, quoted, 84n
Bettelheim, Bruno, Children of the Dream, 215
Blauner, Robert, Alienation and Freedom, 231–2
Boserup, Esther, Women's Role in Economic Development, quoted, 173; 175
Bowlby, John, Child Care and the Growth of Love, 208; Forty-Four Juvenile Thieves, 207
British Institute of Management, 76
British Labour Party Report, Discrimination Against Women, 75
Burundi, 174–5

capitalism, 32, 156. See also industrialization, industrial society
Ceylon, 175
child, children: adopted, 200; attitudes to, in modern industrial society, 31, 67; in pre-industrial Britain, 24–6; in traditional and small-scale societies, 11, 193; battered, 217; in hospital, 204–5, 206, 207; and housework, 102; illegitimate, 200; imitative be-

Dr. Ann Oakley is Research Officer at Bedford College, University of London. She is the author of *Sex, Gender and Society* and *The Sociology of Housework*, is a member of the London Women's Liberation Workshop, and has written many articles about women's roles and situations for various journals and magazines. She is currently working on a study of childbirth in contemporary society.